Jack O'Connell
Seattle
24 March 1988

THE WORLDS
OF JOHN AUBREY

The Worlds
of
John Aubrey

Being a further selection of Brief Lives,
together with excerpts
from his writings on antiquities,
science and folklore

Selected and edited by
RICHARD BARBER

LONDON
THE FOLIO SOCIETY
MCMLXXXVIII

Printed in Great Britain at The Bath Press, Avon

Contents

AUBREY AS BIOGRAPHER
Brief Lives

AUBREY AS ANTIQUARY
Monumenta Britannica and other writings

AUBREY AS LOCAL HISTORIAN
The *Wiltshire Antiquities* and *Natural History of Wiltshire*

AUBREY ON EDUCATION
An Idea of the Education of Young Gentlemen

AUBREY AND THE SUPERNATURAL

Miscellanies

AUBREY ON FOLKLORE AND SUPERSTITION

Sack in their Shoppes. My Grandfather, & severall others, that I knew heretofore, did remember it.

J'aime mon Honneur que ma vie.

1. Aubrey. 2 Danvers.
3. Lyte. 4. as the first

at Christning & feasts.

When I was a Boy (before the late warrs) ye Tabor & Pipe
especially strong & pregnant were commonly used in the Marches of Wales (12 in all Wales)
it is almost lost. The Drumme & Trumpet have put that
able Musiq to silence. I believe 'tis derived from the Rom
Sistrum: [a brasen, or iron Timbrel] Cratalus
Ring of brasse struck with an iron rod: so we play with the
and Tongs.

& Pipe.

The first point-band worne in England, was that a

Aubrey's bookplate, showing the Aubrey coat of arms, quartering Danvers
and Lyte, surrounded with various manuscript jottings

Introduction

The present volume offers a wider view of the world of John Aubrey than the deliberately restricted range of the edition of *Brief Lives* published by The Folio Society in 1976. In that collection, only those lives for which a contemporary and reasonably authentic portrait of the subject could be found were included. Here I have gathered not only the 'unillustrated' *Brief Lives*★, but also glimpses of the other facets of Aubrey's intellectual achievements. We remember him today as a biographer, and in this he was an unrivalled pioneer: but he was also in the forefront of other movements of his time, in the study of antiquities and in the pursuit of natural science. His work in another field was scorned by his contemporaries, but was pioneering indeed, the collection of folklore and tradition.

There is a common thread running through all these activities: an intense conviction of the value of observation and record, whether of apparent idle superstition or of vanished monuments, whether of the natural world or of the men who inhabited it. In this lies Aubrey's novelty and his greatest achievement. Earlier students of natural phenomena had realised the value of writing down apparently trivial data, and from the time when medieval philosophers (though not without controversy and reactionary opposition) had concluded that universal laws must be deduced from observation of particular instances, this had been an accepted working method in astronomy and the more limited studies carried out in the field of physics.

Serious study in 'experimental philosophy' was a very recent phenomenon in Aubrey's time, and he himself noted of the period up to the end of King James's reign that 'things were not then studied. My Lord Bacon first led that dance.' He recorded that 'about the year 1649 . . . Experimental Philosophy was then first cultivated by a Club in Oxford', and at Aubrey's college, Trinity, there were a number of Fellows with scientific interests. The most dramatic scientific discovery of the period was William Harvey's demonstration of the

★Illustrations have now been found for twelve of these, and are therefore included in the appropriate places.

circulation of the blood, and Harvey was both at the centre of this group and later a friend of Aubrey's. From these informal beginnings came the Royal Society, founded in 1660, the year of the Restoration. Aubrey was elected a member in 1663, and was an active participant in its meetings for the rest of his life, although his wide-ranging contributions were sometimes criticised as eccentric or laughable. He was generally in the forefront of speculative thought about scientific matters: despite his acuteness in observation, he lacked the patience and method to follow a single line of enquiry for long, and preferred to dart about the scientific world, offering opinions on geology, education, astrology, chemistry or mathematics. His views were sometimes remarkable – as in his theory of the 'terraqueous world' and its geological history – but often muddled and incoherent, because he collected material piecemeal and without the strictly systematic approach which characterised the best work of other Fellows of the Society. His greatest asset was the lively curiosity that shines through *Brief Lives*: the endlessly repeated note about dubious information, '*Quaere de hoc*' ('make enquiries about this'), might well be his motto. Nor did he ever lose his sense of wonder: he was always capable of 'pure unreflective admiration', as a recent writer puts it. Aubrey's contribution to the advancement of science was in the end relatively slight: the 'Lives of the English Mathematicians' in his biographical notes was a more substantial work than any of his scientific essays, and *The Natural History of Wiltshire*, despite its striking passages on the natural world in general, is valuable chiefly as a record of Aubrey's own knowledge of the county.

In the field of antiquarian studies, Aubrey was more of a pioneer, and his work was more substantial. The one major work which he hoped to publish in his lifetime was the *Monumenta Britannica*: it reached the stage where subscriptions for its publication were invited in 1694, but the disordered state of the manuscript as much as lack of enthusiasm from the public was probably responsible for its non-appearance in print. Yet the *Monumenta* is a real advance in the study of the past, and Aubrey is, in some respects at least, one of the fathers of modern archaeology. His measured and accurate accounts of sites such as Stonehenge are an application of the principles of his scientific colleagues at the Royal Society to a field where a rational and analytic approach had hardly ever been attempted. Although Stonehenge had been the subject of work by the architect Inigo Jones and the scientist Walter Charlton, it had been studied in isolation: Aubrey began similarly with a sight of Stonehenge while out hunting, but soon extended the range of his enquiries, and in 1663 his work on Avebury came to the king's attention.★ He gave the king and the Duke of York a tour of the circle, and in return was commanded to write an account of the site for the king, and a survey of the 'old camp, and barrows on the plains', for the Duke of York. This led to his collection of all the available material on stone circles, fortified camps and dykes which form the bulk of the *Monumenta Britannica*: he searched not only printed sources, such as Camden's *Britannia* and the various county histories which had appeared in the preceding decades, but asked his friends to report any instances they came across, and tried whenever possible to visit the site himself. For earlier antiquaries, such monuments had taken second place to inscriptions and to identifiable remains. Camden, who was Aubrey's most distinguished forerunner in this field, does not even include remains among the features of his work:

In the several counties I have compendiously set down the limits (and yet not exactly by perch and pole to breed questions), what is the nature of the soil, which were the places of greatest antiquity, who have been the dukes, marquesses, earls, viscounts, barons, and some of the most signal and ancient families therein (for who can particulate all?).

The study of coins was the nearest that earlier investigators had come to our modern concept of archaeology, and Aubrey's approach was as novel as his conclusions. He argued that stone circles were neither Danish, as Charlton had claimed, nor Roman, but were the temples of the Druids; and he accordingly entitled the section of the *Monumenta* which dealt with them *Templa Druidum*.

But Aubrey was not the man to specialise in one particular archaeological field. His endless curiosity about the past led him to set out a concept of change, familiar enough to us today, but in his time a rare and novel idea. This is set out in a series of collections of notes at the end of the *Monumenta* which he called Στρωματα sive *Miscellanea*. His notes on architecture are among the first to trace the development of different styles, and to use the results as a means of dating buildings: 'Memorandum: that the fashions of building do last about 100 years or less, the windows the most remarkable thing. Hence one may give a guess about what time the building was.' He was a pioneer in the study of palaeography, the study of ancient scripts which is crucial to the dating of manuscripts, and his enthusiasm for old manuscripts is attested by a famous passage in his autobiographical notes.† He recorded that the shape of shields on tombs varied according to the

★ See p. 150 below.
† *Brief Lives*, p. 26.

date they were erected. And his appetite for information carried him further still, to the world of fashion (*Chronologia Vestiaria*) and new-fangled commodities, which he headed 'Nouvelles' or novelties: a diverse and often surprising list follows. Of these notes, the *Chronologia Vestiaria* and *Nouvelles* are printed here.

If Aubrey's approach to the past was radically different, this did not mean that he rejected the old learning. It is surprising to us to find several important figures among Aubrey's friends interested in astrology; Aubrey was perhaps a greater enthusiast than all save Elias Ashmole and William Lilly, and *Brief Lives* is full of notes for astrological calculations. He spent a great deal of time collecting accurate details of his subject's hour and place of birth so that he could cast their horoscopes, and when his own circumstances were at their most troubled, he believed that astrological influences might be at the root of it. Yet here again Aubrey's interest is largely scientific curiosity: he is attempting to collect data, interpret it by astrological rules, and test the results against what actually happened. As far as he was concerned, astrology was a body of knowledge which could be checked by observation, just as his observations on the correlation of vegetation and different types of soil could be verified. We do not laugh at Aubrey's attempt to use the presence of given species of trees as 'Symptoms of Subterranean Treasure', indicating what minerals lay below ground: and his investigation of astrology is an exact parallel, in that he expected to extract useful information from it. A more superstitious age had seen astrology in terms of spiritual and occult influences: Aubrey was anxious to see if it fitted into the new mechanical view of the world that he and his contemporaries were developing. As always, however, there was a personal side to his enthusiasm: astrology was the scapegoat for his misfortunes, and malign influences were to blame for them, just as his geological observations were going to make his fortune.

Indeed, Aubrey was always hoping to retrieve his estate and make money. He noted down the various schemes in a little volume entitled *Faber Fortunae* (The Smith of Fortune), ranging from the practical information noted above to wild schemes beloved of dreamers in every age. Yet there is a surprisingly down-to-earth element in much of what he writes, and he was interested in ideas such as that of national economic self-sufficiency, particularly in raw materials. What prevented Aubrey from following up these schemes, some of which were perfectly sound? We have to remember that for years at a time he was on the run from lawsuits or creditors, and his cheerfully peripatetic existence was partly a matter of choice. Just as in his notebooks he never treats a single topic for more than a page or two (unless he is quoting someone else), so he seems in everyday life to have been unable to set his hand to any one project for long: there were too many exciting alternatives to tempt him.

In a sense, though, it is precisely Aubrey's magpie, restless mind that makes his notes – for they are rarely more than that – of enduring interest. He gives us something which the formal writing of the scientists of the age, impressive as it often is, cannot recapture: the intense excitement of a time when real discoveries were being made, and when a chance observation might set a whole new train of scientific thought in motion. The same applied in the scholarly world, where historical research had been given a new impetus by the search for legal precedents during the years before the Commonwealth, an impetus which was to result in 'the most prolific movement of historical scholarship which this country has ever seen', in the words of D.C. Douglas. Aubrey was involved, albeit to a lesser extent, in this intellectual movement; he encouraged Thomas Tanner, one of the most industrious scholars of the age, to undertake a history of Wiltshire when it was clear that his own work would never be completed, while Sir William Dugdale, Garter King of Arms and author of much of the *Monasticon Anglicanum*, the great history of English monasteries, was a professed admirer of Aubrey's *Monumenta*. Aubrey himself lacked the temperament for the solid research which lay behind the scholarly enterprises of the age, the patient delving in the dusty records kept in the Tower or perusal of ancient manuscripts in the great library of Sir Robert Cotton, but he was well aware of the value of the work going on around him, and it is against this background that we should view his antiquarian researches, which in a sense tried to unite the worlds of observation and study. His views on education, in his essay *An Idea of the Education of Young Gentlemen*, are surprisingly practical and level-headed, with shrewd criticism of contemporary practices.

In one area, however, Aubrey stood almost alone: that of tradition and the supernatural. He subtitled the one work published during his lifetime, *Miscellanies*, 'A Collection of Hermetick Philosophy'. He contrasted the progress in 'natural philosophy' with a lack of interest in 'hermetic philosophy', and continues: 'It is a subject worthy of serious consideration: I have here, for my own diversion, collected some few remarks within my own remembrance, or within the remembrance of some persons worthy of belief in the age before me.' Here, for once, Aubrey had overstepped the bounds: the one failing of which his contemporaries repeatedly accused him was a love of gossip. John Ray wrote to him: 'I think (if you can give me leave to be free with you) that you are a little too inclinable to credit strange relations', and Aubrey himself reports that Sir William Dugdale said that 'by no means I must not put in writing hearsays.' But just as Aubrey was one of the first to recognise the value of archaeological remains in any exploration of the past, so he realised that oral tradition, used with caution, was well worth recording. Admittedly he excuses such an exercise as a way of illustrating the ignorance of country folk; but elsewhere, in the *Natural History of Wiltshire*, he uses it skilfully to illuminate changes. He is just as concerned to flush out the manners and morals of the past as to describe the political and economic history of the county.

The *Miscellanies* show this interest in tradition in its weakest light, because (as usual) Aubrey's overall train of thought and any kind of critical overview are lacking. He prints the raw material – ghost stories, superstitions, old wives' tales, marvels, prophecies – as his sources provided them, with a bare attempt to set them out in categories and little more. They end by entertaining the reader, but leave him none the wiser as to the possibilities of Aubrey's vaunted 'hermetic philosophy'.

What Aubrey seems to have been after might have shocked his contemporaries even more. There is a strong tendency towards Deism, the search for an impersonal and impartial prime force in the universe, in some of Aubrey's remarks, and it is not unreasonable to assume that his commentary is sometimes absent because it was too sensitive a subject to handle in a scientific way. 'Natural philosophy' had caused enough trouble in religious circles in the past: 'hermetic philosophy' might have looked suspiciously like an attempt at a systematic analysis of religion itself, or at least of territory which came firmly within the scope of the church. Aubrey was mildly anti-clerical; although he mourned the passing of the monasteries, it was only because he perceived that they had a useful social function, not least as a haven for poverty-stricken gentlemen scholars such as himself! Elsewhere, he is all for finding natural explanations for miracles and is dismissive of the power of prayer. In the *Remains of Gentilism and Judaism* he does not hesitate on occasion to treat Christian ritual as just another superstition. When his contemporaries caught wind of this side of his character, they condemned it out of hand. White Kennett depicted him as 'English writer of Mr Hobbes' life (translated by Dr Blackburn), called the corruption carrier to the Royal Society'. Kennett, as a rising cleric, clearly bracketted Aubrey's admiration for Hobbes – whose *Leviathan* advocated the subservience of the church to the state – with his unusual views on other topics.

So, as we read Aubrey's scattered notes – he once called them 'planks from a shipwreck', but they are planks from a ship which never sailed – we can see, beyond the entertaining or curious information they contain, the whole way of thought of an age of intense intellectual curiosity. Just as Pepys has preserved the day-to-day life of Restoration England for us, so, in his disorderly fashion, Aubrey has preserved its spirit of enquiry and pursuit of knowledge.★ And his contribution, however confused or 'maggotty-headed', tells us a great deal about the decades when the foundations of modern scholarship, both in science and the humanities, were being laid.

RICHARD BARBER

★ For a fuller account of Aubrey's intellectual circle, see Michael Hunter, *John Aubrey and the World of Learning* (London 1975), to which the present brief summary is much indebted.

Aubrey as biographer:
Brief Lives

Note: the selection that follows, taken with the previous volume *Brief Lives* (Folio Society 1976, reissued 1988), reproduces the bulk of Aubrey's biographical material: only those lives consisting of an odd line or two, or of no more than an astrological note or record of a funereal inscription, have been excluded. ¶ indicates that the following text is taken from a different section of Aubrey's manuscripts.

Edward Alleyn
1566–1626

Actor and partner in the Fortune Theatre, built in 1600. He specialised in tragic parts.

... Mr Alleyn, being a tragedian, and one of the original actors in many of the celebrated Shakespeare plays, in one of which he played a demon, with six others, and was in the midst of the play, surprised by an apparition of the devil, which so worked on his fancy, that he made a vow, which he performed at this place (Dulwich College) ... Notwithstanding all the solemnity of this deed of gift, the founder lived to change his mind upon a second marriage, when he was very desirous of revoking his charity, but was not allowed to.

Thomas Archer
1554–1630?

Mr Archer, rector of Houghton Conquest, was a good scholar in King James I's days, and one of his majesty's chaplains. He had two thick quarto manuscripts of his own collection; one, jests and tales etc., and discourses at dinners; the other, of the weather. I have desired parson Poynter, his successor, to enquire after them, but I find him slow in it. No doubt there are delicate things to be found there.

Deborah Aubrey
1610–1686

This entry is typical of Aubrey's notes for the purposes of checking a horoscope: 'accidents' are events in the subject's life.

Mrs Deborah Aubrey, my honoured mother, was born at Yatton-Kaynes, commonly West-Yatton, in the parish of Yatton Keynell in the county of Wilts, January 29th 1609, in the morning. In a letter from my mother dated February 3rd 1680 she tells me she was seventy years old last Thursday (29th January), which note.

Her accidents

My mother was married at 15 years old. She fell sick of a burning fever at Langford, Somerset. She was taken ill on June 6th 1675; fever there again in July 1675. She was born on January 29th, in the morning, that is the day before the anniversary day of the king's beheading. She was fifteen years old and as much as from January to June when she was married. She fell from her horse and broke her arm the last day of April (1649 or 50) when I was a suitor to Mrs Jane Codrington.

Letter August 8th, 1681: she was lately ill for three weeks and now her eyes are a little sore.

Memorandum: January 6th, 1683, my mother writes to me that she is 73 years of age.

William Aubrey
1529–1595

John Aubrey's great-grandfather, and the most celebrated of his ancestors

William Aubrey; Doctor of Laws: extracted from a manuscript of funerals, and other good notes, in the hands of Sir Henry St George, Clarenceux King at Arms. I guess it to be the handwriting of Sir Daniel Dun, LLD, who married Joan, third daughter of Dr William Aubrey:

> ... This gentleman in his tender years learned the first grounds of grammar in the college of Brecon, in Brecknock town, and from thence about his age of fourteen years he was sent by his parents to the University of Oxford, where, under the tuition and instruction of one Mr Morgan, a greatly learned man, in a few years he so much profited in the humanities and other recommendable knowledge, especially in rhetoric and history, that he was found to be fit for the study of civil law, and thereupon was also elected into the fellowship of All Souls College in Oxford (where the same law has always much flourished). In which college he earnestly studied and diligently applied himself to the lectures and exercise of the house, so that he there attained the degree of a doctor of civil law at his age of 25 years, and immediately afterwards he had bestowed on him the queen's public lectureship in law in the university; he read his lectures with such success that his fame for learning and

knowledge was spread far abroad and he was esteemed worthy to be called to public office. Wherefore, shortly afterwards, he was made judge marshal of the queen's armies at St Quentin in France. Which wars finished, he returned into England, and he decided, in more peaceable manner and according to his former education, to pass on the course of his life in the exercise of law; he became an advocate in the Court of Arches, and remained so for many years, but with such fame and credit both for his rare skill and knowledge of law, and for his sound judgement and good experience therein, that, among men best qualified to judge, he was generally accounted without equal in that branch of learning. For this reason, when there was occasion to employ a civil lawyer, his service was often used both within the realm and in foreign countries. In which employments he always used such care and diligence and balanced judgement that, as his valour and virtues became more evident each day, so they provided the means to his further advancement, insomuch that he was preferred to be one of the council of the Marches of Wales, and shortly after took his place as Master of the Chancery, and the appointed judge of the Audience, and was made Vicar General to the Lord Archbishop of Canterbury throughout the whole province, and last, by the especial grace of the queen's most excellent majesty, Queen Elizabeth, he was taken into her highness' close service and made one of the Masters of Request in Ordinary. All which titles and offices (except the mastership of Chancery which did not seem compatible with the office of Master of the Rolls) he, by her princely favour, possessed and enjoyed until the time of his death. Besides the great learning and wisdom with which this gentleman was plentifully endowed, Nature had also framed him so courteous of disposition and affable of speech, so sweet of conversation and amiable in behaviour, that there was never anyone in his position better beloved in all his life; nor was he himself more especially favoured of her majesty and the greatest personages in the realm in any part of his life than he was when he drew nearest his death. He was not tall in stature, nor yet overlow; not gross in body, and yet of good habit; somewhat inclining to fatness of face in his youth; round, well favoured, well coloured and handsome; and although in his later years sickness had much impaired his strength and the freshness of his complexion, yet there remained there still to the last in his countenance such comely and decent gravity, that the change added to rather than diminished in any way his former dignity. He left behind him when he died by a virtuous gentlewoman Wilgiford his wife (the first daughter of Mr John Williams of Tainton in the county of Oxford; whom he married very young, as a maiden, and enjoyed to his death, the two of them living together in great love and kindness for the space of forty years) three sons and six daughters, all of them married and having issue . . .

His third son John★, being then of the age of 18 years (or thereabouts) was married to Rachel, one of the daughters of Richard Danvers of Tockenham in the County of Wilts, esquire.

Memorandum: he was one of the delegates (together with Dr Dale etc.) for the trial of Mary Queen of Scots, and was a great stickler for the saving of her life, which kindness was remembered by King James at his coming-in to England, who asked after him, and probably would have made him Lord Keeper, but he died, as we have seen, a little before that good opportunity happened. His majesty sent for his sons, and knighted the two eldest, and invited them to court, which they modestly and perhaps prudently declined. They preferred a country life.

Memorandum: old Judge Atkins (the father) told me that the Portuguese ambassador was tried for his life for killing Mr Greenway in the New Exchange under the commonwealth, on the precedent of the Scottish Bishop of Ross, a trial undertaken on Dr W. Aubrey's advice.

He was a good statesman and Queen Elizabeth loved him and used to call him 'her little Doctor'. Sir Joseph Williamson, principal secretary of state, has told me that in the Letter Office are a great many letters of his to the queen and council.

He sat many times as Lord Keeper, at the queen's pleasure, and made many decrees, which Mr Shuter, etc. told me they had seen.

Memorandum: the *Penkenol*, i.e. chief of the family, is my cousin Aubrey of Llannelly in Brecknockshire, who inherited estates worth about £60 or £80 a year; and the doctor should have used a distinguishing mark on his arms†; for want of which in a badge on one of his servants' blue coats, his cousin William Aubrey, also LLD, who was the chief, plucked it off.

The learned John Dee was his great friend and kinsman, as I find by letters between them in the custody of Elias Ashmole, esq., viz., John Dee wrote a book *The Sovereignty of the Sea*, dedicated to Queen

---

★ (Aubrey's grandfather. *Ed.*) John Whitgift, Archbishop of Canterbury was his guardian, and the doctor's great friend. I have heard my grandmother say that her husband told her that his grace kept a noble house, and did so with admirable order and economy; and that there was not one woman in the household.

† In heraldry, only the eldest son inherits the right to use arms without 'difference'. *Ed.*

Elizabeth, which was published in folio. Mr Ashmole has it, and also the original copy in John Dee's handwriting, and annexed to it is a letter from his cousin to William Aubrey, whose advice he desired in writing on that subject.

He purchased Abercunwrig (the ancient seat of the family) from his cousin Aubrey. He built the great house at Brecknock: his study looks on the river Usk. He could ride nine miles together on his own land in Breconshire. In Wales and England he left £2500 per annum, of which there is now none left in the family. He made one Hugh George (his chief clerk) his executor, who ran away into Ireland and cheated all the legatees, and among others my grandfather (his youngest son), for the addition of whose estate he had contracted for Pembridge castle in Herefordshire, and for which his executor was to have paid. He made a deed of entail in 1594 which is also mentioned in his will, whereby he entails the Brecon estate on the issue male of his eldest son, and in defailer, to skip the second son (for whom he had well provided, and who had married a great fortune) and to come to the third. Edward, the eldest, had seven sons; and so I am heir, being the eighteenth man in remainder★ which puts me in mind of Dr Donne:

> For what doeth it availe
> To be the twentieth man in an entaile?

Old Judge Sir Edward Atkins remembered Dr Aubrey when he was a boy; he lay at his father's house in Gloucestershire; he kept his coach, which was rare in those days. The judge told me that they then (vulgarly) called it a *Quitch*. I have his original picture. He had a delicate, quick, lively and piercing black eye, fresh complexion and a secure eyebrow. The figure in his monument at St Paul's is not like him; it is too big.

The curse of heroes' sons: he used up all the wit of the family, so that none descended from him can pretend to have any. It was a pity that Dr Fuller did not mention him amongst his worthies in that county.

When he lay dying, he desired them to send for a goodman; they thought he meant Dr Goodman, Dean of St Paul's, but he meant a priest†, as I have heard my cousin John Madock say. Captain Pugh used to say that civil lawyers (like most learned gentlemen) inclined naturally to the Church of Rome; and common lawyers, as more ignorant and clownish, to the Church of Geneva.

★ i.e. if seventeen other heirs died in turn without issue, Aubrey would inherit. *Ed.*
† i.e. a Roman Catholic priest. *Ed.*

This Dr William Aubrey was related to the first William, Earl of Pembroke in two ways (as appears by comparing the old pedigree at Wilton with that of the Aubreys); by Melin and Philip ap Elider (the Welshmen are all kin); and it is exceeding probable that the earl was instrumental in his rise. When the Earl of Pembroke was general at St Quentin in France, Dr Aubrey was his judge advocate. In the doctor's will is mention of a great piece of silver plate, the bequest of the right honourable the Earl of Pembroke.

Sir Robert Ayton
1570–1638

A courtier and diplomat under James I and Charles I, whose contemporary reputation as a poet has not stood the test of time.

He is buried in the south aisle of the choir of Westminster Abbey, where there is erected to his memory an elegant marble and copper monument and inscription. His bust is of copper, curiously cast, with a laurel held over it by two figures of white marble.

That Sir Robert was one of the best poets of his time – Mr John Dryden says he has seen verses of his, some of the best of that age, printed with some other verses – enquire for them.

He was acquainted with all the wits of his time in England. He was a great acquaintance of Mr Thomas Hobbes of Malmesbury, whom Mr Hobbes told me he had made use of (together with Ben Jonson) for an Aristarchus [critic and editor] when he made his epistle dedicatory to his translation of Thucydides. I have been told (I think by Sir John himself) that he was eldest brother to Sir John Ayton, Master of the Black Rod, who was also an excellent scholar.

Sir Thomas Badd

Created a baronet in 1642

The happiness a shoemaker has in drawing on a fair lady's shoe; I know a man the height of whose ambition was to be apprenticed to his mistress's shoemaker on condition he could do so. Sir Thomas

Badd's father, a shoemaker, married the brewer's widow of Portsmouth, worth £20,000.

John Barclay
1582–1621

Barclay wrote elegant satires in Latin verse, of which Argenis *is the most famous. Aubrey is wrong about his relationship with Robert Barclay; they were certainly not father and son.*

John Barclay, the Scotsman (from Samuel Butler), was in England some time in the time of King James. He was then an old man, white beard; and wore a hat and a feather, which gave some severe people offence. Dr John Dell tells me that his last employment was library-keeper of the Vatican, and that he was there poisoned.
Memorandum: this John Barclay has a son, now (1688) an old man, and a learned quaker, who wrote a system of the quakers' doctrine in Latin, dedicated to King Charles II, now to King James II. The Quakers mightily value him.

Thomas Batchcroft
d. 1670

Master of Gonville and Caius College, Cambridge, 1625–1670: ejected under the Commonwealth (1649–1660).

Memorandum: in Sir Charles Scarborough's time (he was of Caius College) Dr Batchcroft (the head of that house) would visit the boys' chambers and see what they were studying; and Charles Scarborough's genius led him to mathematics, and he was wont to be reading Clavius on Euclid. The old doctor had found on the title page '. . . . . e Societate Jesu'★ and was much scandalised at it. Said he, 'By all means leave off this author and read Protestant mathematical books.' Someone sent this doctor a pigeon pie from Newmarket or thereabouts, and he asked the bearer whether it was hot or cold. He did outdo Dr Kettle.

★ i.e. Clavius was a Jesuit. *Ed.*

Sir Henry Billingsley
d. 1606

This is one of Aubrey's projected Lives of English Mathematicians. Billingsley studied at Cambridge and went on to make a successful career in the City: he was Lord Mayor in 1596, and MP in 1603–4.

This Sir Henry Billingsley was one of the learnedest citizens that London has bred. This was he that put forth all Euclid's *Elements of Geometry* in English with learned notes and a preface by Mr John Dee, and learned men say it is the best Euclid. He had been Sheriff and Lord Mayor of the City of London. His house was the fair house in Fenchurch Street, where now Jacob Luce lives, a merchant.

Memorandum: P. Ramus in his *Scholia* says that the reason why mathematics did most flourish in Germany was that the best authors were rendered into their mother tongue, and that public lectures of it were also read in their own tongue.

Memorandum: when I was a boy Sir ... Billingsley had a very pleasant seat with an oak wood adjoining it, about one and a half miles east of Bristol; enquire if he was Sir Henry's descendant.

See on Sir Thomas Billingsley; enquire if descended from Sir Henry.

¶ (Sir Thomas Billingsley was the best horseman in England, and out of England no man exceeded him. He taught the Earl of Dorset and his thirty gentlemen to ride the great horse. He taught the Elector Palatine of the Rhine and his brothers⋆. He ended his days at the Countess of Thanet's, the earl's daughter; died praying on his knees.)

¶ In those days merchants travelled much abroad into Italy and Spain. Ask Mr Abraham Hill of what Company he was. Probably good memorials may be there found of his generous and public spirit. He answers: he was of the Goldsmith's Company, where there is a good picture of him.

Robert Billingsley teaches arithmetic and mathematics; he has printed a very pretty little book of arithmetic and algebra. He was Sir Henry's great-grandson – from Mr Abraham Hill, FRS.

¶ Many years since, Mr Abraham Hill, FRS, citizen, told me that Sir Henry Billingsley was one of the Goldsmith's Company, and that his picture was in Goldsmith's Hall, which I went lately to see. No picture of him, and besides the clerk of the Company told me he is sure he was never of that company. But Mr Hill tells me since that in

---

⋆ Charles-Louis and his brothers Prince Rupert and Prince Maurice. *Ed.*

Stowe's Survey you may see of what company all the Lord Mayors were.

¶ Friar Whitehead, of Austin Friars (now Wadham College) did instruct him. He (i.e. Billingsley) kept him at his house, and there I think he died.

Sir John Birkenhead

As founder of Mercurius Aulicus, *Birkenhead ranks as one of the first journalists of distinction. He went with Charles II into exile, but moved between France and England under the Commonwealth.*

Sir John Birkenhead, knight, was born at Northwich in Cheshire. His father was a saddler there, and he had a brother, a saddler, who was a trooper in Sir Thomas Ashton's regiment, who was quartered at my father's, who told me so.

He went to Oxford University at fifteen years old, and was first a servitor at Oriel College. Mr Gwyn, minister of Wilton, was his contemporary there, who told me he wrote an excellent hand, and in 1637 or 8, when William Laud, Archbishop of Canterbury was last there, he had occasion to have some things well transcribed, and this Birkenhead was recommended to him who performed his business so well, that the archbishop recommended him to All Soul's College to be a fellow, and he was accordingly elected.

After Edgehill fight, when King Charles I had his court at Oxford, he was chosen as someone fit to write the news; the Oxford newspaper was called *Mercurius Aulicus*★ which he wrote wittily enough till the surrender of the town (which was on June 24th, 1646). He left a collection of all his *Mercurius Aulicus*'s and all his other pamphlets, which his executors (Sir Richard Mason and Sir Muddiford Bramston) were ordered by the king to give to the Archbishop of Canterbury's library.

After the surrender of Oxford, he was put out of his fellowship by the Visitors, and had to shift for himself as well as he could. The most part of his time he spent in London, where he met with several persons of quality who loved his company, and made much of him.

He went over into France, where he stayed some time, not long, I think. He received grace there from the Duchess of Newcastle, I remember he told me.

★ Roughly, *The Court Messenger. Ed.*

He got many forty shillings (I believe) by writing pamphlets such as that of 'Col. Pride' and 'The Last Will and Testament of Philip Earl of Pembroke' etc.

At the restoration of his majesty, he was made Master of the Faculties, and afterwards one of the Masters of Requests. He was exceedingly confident, witty, not grateful to his benefactors, would lie damnably. He was of middling stature, great goggly eyes, not of a sweet aspect.

He was chosen a burgess of parliament at Wilton in Wiltshire in 1661, i.e. of the King's long parliament. In 1679, on the choosing of this present parliament, he went down to be elected and at Salisbury heard how he was scorned and mocked at Wilton (where he was going), and called *Pensioner* etc.; he went not to the borough where he intended to stand, but returned to London and took it so to heart that he gradually decayed and pined away; and so died at his lodgings in Whitehall in December 1679, and was buried on Saturday December 6 in St Martin's Churchyard in the Fields★.

He had the art of remembering places; and his surroundings were the chambers of All Souls College (about 100), so that for a hundred errands he would easily remember. He was created DCL because he had been with the king. His library was sold to Sir Robert Atkins for £200, his manuscripts, (chiefly copies of records) for £900.

Henry Birkenhead
1617–1696

Remembered as a writer of Latin verse, and founder of the professorship of poetry at Oxford, which was established in 1708 from funds bequeathed by him.

From a letter to Thomas Tanner, November 21, 1696:

My old acquaintance, Dr Henry Birkenhead, formerly fellow of your college (but first was commoner of Trinity College, Oxford), was an universally beloved man. He had his school education under Mr Farnaby, and was his beloved disciple. He died at the Bird-Cage (at his sister's, Mrs Knight, the famous singer) in St James's Park on Michaelmas eve 1696, aged almost 80.

★ His reason (for not being buried in the church as a man of rank – *Ed*.) was because he said they removed the bodies out of the church.

He was born in London at the Paul's head tavern (which his father kept) in Paul's chain in St Paul's churchyard in 1617; he was baptized on the 25th September. John Gadbury has [astrological details of] his nativity from him.

I will ask his sister (Mrs Knight) for a very ingenious diatribe that he wrote on Martial's epigram *'Jura verpe, per Anchialum'* which he has made clear beyond his master Farnaby, Scaliger or any other. 'Scaliger', he said, 'speaks the truth, but not the whole truth.' 'Tis pity it should be lost, and I would deposit it in the Ashmolean Museum.

I gave my Holyoke's Dictionary to the Museum. Pray look on the blank leaves at the end of it, and you will find a thundering copy of verses that he gave me, in the praise of this king (Louis XIV) of France. Now he is dead, it may be looked upon.

Robert Blake
1599–1657

Admiral under the Commonwealth. He made his reputation as a commander on land in 1642–4, culminating in his defence of Lyme in Dorset and capture of Taunton in 1644, which he held during a year's siege in 1644–5. He was commander of the fleet from 1649 onwards, and fought the Dutch under van Tromp; he campaigned in the Mediterranean from 1655 until 1657, culminating in a great victory over the Spanish at Santa Cruz in the three months before his death on the voyage home.

Robert Blake, admiral, was born in Somerset; he was at St Alban Hall in Oxford. He was there a young man of strong body, and good parts. He was an early riser, and studied well, but also took his robust pleasures of fishing, fowling etc. He would steal swans – from H. Norborne, BD, his contemporary there.

He served in the House of Commons for Bridgewater in 1640. In 1649, he was made admiral. He did the greatest actions at sea that were ever done.

Blake died in 1657, and was buried in King Henry VII's chapel; but upon the return of the king, his body was taken up again and removed; Mr Wells had this done, and where it is now, I know not. Ask Mr Wells of Bridgewater.

James Bovey
1622–?

James Bovey esq. was the youngest son of Andrew Bovey, merchant, cash-keeper to Sir Peter Vanore in London. He was born in the middle of Mincing Lane, in the parish of St Dunstan's in the East, London in 1622, on May 7th, at six o'clock in the morning. Went to school at Mercers' Chapel under Mr Augur. At 9 he was sent into the Low Countries; then returned, and perfected himself in the Latin and Greek. At 14, travelled into France and Italy, Switzerland, Germany and the Low Countries. Returned into England at 19; then lived with one Hoste, a banker, 8 years, was his cashier for 8 or 9 years. Then he traded for himself, aged 27, till he was 31; then married the only daughter of William de Vischer, a merchant; lived 18 years with her, then continued single. Left off trade at 32, and retired to a country life, by reason of his indisposition, the air of the city not agreeing with him. Then, in this retirement, he wrote *Negotiative Philosophy* [i.e. a manual on business practice] (a thing not done before) wherein are enumerated all the arts and tricks practised in negotiation, and how they were to be balanced by precautionary rules.

While he lived with Mr Hoste, he kept the cash of the ambassadors of Spain that were here; and the agents called by them *Assentists*, who supplied the Spanish and Imperial armies in the Low Countries and Germany; and also many other large sums of cash, such as that of Sir Theodore Mayerer, etc.; his dealing being altogether in money matters; by which means he became acquainted with the ministers of state both here and abroad.

When he was abroad, his chief employment was to observe the affairs of the state and their judicature and to survey the politics in the countries he travelled through, more especially in relation to trade. He speaks Dutch, German, French, Italian, Spanish, dialects and Latin, besides his own language.

When he retired from business he studied merchant law and admitted himself to the Inner Temple, London, about 1660. His judgement has been taken in most of the great causes of his time in points concerning the merchant law. As to his person, he is about 5 foot tall, slender, straight, hair exceeding black and curling at the end, a dark hazel eye, of a middling size, but the most sprightly that I have beheld. Brows and beard of the same colour as his hair. A person of great temperance and deep thoughts, and a working head, never idle. From 14 he had a candle burning by him all night, with pen, ink and paper, to write down thoughts as they came into his head; that in this way he might not lose a thought. He was ever a great lover of natural philosophy. His whole life has been perplexed by law-suits (which has made him expert in human affairs), in which he always overcame. He had many lawsuits with powerful adversaries; one lasted 18 years. Red-haired men never had any kindness for him. He used to say 'Beneath a red head there is never a mind without malice'. In all his travels he was never robbed.

He has one son, and one daughter who resembles him. From 14 he began to take notice of all the rules for prudent conduct that came his way, and wrote them down, and so continued to this day, September 28, 1680, being now in his 59th year. As to his health, he never had it very well, but indifferently, always a weak stomach, which proceeded from the agitation of the brain. His diet was always fine diet; much chicken.

He made it his business to advance the trade of England, and many men have printed his conceptions.

William, Lord Brereton
1631–1680

William, Lord Brereton of Leighton: this virtuous and learned lord (who was my most honoured and obliging friend) was educated at Breda, by John Pell, DD, then mathematics professor there of the Prince of Orange's 'illustrious school'. Sir George Goring, Earl of Norwich (who was my lord's grandfather), did send for him to go over there, where the doctor (then Mr John Pell) took great care of him and made him a very good algebrist.

He was an excellent musician and also a good composer.

Edward Brerewood
1565?–1613

Antiquary and mathematician

He was of Brasenose College in Oxford. My old cousin Whitney, a fellow there long since, told me, as I remember, that his father was a citizen of West Chester; that (I have now forgotten on what occasion, whether he had run through his allowance from his father, or what) but he was for some time in straits in the College: that he went not out of the College gates in a good while, nor (I think) out of his chamber, but was in slippers, and wore out his gown and clothes on the board and benches of his chamber, but profited in knowledge wonderfully. He was astronomy professor at Gresham College, London.

'Tis pity I can pick up no more of him.

Henry Briggs
1561–1630

Mathematician

He was first of St John's College in Cambridge. Sir Henry Saville sent for him and made him his geometry professor. He lived at Merton College in Oxford, where he made the sundials at the buttresses of the east end of the chapel with a bullet for the axis.

He travelled into Scotland to commune with the honourable John Napier of Merchiston about making the logarithmical tables.

Looking once on the map of England, he observes that the two rivers, the Thames and that Avon which runs to Bath and so to Bristol, were not far distant, i.e. about 3 miles – see the map. He sees 'twas but about 25 miles from Oxford; gets a horse and views it and finds it to be a level ground and easy to be digged. Then he considers the charge of cutting between them and the convenience of making a marriage between those rivers which would be of great consequence for cheap and safe carrying of goods between London and Bristol, and though the boats go slowly and with meanders, yet considering they go day and night, they would be at their journey's end almost as soon as the waggons, which are often overthrown and liquors spilt and other goods broken. Not long after this he died and the civil wars broke out. It happened by good luck that one Mr Matthews of Dorset had some acquaintance with this Mr Briggs and had heard him discourse on it. He was an honest simple man, and had spent all his inheritance, and this project did much run in his head. He wanted to revive it (or else it had been lost and forgotten) and went into the country to make an ill survey of it (which he printed) but with no great encouragement from the people of the country or others. Upon the restoration of King Charles II, he renewed his design, and applied himself to the king and council. His majesty espoused it more (he told me) than anyone else. In short, for want of management and his non-ability, it came to nothing and he is now dead of old age. But Sir Jonas Moore (an expert mathematician and a practical man) being sent to survey the manor of Dauntsey in Wilts (which was forfeited to the crown by Sir John Danvers's foolery), went to see these streams and distances. He told me the streams were too small except in winter; but if some prince or the parliament would raise money to cut through the hill by Wooton Bassett, then there would be water enough and streams big enough. He worked out the cost, which I have forgotten, but I think it was about £200,000.

Elizabeth Broughton

Mrs Elizabeth Broughton was daughter of an ancient family in Herefordshire. Her father lived at the manor house at Canon Pyon. Whether she was born there or not, I know not; but there she lost her maidenhead to a poor young fellow, then, I believe, handsome, but, in 1660, a pitiful poor old weaver, clerk of the parish. He had fine curled hair, but grey. Her father at length discovered her inclinations, and locked her up in a turret of the house; but she gets down by a rope; and away she got to London, and did set up for herself.

She was a most exquisite beauty, as finely shaped as nature could frame; and had a delicate wit. She was soon taken notice of at London, and her price was very dear – a second Thais*. Richard, Earl of Dorset, kept her (whether before or after Venetia†, I know not, but I guess before). At last she grew commoner and infamous, and got the pox, of which she died.

I remember this much of an old song of those days which I have seen in a collection – 'twas by way of litany:

> From the watch at twelve o'clock
> And from Bess Broughton's buttoned smock‡
> > > Good Lord, deliver us.

* The famous courtesan of Alexander. *Ed.*
† Venetia Stanley (*later* Digby). *Ed.*
‡ Barbara (Countess of Castlemaine) had such a one; my sempstress helped to work it.

In Ben Jonson's execrations against Vulcan, he concludes thus:

> Pox take thee, Vulcan! May Pandora's pox
> And all the ills that flew out of her box
> Light on thee. And if those plagues will not do
> Thy wife's pox take thee, and *Bess Broughton's* too.

In the first octavo edition her name is thus at length [given in full].

I see there have been famous women before our times.

> Many strong men lived before Agamemnon
> Horace, *Odes* iv, 9

I do remember her father (1646), nearly 80, the handsomest shaped man that ever my eyes beheld, a very wise man and of an admirable elocution. He was a committee man in Herefordshire and Gloucestershire. He was commissary to Colonel Massey. He was of the Puritan party heretofore; had a great gift in praying, etc. His wife (I have heard my grandmother say, who was her neighbour) was as talented as him. He was the first that used to improve his land by spreading soap-ashes, when he lived at Bristol, where they threw them away at that time.

William Brouncker
1620–1684

Mathematician and founder-member of the Royal Society in 1662 of which he was president from the beginning. He was a friend of Evelyn, and worked with Pepys at the Navy Office from 1664–1679

William Brouncker, Lord Viscount of Castle Lyons in Ireland: he lived in Oxford when 'twas a garrison for the king; but he was of no university, he told me. He addicted himself only to the study of the mathematics, and was a very great artist in that learning.

His mother was an extraordinary great gamester, and played all games, gold play [for stakes in gold]; she kept the box [bank?] herself.

Mr Arundel (brother of the Lord Wardour) made a song of the characters of the nobility. Among others, I remember this:

Here's a health to my Lady Brouncker, and the best card in her hand,
And a health to my lord her husband, with ne'er a foot of land.

He was president of the Royal Society about fifteen years. He was of the Navy Office.

He died April 5th 1684; buried the 14th following in the middle of the choir of St Katherine's near the Tower, of which he was a governor. He gave a fine organ to this church a little before his death; and whereas it was a noble and large choir, he divided it in the middle with a good screen (at his own charge) which has spoiled it.

Sir Richard Bulkeley
1644–1710

Fellow of the Royal Society

He was a gentleman of large estate in Ireland; but unhappily plunged into debt, by supporting a set of enthusiastic pretenders to prophecy, whose first spawn appeared amongst the seditious and rebellious French Camisards and Huguenots, with whom he engaged so deeply, that not only his estate partly supplied their extravagances, but he prostituted his excellent pen in defence of their frenzy, and misapplied a great capacity and good sense, by submitting them to their groundless delusions.

Robert Burton
1577–1640

The author of The Anatomy of Melancholy, *a brilliant if eccentric book which defies classification.*

Mr Robert Hooke of Gresham College told me that he lay in the chamber in Christ Church that was Mr Burton's, of whom 'tis whispered that notwithstanding all his astrology and his book of melancholy, he ended his days in that chamber by hanging himself.

Sir Edward Bysshe
1615?–1679

Garter King of Arms under the Commonwealth. He was forced to resign at the Restoration, but became Clarenceux King of Arms instead.

Smallfield is a fair, well built house of freestone, situated by the common and (1672) belonging to Sir Edward Bysshe, Clarenceux King at Arms, by whose father Edward Bysshe, a councillor at law, and bencher of Lincoln's Inn, it was built. This gentleman was a great practiser in the court of wards, where he got his estate, and was wont to say jestingly 'That he built that fine house with woodcocks' heads'. His son Sir Edward complied, and was active in the iniquity of the times, ate the bread of Royalists and accepted of a pension of £600 per annum from sequestrators. In the windows of the house are abundance of late escutcheons of Bysshe, and some matches [quarterings by marriage]; these I have neglected to insert, because it appears from the Heralds' books that they are all false and forged. His true coat is *Ermine on a chief embattled*. During the usurpation, he assumed the coat of de la Bishe, with which he quartered some of the most ancient and noble quarterings of England, to which he had no pretence, to the great scandal of the College of Heralds, who speak hardly of him. I cannot also but term this silly as well as base, because, (notwithstanding all his vaunting, pompous escutcheons in his hall) the descent and arms of his family are well known by the inhabitants here, who call it a new raised, upstart family, of yesterday's growth, and that the bencher's father or grandfather, was a miller; and that there are several Goodman Bysshes in this parish of Tilburstow.

William Canynges
1399?–1474

Five times Mayor of Bristol. Most of his trade seems in fact to have been with northern Europe.

The antiquities of the city of Bristol do very well deserve some antiquary's pains (and the like for Gloucester). There were a great many religious houses. The collegiate church (Augustinian priory) is a very good building, especially the gate-house. The best built churches of any city in England, before these new ones at London since the conflagration.

St Mary Radcliffe church (which was intended as a chapel) is an admirable piece of architecture of about Henry VII's time. It was built by Alderman Canynges, who had fifteen or sixteen ships of his own. He got his estate chiefly by carrying pilgrims to Santiago de Compostela. He had a fair house in Radcliffe Street that looks towards the water side, ancient Gothic buildings, a large house that, 1656, was converted to a glass-factory. See the annotations on Norton's Ordinal in *Theatrum Chemicum*, where 'tis said that Thomas Norton of Bristol got the secret of the philosopher's stone from Alderman Canynges' widow.

This Alderman Canynges did also build and well endow the religious house at Westbury or Henbury (see Speed's map and chronicle); 'tis about two or three miles from Bristol on the road to Aust ferry. In his old age he retired to this house and entered into that order.

Sir Charles Cavendish
d. 1652

(From Mr John Collins, mathematician). Sir Charles Cavendish was the younger brother to William, Duke of Newcastle. He was a little, weak, crooked man, and nature not having adapted him for the court nor the camp, he betook himself to the study of the mathematics, wherein he became a great master. His father left him a good estate, the revenue whereof he expended on books and on learned men.

He had collected in Italy, France, etc. with no small charge, as many manuscript mathematical books as fill a hogshead [barrel], which he intended to have printed; which if he had lived to have done, the growth of mathematical learning had been thirty years or more forwarder than it is. But he died of the scurvy, contracted by hard study, about 1652, and left an attorney of Clifford's Inn as his executor, who shortly after died, and left his wife as executrix, who sold this incomparable collection aforesaid by weight to the paste-board makers for waste paper. A good caution for those that have good manuscripts to take care to see them printed in their lifetimes.

William Cecil, Lord Burghley
1520–1598

Secretary of State to Elizabeth I from her accession in 1558 until 1572, and then Lord High Treasurer until his death. When she appointed him, Elizabeth said: 'This judgement I have of you, that you will not be corrupted by any gifts, and that you will be faithful to the state.' His career amply bore out her prediction: his greatest success, though won through dubious means, was to secure Elizabeth's Protestant kingdom against Roman Catholic subversion.

The first Lord Burghley (who was Secretary of State) was at first but a country schoolmaster, and (I think Dr Thomas Fuller says, vide *Holy State*) born in Wales.

I remember (when I was a schoolboy at Blandford) Mr Basket, a reverend divine, who was wont to beg us play-days, would always be uncovered [keep his hat off, as a mark of respect] and said that it was the Lord Burghley's custom, *for* (said he) *here is my Lord Chancellor, my Lord Treasurer, my Lord Chief Justice etc., predestinated* [of the future].

'He made Cicero's Epistles his glass, his oracle and his ordinary pocket-book.' (Dr J. Webb in preface of his translation of Cicero's *Familiar Epistles*.)

¶ I have often admired, that so wise man as the Lord Burghley and his sons were, would so vainly change their name, that is to that of Sitsilt, of Monmouthshire, a family of great antiquity; there are yet of that name there, but the estate is much decayed, and became small. I was in Monmouth church in 1656; and there was in a sash window of the church a very old escutcheon, as old as the church, belonging to the aforesaid family: it did hang a little dangerously, and I fear 'tis now spoiled. They are vulgarly called Seysil. And Mr Verstegan (otherwise an exceeding ingenious gentleman) to flatter this family, would have them to be derived from the Roman *Caecilii*; whereas they might as well have been contented with the real antiquity of this and Monmouthshire, and needed not to have gone as far as Italy for it. In like manner, and about the same time, Skydmore of Herefordshire changed his name to Scudamore; and took his motto *Scutum Amoris* [Love's shield] when Spenser's *Faerie Queene* came out, wherein he has a very fine character of (called) Sir Scudamore.

Thomas Chaloner
1595–1661

Thomas Chaloner's anti-monarchist ideas seem to have been the result of foreign travel, combined with the injustice done to his father over the Yorkshire mines. He became a member of Parliament in 1645, and quickly became a leading anti-Royalist. He failed to make his peace at the Restoration, and died in Holland, an exile, in 1661.

Thomas Chaloner esq. was the son of Dr Chaloner, who was tutor (i.e. *informator* [instructor] to Prince Henry (or Prince Charles – vide Bishop Hall's Letters about this).

He was a well-bred gentleman, and of very good natural parts, and of an agreeable humour. He had the accomplishments of studies at home, and travels in France, Italy and Germany.

About the year [1600] (ask John Collins) riding a-hunting in Yorkshire (where the alum works now are), on a common, he took notice of the soil and herbage, and tasted the water, and found it to be like that where he had seen the alum works in Germany. Whereupon he got a patent of the king (Charles I) for an alum work (which was the first that ever was in England) which was worth to him two thousand pounds per annum or better: but in the time of Charles I some courtiers did think the profit too much for him, and prevailed so with the king, that notwithstanding the patent aforesaid, he granted a half share, or more, to another (a courtier) which was the reason that made Mr Chaloner so interest himself for the Parliament cause, and, in revenge, to be one of the king's judges.*

He was as far from puritan as the East from the West. He was of the natural religion, and one of Henry Martyn's gang, and one who loved to enjoy the pleasures of this life. He was (they say) a good scholar, but he wrote nothing that I hear of, only an anonymous pamphlet, octavo, *An account of the Discovery of Moyses's Tombe*; which was written very wittily. It was about 1652. It did set the wits of all the Rabbis of the Assembly then to work, and 'twas a pretty while before the sham was detected.

He had a trick sometimes to go into Westminster Hall in a morning in the law term, when courts were sitting and tell some strange story (sham), and would come thither again about 11 or 12 to have the pleasure to hear how it spread; and sometimes it would be altered, with additions, he could scarce know it to be his own. He was neither proud nor covetous, nor a hypocrite: not apt to do injustice, but apt to revenge.

After the restoration of King Charles the Second, he kept the castle at the Isle of Man†, where he had a pretty wench that was his concubine. Where, when news was brought him that there were some come to the castle to demand it for his majesty, he spake to his girl to make him a posset, into which he put, out of a paper he had, some poison, which did, in a very short time, make him fall a-vomiting exceedingly; and after some time vomited nothing but blood. His retchings were so violent that the standers by were much grieved to behold it. Within three hours he died. The men who had demanded the castle came and saw him dead; he was swollen so extremely that they could not see any eye he had, and no more than of his nose than the tip of it, which showed like a wart, and his cods were swollen as big as one's head. This account I had from George Estcourt DD, whose brother-in-law, Hotham, was one of those that saw him.

---

* Aubrey has confused Sir Thomas Chaloner, Thomas Chaloner's father, and Thomas Chaloner himself. It was the father who discovered the mines, the son who was one of Charles I's judges. *Ed.*

† This is a mistake. E.W. esq. assures me that 'twas James Chaloner that died in the Isle of Man; and that Thomas Chaloner died or went beyond the sea; but which of them was the elder brother he knows not, but he guesses James to be the elder because he had £1500 per annum (about) which Thomas had not.

Geoffrey Chaucer
1328–1400

Sir Hamon L'Estrange had his works in MS, a most curious piece, most rarely written and illuminated, which he valued at £100. His grandson and heir still has it from Mr Roger L'Estrange. He taught his son the use of the astrolabe at 10; see his treatise on the astrolabe. Dunnington Castle, near Newbury, was his; a noble seat and strong castle, which was held by the king, Charles I, (who was governor?) but since dismantled.

Near this castle was an oak, under which Sir Geoffrey was wont to sit, called Chaucer's oak, which was cut down under Charles I; and so it was, that the culprit was called into the star chamber, and was fined it. Judge Richardson harangued against him for a long time, and like an orator, had topics from the Druids etc. This information I had from an able attorney that was at the hearing.

One Mr Goresuch of Woodstock dined with us at Romney Marsh, who told me that at the old Gothic-built house near the park gate at Woodstock, which was the house of Sir Geoffrey Chaucer, that there is his picture which goes with the house from one owner to another – which see.

Henry Clifford, fifth Earl of Cumberland
1591–1643

A friend of Strafford; neither his political career nor his military exploits in the Royalist cause were particularly distinguished: with him the line of the earls of Cumberland came to an end.

Henry, Earl of Cumberland, was a poet: the countess of Cork and Burlington has still his verses. He was of Christ Church, Oxford. Nicholas, Earl of Thanet, was wont to say that the mare of Fountains Abbey did dash, meaning that since they got that estate (given to the church) they did never thrive, but still declined.

¶ He was an ingenious gentleman for those times and a great acquaintance of the Lord Chancellor Bacon's; and often wrote to one another, which letters the countess of Cork and Burlington, my Lady Thanet's mother, daughter and heir of that family, keeps as reliques; and a poem in English that her father wrote upon the Psalms and many other subjects, and very well, but the language now being something out of fashion, like Sir Philip Sidney's, they will not print it.

John Cleveland
1613–1658

Cavalier poet

John Cleveland was born in Warwickshire. He was a fellow of St John's College in Cambridge, where he was more taken notice of for his being an eminent debater than a good poet. Being turned out of his fellowship for a malignant (being a Royalist) he came to Oxford, where the king's army was, and was much caressed by them. He went thence to the garrison at Newark upon Trent, where upon some occasion when articles were drawn up, or some other writing, he would needs add a short conclusion, 'and hereunto we annex our lives, as a label to our trust'. After the king was beaten out of the field, he came to London and retired in Grays Inn. He and Samuel Butler etc of Gray's Inn, had a club [drinking bout] every night. He was a comely plump man, good curled hair, dark brown.

Henry Coley
1633–1695?

My friend Mr Henry Coley was born in Magdalen parish in the city of Oxford, October 18, 1633. His father was a joiner, with a shop over against the Theatre. He is a tailor in Gray's Inn Lane. He is a man of admirable parts, and more to be expected from him every day; and as good a natured man as can be. And comes by his learning merely by the strong impulse of his genius. He understands Latin and French; yet never finished learning his grammar.

He was a women's tailor: took to the love of astrology, in which he grew in a short time to a good proficiency; and in Mr W. Lilly's later time, when his sight grew dim, was his amanuensis. He has great practice in astrology, and teaches mathematics. He has published *The Key to Astrology*, wherein he has compiled clearly the whole science out of the best authors.

Thomas Cooper
1517?–1594

Dr Edward Davenant told me that this learned man had a shrew to his wife, who was irreconcilably angry with him for sitting up so late at night, compiling his Latin dictionary. When he had half-done it, she had the opportunity to get into his study, took all his pains out in her lap, and threw it into the fire and burnt it. Well, for all that, that good man had so great a zeal for the advancement of learning, that he began it again, and went through with it to that perfection that he hath left it to us a most useful work. He was afterwards made Bishop of Winchester.

Thomas Cromwell
?1485–1540

Cromwell rose from being a clothier and lawyer, through service under Cardinal Wolsey, to being Henry VIII's chief minister. He was an architect of the Act of Supremacy (1534) by which the king became head of the English Church.

Over against Fulham, on the bank of the River Thames, is situated Putney, a small village, and famous for little, but giving birth to that remarkable instance of the inconstancy of fortune, Thomas Cromwell, son of a blacksmith of this place, raised from the anvil, and forge to the most beneficial places and highest of honours in the nation, insomuch that though a layman, he presumed to exercise an ecclesiastical authority over the clergy, and assumed an office, which began and ended in him; to his advice we owe the destruction of religious houses in this nation, and the sacrilegious alienations consequent on it. But the justice of divine providence soon overtook

this favourite of fortune, and not only despoiled him of his upstart honours, but of his life, and so for some time retarded the happy Reformation, begun upon so bad principles.

Madam Curtin

Madam Curtin, who had a good fortune of £3000, daughter of Sir William Curtin, the great merchant, lately married her footman, who not long after marriage, beats her, gets her money, and ran away.

Edward Davenant
d. 1680

Edward Davenant, Doctor of Theology, was the eldest son of Mr Davenant, merchant of London, who was elder brother to the right reverend father in God, the learned John Davenant, Bishop of Salisbury.

I will first speak of the father, for he was a rare man in his time, and deserves to be remembered. He was of a healthy complexion, rose at 4 or 5 in the morning, so that he followed his studies till 6 or 7, the time that other merchants go about their business; so that, stealing so much and so quiet time in the morning, he studied as much as most men. He understood Greek and Latin perfectly, and was a better Grecian than the bishop. He wrote as rare a Greek character as ever I saw. He was a great mathematician, and understood as much of it as was known in his time. Dr Davenant, the son, has excellent notes of his father's, in mathematics, as also in Greek, and it was no small advantage to him to have such a learned father to imbue arithmetical knowledge into him when a boy, night times when he came from school (Merchant Taylors').

He understood trade very well, was a sober and good manager, but the winds and seas crossed him. He had such great losses that he went bankrupt, but his creditors knowing that it was no fault of his, and also that he was a person of great virtue and justice, used not extremity towards him; but I think gave him more credit, so that he went into Ireland, and did set up a fishery for pilchards at Wythy Island, in Ireland, where in some years he got £10,000; he satisfied and paid his creditors; and over and above left a good estate to his son. His picture bespeaks him to be a man of judgement and parts, and gravity extraordinary. He slipped coming down the stone stairs at the palace at Salisbury, which bruise caused his death. He lies buried in the south aisle of the choir in Salisbury Cathedral behind the bishop's stall.

Dr Edward Davenant was born at his father's house at Croydon in Surrey (the farthest handsome great house on the left hand as you ride to Banstead Downs). I have heard him say, he thanked God his father did not know the hour of his birth, for that it would have tempted him to have studied astrology, for which he had no esteem at all.

He went to school at Merchant Taylors' school, from thence to Queen's College in Cambridge, of which house his uncle, John Davenant (after Bishop of Salisbury) was master, where he was fellow.

When his uncle was preferred to the church of Salisbury, he made his nephew treasurer of the church, which is the best dignity, and gave him the vicarage of Gillingham in Dorset, and then Paulsholt parsonage, near Devizes, which last in the late troubles [under the Commonwealth] he resigned to his wife's brother, William Grove.

He was to his dying day of great diligence in study, well versed in all kinds of learning, but his genius did most strongly incline him to the mathematics, wherein he has written, (in a hand as legible as print) manuscripts in quarto, a foot high at least. I have often heard him say (jestingly) that he would have a man knocked on the head that should write anything in mathematics that had been written of before. I have heard Sir Christopher Wren say that he does believe he was the best mathematician in the world about thirty or thirty five years ago. But being a divine he was unwilling to print, because the world should not know how he had spent the greatest part of his time.

He very rarely went any farther than the church, which is hard by his house. His wife was a very discreet and excellent housewife, so that he troubled himself about no mundane affairs, and it is a private place, so that he was but little diverted with visits.

I have written to his executor, that we may have the honour and favour to conserve his manuscripts in the Library of the Royal Society, and to print what is fit. I hope I shall obtain my desire. And the Bishop of Exeter (Lamplugh) married the doctor's second daughter Katherine, and he was tutor to Sir Joseph Williamson, our President. He had a noble library, which was the aggregate of his father's, the bishop's and his own.

He was of middling stature, somewhat spare; and weak, feeble legs; he had sometimes the gout; was always of great temperance, he always drank his beer at meals with a piece of toast, winter and summer, and said it made the beer better.

He was not only a man of vast learning, but of great goodness and charity; the parish and all his friends will have a great loss in him. He took no interest for money upon bond. He was my singular good friend, and to whom I have been more obliged than to anyone besides; for I borrowed five hundred pounds of him for a year and a half, and I could not fasten any interest on him.

He was very ready to teach and instruct. He did me the favour to inform me first in algebra. His daughters were algebrists.

His most familiar learned acquaintance was Lancelot Morehouse, parson of Pertwood. I remember when I was a young Oxford scholar, that he could not endure to hear of the *New* (Cartesian etc.) *Philosophy*; 'for,' said he, 'if a new philosophy is brought in, a new divinity will shortly follow' (or 'come next'); and he was right.

He died at his house at Gillingham aforesaid, where he and his predecessor, Dr Jessop, had been vicars one hundred and more years, and lies buried in the chancel there.

He was heir to his uncle, John Davenant, bishop of Salisbury. Memorandum: when bishop Coldwell came to this bishopric (1591–6), he did let long leases which were but newly expired when bishop Davenant came to this see; so that there tumbled into his coffers vast sums. His predecessor Dr Tounson married Davenant's sister, continued in the see but a little while, and left several children unprovided for, so the king or rather the Duke of Buckingham gave Bishop Davenant the bishopric out of pure charity. Sir Antony Weldon says (in his *Court of King James*) it was the only bishopric that he disposed of without simony, all others being made merchandise of for the advancement of his kindred. Bishop Davenant being invested, married all his nieces to clergymen, so he was at no expense for their preferment. He granted to his nephew (this Doctor) the lease of the great manor of Poterne, worth about £1000 per annum; made him treasurer of the church of Salisbury, of which the endowment is the parsonage of Calne, which was esteemed to be of like value. He made several purchases of property, all which he left him; insomuch as the churchmen of Salisbury say, that he gained more by this church than ever any man did by the church since the Reformation, and take it very unkindly that, at his death, he left nothing (or but £50) to that church which was the source of his estate. How it happened I know not, or how he might be worked on in his old age, but I have heard several years since, he had set down £500 in will for the Cathedral Church of Sarum.

He had six sons and four daughters. There was a good school at Gillingham: at winter nights he taught his sons arithmetic and geometry; his two eldest daughters, especially Mrs Ettrick, were notable algebrists.

Memory: he had an excellent way of improving his children's memories, which was thus: he would make one of them read a chapter or etc, and then they were at once to repeat what they remembered, which did exceedingly profit them; and so for sermons, he did not let them write notes (which jaded their memory), but gave a verbal account. When his eldest son, John, came to Winchester school (where the boys were enjoined to write sermon-notes) he had not written (any); the master asked him for his notes – he had none, but said, 'If I do not give you as good an account of it as they that do, I am much mistaken.'

Michael Davy
d. 1679

Michael Davy, mathematician, and a gunner of the Tower (by profession, a tobacco-cutter) an admirable algebrician, was buried in the churchyard near Bedlam on May Day 1679. With writing in the frosty weather, his fingers rotted and gangrened.

Gideon de Laune
1505–1569

He was apothecary to Mary the queen mother [?Henrietta Maria]. He was a very wise man, and as a sign of it left an estate of £80,000.

Sir William Davenant was his great acquaintance, and told me of him, and after his return into England he went to visit him, being then in his eighties, and very decrepit with the gout, but had his sight and understanding. He had a place made for him in the kitchen chimney; and even though he was master of such an estate, Sir William saw him slighted not only by his daughter-in-law, but by the cook-maid, which much affected him – misery of old age.

He wrote a book of prudent advice, in English verse, which I have seen, and there are good things in it.

Michael Drayton
1563–1631

Drayton's reputation as a poet stood very high with his contemporaries, but has varied from total neglect to a more modest place among the Elizabethan and Jacobean poets since then. His chief works were historical and patriotic poems, the most famous being Poly-Olbion, a description of England. He also contributed texts for many of the Jacobean masques.

Michael Drayton esq., born in Warwickshire at Atherston on Stour (ask Thomas Mariett). He was a butcher's son. Was a squire, that is, one of the esquires to Sir Walter Aston, Knight of the Bath, to whom he dedicated his poem. Sir J. Brawne was a great patron of his. He lived at the bay-window house next to the east end of St Dunstan's church in Fleet Street.

Sir Edward Bysshe, Clarenceux herald, told me he asked Mr Selden once (jestingly) whether he wrote the commentary to his 'Polyolbion' and 'Epistles' or Mr Drayton made these verses to his notes.

See his inscription (on his monument in Westminster Abbey) given by the Countess of Dorset. Mr Marshal, the stone-cutter, of Fetter Lane, told me that these verses were made by Mr Francis Quarles, who was his great friend, and whose head he wrought curiously in plaster, and valued for his sake. 'Tis pity it should be lost. Mr Quarles was a very good man.

Saint Dunstan
924–988

Dunstan, son of a Somerset nobleman, became a monk at Glastonbury, though he retained close connections with the court. As abbot of Glastonbury, he reformed the monastery, while as Archbishop of Canterbury he played an important role in political life.

I find in Mr Selden's verses before Hopton's *Concordance of Years* that he was a Somersetshire gentleman. He was a great chemist.

The story of his pulling the devil by the nose with his tongs as he was in his laboratory, was famous in church windows.

He was a Benedictine monk at Glastonbury, where he was afterwards abbot, and after that was made Archbishop of Canterbury. He preached the coronation sermon at Kingston, and crowned King Edwy. In his sermon he prophesied, which the Chronicle mentions.

Mr Meredith Lloyd tells me that there is a book in print of his on the philosopher's stone; ask its title.

Edwardus Generosus give a good account of him in a manuscript which Mr Ashmole has.

Meredith Lloyd had, about the beginning of the civil wars, a manuscript of this saint's concerning chemistry, and says that there are several manuscripts of his up and down in England: ask Mr Ashmole.

Edwardus Generosus mentions that he could make a fire out of gold, with which he could set any combustible matter on fire at a great distance.

Meredith Lloyd tells me that, three or four hundred years ago, chemistry was in a greater perfection much, than now; their process was then more seraphic and universal: now they look only after medicines.

Several churches are dedicated to him: two at London: ask if one at Glastonbury.

Sir John Dunstable

He calls the cellar his library. Parliament men prepare themselves for the business of the nation with ale in the morning. Some justices sleep on the bench every assizes.

At Chippenham the deputy lieutenants met to see the order of the militia, but there were as many deputy lieutenants as officers. After a lengthy sitting (at dinner and drinking after dinner) the drums beat and the soldiers went to march before the window to be seen by the deputy lieutenant. Sir John Dunstable (colonel) had not marched before them many yards, but down he falls full length in the dirt. His myrmidons [troops], with much effort, heaved him up, and then he cried out, 'Some drink, ho!' and so there was an end of that business.

Sir Edward Dyer
d. 1607

Sir Edward Dyer of Somersetshire (Sharpham Park, etc.) was a great wit, poet and acquaintance of Mary, Countess of Pembroke, and Sir Philip Sidney. He is mentioned in the preface of the *Arcadia*. He had four thousand pounds income per annum, and was left £80,000 in money; he wasted it almost all. This I had from Captain Dyer, his great-grandson or brother's great-grandson. I thought he was the son of Lord Chief Justice Dyer, as I have inserted in one of these papers, but that was a mistake. The judge was of the same family, the captain tells me.

Thomas Egerton, Lord Ellesmere
1540–1617

Lord Keeper under Elizabeth and James I (1596–1604) and Lord Chancellor 1604–1617.

Sir Thomas Egerton, Lord Chancellor, was the natural son of Sir Richard Egerton of Ridley in Cheshire. This information I had thirty years since from Sir John Egerton, of Egerton in Cheshire, baronet, the chief of that family.

He was of Lincoln's Inn, and I have heard Sir John Danvers say that he was so hard a student that for three or four years he was not out of the house. He had good parts (a good mind), and early came into good practice.

My old father, Colonel Sharington Talbot★, told me that (Gilbert, I think) Earl of Shrewsbury, desired him to buy that noble manor of Ellesmere for him, and delivered him the money. Egerton liked the bargain and the seat so well, that truly he even kept it for himself, and afterwards made it his barony (took his title from it), but the money he restored to the Earl of Shrewsbury again.

He was a great patron to Ben Jonson, as appears by several epistles to him.

His son and heir, since Earl of Bridgewater, was an indefatigable bell-ringer – see the ballad.

George Feriby
b. 1573

In King James's time, one Mr George Feriby was parson of Bishop Cannings in Wiltshire: an excellent musician, and no ill poet. When Queen Anne† came to Bath, her way led to traverse the famous Wansdyke, which runs through his parish. He made several of his neighbours (good musicians) to play with him in consort and to sing. Against her majesty's coming, he made a pleasant pastoral, and gave her an entertainment, with his fellow songsters in shepherds' weeds and bagpipes, he himself like an old bard. After that wind music was over, they sang their pastoral eclogues (which I have, to insert in the other book).

★ He had, I believe, 200 adopted sons.
† Wife of James I. *Ed.*

He was one of the king's chaplains. 'Twas he caused the eight bells to be cast there, being a very good ringer.

He has only one sermon in print that I know of, at the funeral of Mr Drew of Devizes, called *Life's Farewell*. He was demy [scholar], if not fellow, of Magdalen College, Oxford.

He gave another entertainment in Cotefield to King James, with carters singing, with whips in their hands; and afterwards a football play. This parish would have challenged all England for music, ringing and football play.

Sir William Fleetwood
1535–1594

An energetic administrator, recorder of London from 1571 to 1591. Aubrey seems to have confused him with Sir Miles Fleetwood, receiver of the court of wards (d. 1641), as the dates given (1603, 1646) are clearly impossible.

Sir William Fleetwood, Recorder of London, was of the Middle Temple; was Recorder of London, when King James came into England; made his harangue to the City of London: 'When I consider your wealth, I do admire your wisdom, and when I consider your wisdom I do admire your wealth.' It was a two-handed piece of rhetoric, but the citizens took it in the best sense.

He was a very severe hanger of highwaymen, so that the fraternity was resolved to make an example of him: which they executed in this manner. They lay in wait for him not far from Tyburn, when he was coming from his house in Buckinghamshire; had a halter in readiness; brought him under the gallows, fastened the rope about his neck and on the tree, his hands tied behind him (and servants bound) and then left him to the mercy of his horse★, which he called Ball. So he cried 'Ho, Ball!' and it pleased God that his horse stood still, till somebody came along, which was half a quarter of an hour or more. He ordered that this horse should be kept as long as he would live, and it was so – he lived till 1646 – from Mr Thomas Bigge, of Wycombe.

One day, going on foot to the guildhall with his clerk behind him, he was surprised in Cheapside with a sudden and violent looseness, near the Standard. He turned up his breech against the Standard and bade his man hide his face; 'For they shall never see my arse again,' said he.

★ i.e. standing on his horse's back. *Ed.*

John Fletcher
1579–1625

Mr John Fletcher, poet: in the great plague, 1625, a knight of Norfolk
(or Suffolk) invited him into the country. He stayed but to make
himself a suit of clothes, and while it was making, fell sick of the
plague and died. This I had (1669) from his tailor, who is now a very
old man and clerk of St Mary Overy's.

Samuel Foster
?d. 1652

From Mr Beyes, the watchmaker, his nephew: Mr Samuel Foster,
was born at Coventry (as I take it); he was sometime usher of the
school there. Was professor at Gresham College, London: where, in
his lodging, on the wall in his chamber, is, of his own hand drawing,
the best sundial I do verily believe in the whole world. Among other
things it shows you what o'clock 'tis at Jerusalem, Gran Cairo etc. It is
drawn very skilfully.

Thomas Fuller
1608–1661

Fuller was one of the first authors to make an income by writing: he published more than twenty books, both religious and historical, the most famous being The History of the Worthies of England, *printed after his death.*

Thomas Fuller, DD, born at Orwincle* in Northamptonshire. His father was minister there, and married one of the sisters of John Davenant, Bishop of Salisbury. From Dr Edward Davenant.

He was a boy of pregnant wit, and when the bishop and his father were discoursing, he would be nearby and hearken and now and then join in, and sometimes beyond expectation, or his years (what would be expected of someone his age).

He was of a middle stature; thickset; curled hair; a very working head, in so much that, walking and meditating before dinner, he would eat up a penny loaf, not knowing that he did it. His natural memory was very great, to which he had added the art of memory: he would repeat to you forwards and backwards all the signs from Ludgate to Charing Cross.

He was a fellow of Sidney Sussex College in Cambridge, where he wrote his *Divine Poems*. He was first minister of Broad Windsor in Dorset, and prebendary of the church of Salisbury. He was sequestered, being a royalist, and was afterwards minister of Waltham Abbey, and preacher of the Savoy, where he died, and is buried.

William Gascoigne
1612?–1644

A brilliant astronomer, and inventor of the micrometer as used in astronomy.

There was a most gallant gentleman that died in the late wars, one Mr Gascoigne, of good estate in Yorkshire; from whom Sir Jonas Moore acknowledged to have received most of his knowledge. He was bred up by the Jesuits. I thought to have taken memoirs of him; but deferring it, death took away Sir Jonas. But I will set down what I remember.

*J. Dryden, poet, was born here.

William Gascoigne esq., of Middleton, near Leeds, Yorkshire, was killed at the battle of Marston Moor, about the age of 24 or 25 at most.

Mr Towneley, of Towneley in Lancashire, esquire, has his papers. From Mr Edmund Flamsteed★ who says he found out the way of improving telescopes before Descartes.

Mr Edmund Flamsteed tells me, September 1682, that 'twas at York fight he was slain.

Henry Gellibrand
1597–1637

Henry Gellibrand was born in London. He was of Trinity College in Oxford. Dr Potter and Dr William Hobbes knew him. Dr Hannibal Potter was his tutor, and preached his funeral sermon in London. They told me that he was good for little a great while, till at last it happened accidentally that he heard a geometry lecture. He was so taken with it that he immediately fell to studying it, and quickly made great progress in it. The fine sundial over the College Library is of his own doing. He was astronomy professor in Gresham College, London. He being one time in the country showed the tricks of drawing what card you touched, which was by combination with his confederate, who had a string that was tied to his leg, and the leg of the other, by which his confederate gave him notice by the touch; but by this trick he was reported to be a conjuror.

See *Canterbury's Doom* about Protestant martyrs, inserted in the almanac: he held prayer-meetings in Gresham College.

Adrian Gilbert

According to a pedigree given by Aubrey, he was Sir Walter Raleigh's half-brother.

This Adrian Gilbert was an excellent chemist, and a great favourite of Mary, Countess of Pembroke, with whom he lived and was her assistant in the laboratory. He was a man of great parts, but the

★ The Astronomer Royal. *Ed.*

greatest buffoon in England; cared not what he said to man or woman of what quality soever. 'Twas he that made the curious wall about Rollington Park at Wilton.

Alexander Gill

There were two men of this name, father and son, who were high master of St Paul's from 1608–1635 and 1635–9 respectively. Although Aubrey appears to impute the whipping stories to the father, it was in fact the son who was renowned for this, and was finally dismissed for maltreating a boy.

Dr Gill, the father, was a very ingenious person, as may appear by his writings. Notwithstanding, he had moods and humours, as particularly his whipping fits:

> As pedants out of schoolboys' breeches
> Do claw and curry their own itches
> Samuel Butler, *Hudibras*

This Dr Gill whipped Duncombe, who was not long after a colonel of dragoons at Edgehill-fight, taken pissing against the wall. He had his sword by his side, but the boys surprised him: somebody had thrown a stone in at the window; and they seized on the first man they lighted on. I think his name was Sir John Duncombe (Sir John Denham told me the story), and he would have cut the doctor, but he never went abroad except to church, and then his army went with him. He complained to the council, but it became ridicule and his revenge sank.

Dr Triplett came to give his master a visit, and he whipped him. The Dr (i.e. Triplett) got Pitcher of Oxford, who had a strong and a sweet bass, to sing a song against him under the school windows, and got a good guard to secure him with swords, and he was preserved from the test of the little myrmidons [troops] which issued out to attack him; but he was so frightened that he beshit himself most fearfully.

¶ At Oxford (and I do believe the like at Cambridge) the rod was frequently used by the tutors and deans on their pupils, till (they were) bachelors of arts; even gentle commoners. One Dr I knew (Dr Hannibal Potter, Trinity College, Oxford) right well that whipped his scholar with his sword by his side when he came to take his leave of him to go to the Inns of Court.

Robert Glover
1544–1588

Somerset herald and one of the greatest collectors of heraldic and genealogical material in the Elizabethan period.

I have heard Sir William Dugdale say that, thought Mr Camden had the name, yet Mr Glover was the best herald that did ever belong to the office. He took a great deal of pains in searching the antiquities of several counties. He wrote a most delicate hand and portrayed [drew] finely.

There is (or late was) at a coffee-house at the upper end of Bell Yard (or Shire Lane) in his own hand, a visitation of Cheshire, a most curious piece, which Sir William Dugdale wished one to see; and he told me that at York, at some ordinary house (I think a house of entertainment) he saw a similar elaborate piece on Yorkshire. But several counties he surveyed, and that with great exactness, but after his death they were all scattered abroad, and fell into ignorant hands.

Jonathan Goddard
1617–1675

Physician to Oliver Cromwell, and warden of Merton College during the Commonwealth. He was on the council of the Royal Society from its foundation in 1663.

Jonathan Goddard, MD, born at Greenwich (or Rochester, where his father commonly lived; but to my best remembrance, he told me at the former). His father was a ship-carpenter.

He was of Magdalen Hall, Oxford. He was one of the College of Physicians in London; Warden of Merton College, Oxford during the Commonwealth; physician to Oliver Cromwell, protector; went with him into Ireland. Enquire if not also sent to him into Scotland, when he was so dangerously ill there of a kind of high fever, which made him mad that he pistolled one or two of his commanders that came to visit him in his delirious rage.

He was professor of medicine at Gresham College; where he lived and had his laboratory for chemistry. He was an admirable chemist.

He had three or four medicines wherewith he did all his cures; a great ingredient was serpent's root. From Mr Michael Weeks, who looked after his stills.

He intended to have left his library and papers to the Royal Society, had he made his will, and had not died so suddenly. So that his books (a good collection) are fallen into the hands of a sister's son, a scholar at Caius College, Cambridge. But his papers are in the hand of Sir John Bankes, fellow of the Royal Society. There were his lectures at Surgeons' Hall; and two manuscripts, thick volumes, ready for the press. One was a kind of Pharmacopoeia (his nephew has this). 'Tis possible his invaluable universal medicines aforesaid might be retrieved amongst his papers. My Lord Brouncker has the recipe but will not impart it.

He was fellow of the Royal Society, and a zealous member for the improvement of natural knowledge amongst them. They made him their drudge, for when any curious experiment was to be done they would lay the task on him.

He loved wine and was most curious in his wines; was hospitable; but drank not to excess; but it happened that coming from his club at the Crown tavern in Bloomsbury, on foot, eleven o'clock at night, he fell down dead of an apoplexy in Cheapside, at Wood Street End, March 24, Anno Domini 1675, age 56.

Thomas Goffe
1591–1629

Goffe's reputation was as an orator and playwright rather than poet; three of his plays survive.

Thomas Goffe the poet was rector here; his wife, it seems, was not so kind. His wife pretended to fall in love with him, by hearing of him preach: upon which said one Thomas Thimble (one of the esquire beadles in Oxford [a university officer] and his confidant) to him: 'Do not marry her: if thou dost, she will break thy heart.' He was not obsequious [did not follow] to his friend's sober advice, but for her sake altered his condition, and cast anchor here. One time some of his Oxford friends made a visit to him; she looked upon them with an ill eye, as if they had come to eat her out of her house and home (as they say); she provided a dish of milk and some eggs for supper and nothing more. They perceived her niggardliness, and that her husband was inwardly troubled at it, (she wearing the breeches) so they were resolved to be merry at supper, and talk all in Latin, and laughed exceedingly. She was so vexed at their speaking Latin, that she could not hold, but fell out a-weeping, and rose from the table. The next day, Mr Goffe ordered a better dinner for them, and sent for some wine: they were merry, and his friends took their final leave of him. 'Twas no long time before this *Xantippe*★ made Mr Thimble's prediction good: and when he died the last words he spoke were: 'Oracle, oracle, Tom Thimble,' and so he gave up the ghost.

John Graunt
1620–1674

One of the first students of statistics.

He was born at the Seven Stars in Burchin Lane, London, in the parish of St Michael's, Cornwall. He wrote *Observations on the bills of mortality* very ingeniously (but I believe, and partly know, that he had his hint from his intimate and familiar friend Sir William Petty), to which he made some *Additions*, since printed. And he intended, had he lived, to have written more on the subject.

He wrote also some *Observations on the advance of excise*, not printed; ask his widow for them.

To give him his due praise, he was a very ingenious and studious person, and generally beloved, and rose early in the morning to his study before shoptime. He understood Latin and French. He was a pleasant facetious companion, and very hospitable.

He was brought up (as the fashion then was) in the Puritan way; wrote shorthand dextrously; and after many years constant hearing and writing sermon notes, he fell to buying and reading of the best Socinian books, and for several years continued of that opinion. At last he turned a Roman Catholic; of which religion he died a great zealot.

He was admitted a fellow of the Royal Society, about 1663.

He went bankrupt. He had one son, a man, who died in Persia; one daughter, a nun at, I think, Ghent. His widow yet alive.

He was by trade a haberdasher of small wares, but was freeman of the drapers' company. A man generally beloved; a faithful friend.

★Socrates's wife, legendary for her ill-treatment of her husband. *Ed.*

Often chosen for his prudence and justness to be an arbitrator; and he was a great peacemaker. He had an excellent working head, and was very facetious and fluent in his conversation.

He had gone through all the offices of the city so far as common council man. He was a common council man for two years. Captain of the trained band, several years; major of it, two or three years, and then laid down trade and all other public employment for his religion, being a Roman Catholic.

He was my honoured and worthy friend – God have mercy on his soul, Amen. His death is lamented by all good men that had the happiness to know him; and a great number of ingenious persons attended him to his grave. Among others, with tears, was that ingenious great virtuoso, Sir William Petty, his old and intimate acquaintance, who was sometime a student at Brasenose College.

Edward Gunter
1581–1626

Captain Ralph Greatorex, mathematical instrument maker in London, said that he was the first that brought quadrant, sector, and cross-staff; did open men's understandings and made young men in love with that study. Before, the mathematical sciences were locked up in the Greek and Latin tongues and so lay untouched, kept safe in some libraries. After Mr Gunter published his book, these sciences sprang up amain, more and more to that height it is at now (1690).

When he was a student at Christ Church, it fell to his lot to preach the Good Friday sermon, which some old divines that I knew did hear, but they said that 'twas said of him then in the University that our Saviour never suffered so much since his passion as in that sermon, it was such a lamentable one –

we cannot all do all things.

The world is much indebted to him for what he has done well.

Gunter is originally a Brecknockshire family, of Tregunter. They came thither under the conduct of Sir Bernard Newmarch, when he made the conquest of that county (Camden says). 'Aubrey, Gunter, Waldbeof, Harvard, Pichard' (which is falsely expressed in all Mr Camden's books as Prichard, which is nonsense).

Francis Hall
1595–1675

Professor of Hebrew and mathematics at the Jesuit college at Liège. He was in England from 1656–1672 as a missionary priest.

Father Franciscus Linus, i.e. Hall, was born in London – which Captain Robert Pugh, SJ, assured me, who was his acquaintance.

He was of the Society of Jesus and lived most at Liège, where he died.

He wrote a learned discourse, on colours, which Sir Kenelm Digby quotes with much praise in his philosophy.

He printed a discourse of sundials in quarto, Latin, and made the Jesuits' College there the finest dials in the world, which are described in that book. The like dials he made (which resemble something a branch of candlesticks) in the garden at Whitehall which were one night, in 1674 (as I take it), broken all to pieces (for they were of glass spheres) by the Earl of Rochester, Lord Buckhurst, Fleetwood Sheperd, etc., coming in from their revels. 'What!' said the Earl of Rochester, 'dost thou stand here to tell time?' Dash, they fell to work. There was a watchman always stood there to guard it.

He wrote a piece of philosophy in Latin in octavo, called . . .

He had great skill in the optics, and was an excellent philosopher and mathematician, and a person of exceeding suavity, goodness and piety, insomuch that I have heard Father Manners, SJ, say that he deserved canonisation.

Memorandum: he wrote a little tract, about half a sheet or not much more, of Transubstantiation, proving it metaphysically and by natural reason – which I have seen.

Thomas Hariot
1560–1621

Mathematician, astronomer and explorer

Sir Robert Moray (from Francis Stuart) declared at the Royal Society – 'twas when the comet appeared before the Dutch war – that Sir Francis had heard Mr Hariot say that he had seen nine comets, and predicted seven of them, but did not tell them how. 'Tis very strange; let the astronomers work it out.

Mr Hariot went with Sir Walter Raleigh into Virginia, and has written the Description of Virginia which is since printed in Mr Purchas's Pilgrims.

Dr Pell tells me that he finds among his papers (which are now, 1684, in Dr Busby's hands) an alphabet he had contrived for the American language, like devils.★

When Henry Percy, ninth Earl of Northumberland and Sir Walter Raleigh were both prisoners in the Tower, they grew acquainted, and Sir Walter Raleigh recommended Mr Hariot to him, and the earl settled an annuity of two hundred pounds a year on him for life, which he enjoyed. But to Hues (who wrote *On the Use of Globes*) and to Mr Warner, he gave an annuity of but sixty pounds per annum. These three were usually called '*the Earl of Northumberland's three Magi*'. They had a table at the earl's expense, and the earl himself had them to converse with, singly or together.

★ Andrew Clark noted in his edition of 1898: 'Perhaps because the letters ended in tridents' (like devils' traditional pitchforks). *Ed.*

He was a great acquaintance of Master Ailsbury, to whom Dr Corbet sent a letter in verse, December 9, 1618, when the great blazing star appeared:

> Now for the peace of Gods and men advise,
> (Thou that hast wherewithal to make us wise),
> Thine own rich studies, and deep Harriot's mine,
> In which there is no dross, but all refine.

The Bishop of Salisbury (Seth Ward) told me that one Mr Haggar (a fellow-countryman of his), a gentleman and a good mathematician, was well acquainted with Mr Thomas Hariot, and was wont to say, that he did not like (or valued not) the old story of the Creation of the World. He could not believe that old position; he would say 'Nothing is made out of nothing.' But, Mr Haggar, a nothing killed him at last; for in the top of his nose came a little red speck (exceeding small) which grew bigger and bigger, and at last killed him. I suppose it was that which surgeons call a *noli me tangere*.

He made a philosophical theology, wherein he cast off the Old Testament, and then the New one would (consequently) have no foundation. He was a Deist. His doctrine he taught to Sir Walter Raleigh, Henry, Earl of Northumberland, and some others. The divines of those times looked on his manner of death as a judgement upon him for valuing the Scripture at nothing.

Richard Head
?1637–?1686

Mr Meriton – his true name was Head. Mr Bovey knew him. He was a bookseller in Little Britain (in London).

He had been amongst the gipsies. He looked like a knave with his goggling eyes. He could transform himself into any shape. Went bankrupt two or three times. Was at last a bookseller, or towards his later end. He maintained himself by scribbling. He was paid 20s. per [printed] sheet. He wrote several pieces, viz *The English Rogue, The Art of Wheedling* etc.

He was drowned going to Plymouth by the long sea route about 1676, being about fifty years of age.

William Herbert, 3rd Earl of Pembroke
1580–1630

Courtier, poet, patron of the arts and supporter of several expeditions to America. He was banished from the court by Elizabeth for seducing one of her ladies. The first Folio of Shakespeare's works is dedicated to him and his brother Philip.

His nativity was calculated by old Mr Thomas Allen: his death was foretold, which happened true at the time foretold. Being well in health, he made a feast; ate and drank plentifully; went to bed; and found dead in the morning.

He was a most magnificent and brave peer, and loved learned men. He was a poet. There is a little book which contains his wife's and Sir Benjamin Rudyer's (verses) who was his friend and contemporary.

¶ As I remember he was Lord High Steward of his majesty's Household, Justice in Eyre of all his majesty's Forests, etc. on this side Trent, Chancellor of the University of Oxford, one of his majesty's Privy Council, and Knight of the Garter. He was a most noble person, and the glory of the court in the reigns of King James and King Charles. He was handsome, and of an admirable presence. He was the greatest Maecenas [patron] to learned men of any peer of his time or since. He was very generous and open handed. He gave a noble collection of choice books and manuscripts to the Bodleian Library at Oxford, which remain there as an honourable monument of his munificence. 'Twas thought, had he not been suddenly snatched away by death, to the grief of all learned and good men, that he would have been a great benefactor to Pembroke College in Oxford, whereas there remains only from him a great piece of plate that he gave there. His lordship was learned, and a poet; there are yet remaining some of his lordship's poetry in a little book of poems written by his lordship and Sir Benjamin Rudyer. He had his nativity calculated by a learned astrologer, and died exactly according to the time predicted therein, at his house at Baynard's Castle in London. He was very well in health, but because of the fatal direction which he lay under, he made a great entertainment (a supper) for his friends, and died in his sleep, April 10, 1630.

He was of an heroic and public spirit, bountiful to his friends and servants, and a great encourager of learned men.

John Heydon
1629–?

From Elias Ashmole esq.: he had the book called *The way to bliss* from his adoptive father Backhouse at Swallowfield in Berkshire, a manuscript written in Queen Elizabeth's time, hand and style anonymous.

Mr Heydon married Nicholas Culpepper's widow, and lights there (among Culpepper's papers) on the aforesaid manuscript, and prints a book with a great deal of *The way to bliss* word for word, and verses that are printed in the commendation of other books; and instead of such and such old philosophers (named in the MS) he puts down John Barker's and William Lilly's name, which they never heard of; and is so impudent in one of his books since as to say Mr Ashmole borrowed of him.

Nicholas Hill
1570–?1610

This Nicholas Hill was one of the most learned men of his time: a great mathematician and philosopher and traveller, and a poet. His writings had the usual fate of those not printed in the author's lifetime. He was so eminent for knowledge that he was the favourite of the great Earl of Oxford★, who had him to accompany him on his travels (he was his steward), which were so splendid that he kept at Florence a greater court than the Grand Duke. This earl spent in travelling the inheritance of ten or twelve thousand pounds per annum.

Old Serjeant Hoskins (the poet, grandfather to the present Sir John Hoskins, baronet, my honoured friend) knew him (was well acquainted with him) by which means I have this tradition which otherwise had been lost.

I fancy this his picture (i.e. head) is at the end of the Long Gallery of pictures at Wilton; it has the most philosophical aspect that I have seen, very much of Mr T. Hobbes of Malmesbury, but rather in the antique fashion. 'Tis pity that in noblemen's galleries the names are not written on, or behind, the pictures.

★'Twas that Earl of Oxford that let the f . . . before Queen Elizabeth; whereupon he travelled.

In his travels with his lord (I forget whether in Italy or Germany, but I think the former) a poor man begged him a penny. 'A penny!' said Mr Hill, 'what do you say to ten pounds?' 'Ah, ten pounds,' said the beggar, 'that would make a man happy.' Mr Hill gave him immediately £10, and put it down in the accounts: 'Item, to a beggar, ten pounds, to make him happy.'

Mr Thomas Henshaw bought from Nicholas Hill's widow, in Bow Lane, some of his books; among which is a manuscript *On the Infinity and Eternity of the World*. He finds by his writings that he was (or leaning) a Roman Catholic. Mr Henshaw believes he died about 1610; he died an old man. He flourished in Queen Elizabeth's time. I will search the register at Bow.

I have searched the register at Bow, where I did not find Nicholas Hill.

Hugh Holland
d. 1633

From Sir John Penrudock: Hugh Holland, poet: he was descended of the family of the earls of Kent, etc., and was a Roman Catholic. The Lady Elizabeth Hatton (mother to the Lady Purbeck) was his great patroness (see Ben Jonson's masque of the Gipsies for these two beauties).

Sir J.P. asked him his advice as he was dying (or he then gave it) that, the best rule for him to govern his life was to read St Jerome's Epistles.

He was of a Lancashire family.

Philemon Holland
1552–1637

He is best known for his translations of Pliny, Suetonius and of William Camden's Britannia.

Philemon Holland was schoolmaster of the free school at Coventry, and that for many years. He made a great many good scholars. He translated Livy with one and the same pen, which the Lady (see at the end of his translation of Suetonius) embellished with silver, and kept amongst her rare pieces (heirlooms). He wrote a good hand, but a rare Greek character; witness the manuscript of Euclid's *Harmonics* in the library belonging to the school. He translated several Latin authors, e.g. Livy, Pliny's *Natural History*, Suetonius Tranquillus.

One made this epigram on him:

> Philemon with 's translations doeth so fill us
> He will not let Suetonius be Tranquillus.

Robert Hooke
1635–1703

Aubrey's life needs little additional explanation: Hooke was probably the best experimental scientist among the first Fellows of the Royal Society, and certainly one of the most wide-ranging of the 'philosophers'.

Mr Robert Hooke, curator of the Royal Society at London, was born at Freshwater in the Isle of Wight; his father was minister there, and of the family of the Hookes of Hooke in Hants, in the road from London to Salisbury, a very ancient family and in that place for many (three or more) hundred years. His father, Mr John Hooke, had two or three brothers, all ministers.

John Hoskyns, the painter, being at Freshwater, to draw pictures, Mr Hooke* observed what he did, and, thought he, 'Why cannot I do so too?' So he gets him chalk, and red ochre, and coal, and grinds them, and puts them on a trencher [flat wooden plate] got a pencil, and to work he went, and made a picture: then he copied (as they hung up in the parlour) the pictures there, which he made like. Also, being a boy there, at Freshwater, he made a sundial on a round trencher; never having had any instruction. His father was not mathematical at all.

When his father died, his son Robert was but 13 years old, to whom he left one hundred pounds, which was sent up to London with him, with an intention to have him bound to Mr Lely† the painter, with whom he was a little while upon trial; who liked him very well, but

---

* This episode refers to Hooke's boyhood: Aubrey meant to give his age, but left a blank for it to be inserted later. *Ed.*

† i.e. Sir Peter Lely. *Ed.*

Mr Hooke quickly perceived what was to be done, so, thought he, 'why cannot I do this by myself and keep my hundred pounds?' He also had some instructions in drawing from Mr Samuel Cooper (prince of portrait painters of this age); but whether from him before or after Mr Lely, query?

Query when he went to Mr Busby's the schoolmaster of Westminster, at whose house he was; and he made very much of him. With him he lodged his hundred pounds. There he learned to play twenty lessons on the organ. He there in one week's time made himself master of the first six books of Euclid, to the admiration of Mr Busby (now doctor of theology), who introduced him. At school here he was very mechanical, and (amongst other things) he invented thirty different ways of flying, which I have not only heard him say but also Dr Wilkins (at Wadham College at that time), who gave him his *Mathematical Magic*, which did him a great kindness. He was never a King's Scholar [i.e. at Westminster School] and I have heard Sir Richard Knight (who was his schoolfellow) say that he seldom saw him in the school.

In 1658 he was sent to Christ Church in Oxford, where he had a chorister's place (in those days when the church music was put down*), which was a pretty good maintenance. He was there assistant to Dr Thomas Willis in his chemistry; who afterwards recommended him to the honourable Robert Boyle esq., to be useful to him in his chemical operations. Mr Hooke then read to him (i.e. Robert Boyle) Euclid's *Elements* and made him understand Descartes's philosophy.

In 1662 Mr Robert Boyle recommended Mr Robert Hooke to be Curator of the experiments of the Royal Society, wherein he did an admirable good work to the commonwealth of learning in recommending the fittest person in the world to them. In 1664 he was chosen geometry professor at Gresham College. Sir John Cutler, knight, endowed a lecture on mechanics, which he read.

In 1666 the great conflagration of London happened, and then he was chosen one of the two surveyors of the city of London; by which he has got a great estate. He built Bedlam, the Physician's College, Montagu House, the Monument on Fish Street Hill, and Theatre there; and he is much made use of in designing buildings.

He is but of middling stature, something crooked, pale faced, and his face but little below, but his head is large; his eye full and popping, and not quick; a grey eye. He has a delicate head of hair, brown, and of an excellent moist curl. He is and ever was very temperate, and moderate in diet etc.

* i.e. suppressed under the Commonwealth. *Ed.*

As he is of a prodigious inventive head, so he is a person of great virtue and goodness. Now when I have said his inventive faculty is so great, you cannot imagine his memory to be excellent, for they are like two buckets, as one goes up, the other goes down. He is certainly the greatest expert on mechanics this day in the world. His head lies much more to geometry than to arithmetic. He is a bachelor, and, I believe, will never marry. His elder brother left one fair daughter, which is his heir. In fine, (which crowns all) he is a person of great suavity and goodness.

It was Mr Robert Hooke that invented the pendulum watches, so much more useful than the other watches.

He has invented an engine for the speedy working out of division, etc. or the speedy and immediate finding out of the divisor.

(From a letter to Anthony Wood):* About nine or ten years ago, Mr Hooke wrote to Mr Isaac Newton of Trinity College, Cambridge, to make a demonstration of this theory (of gravity), not telling him, at first, the proportion of the gravity to the distance, nor what was the curved line that was thereby made. Mr Newton, in his answer to this letter, did express that he had not known of it; and in his first attempt about it, he calculated the curve by supposing the attraction to be the same at all distances: upon which, Mr Hooke sent, in his next letter, the whole of his hypothesis, that is, that the gravitation was reciprocal to the square of the distance . . . which is the whole celestial theory, concerning which Mr Newton has a demonstration, not at all owning he received the first intimation of it from Mr Hooke. Likewise Mr Newton has in the same book printed some other theories and experiments of Mr Hooke's, as that about the oval figure of the earth and sea: without acknowledging from whom he had them. . . .

Mr Wood! This is the greatest discovery in nature that ever was since the world's creation. It never was so much as hinted by any man before. I know you will do him right. I hope you may read his hand. I wish he had written plainer and afforded a little more paper.

Yours
J. Aubrey

Before I leave this town, I will get of him a catalogue of what he has written; and as much of his inventions as I can. But there are many hundreds; he believes not fewer than a thousand. It is such a hard matter to get people to do themselves right.

* The letter was corrected by Robert Hooke, and some of his technical details have been omitted.

John Hoskyns
1566–1638

John Hoskyns, serjeant-at-law, was born at Monnington in the
county of Hereford. Monnington belonged to the priory of Llantony
near Gloucester, where his ancestors had the office of cupbearer (or
'pocillator') to the prior. I have heard there was a window given by
one Hoskyns there, as by the inscription did appear.

Whether the serjeant were the eldest brother or no, I have
forgotten; but he had a brother, John, DD, a learned man, rector of
Ledbury and canon of Hereford, who, I think, was eldest, who was
designed to be a scholar, but this John (the serjeant) would not be
quiet, but he must be a scholar too. In those days boys were seldom
taught to read that were not to be of some learned profession. So,
upon his insistence, being then ten years of age, he learned to read,
and, at the year's end, entered into his Greek grammar. This I have
heard his son, Sir Benet Hoskyns, knight and baronet, several times
say. Charles Hoskyns was brother to the serjeant and the doctor, a
very ingenious man, who would not have been inferior to either, but
killed himself with hard study.

He was of a strong constitution, and had a prodigious memory. He
went to Winchester school, where he was the flower of his time. I
remember I have heard that one time he had not made his exercise
[verse] and spoke to one of his form to show him his, which he saw.
The schoolmaster presently calls for the exercises, and Hoskyns told
him that he had written it out but lost it, but he could repeat it, and
repeated the other boy's exercise (I think twelve or sixteen verses)
having read them once only. When the boy who really had made
them showed the master the same, and could not repeat them he was
whipped for stealing Hoskyns's exercise. I think John Owen and he
were schoolfellows. There were many pretty stories of him when a
schoolboy, which I have forgotten. I have heard his son say that he
was a year at Westminster; and not doing well there, he was sent to
Winchester.

The Latin verses in the quadrangle at Winchester College, at the
taps where the boys wash their hands, were of his making, where
there is the picture of a good servant, with hind's feet, asses' ears, a
padlock on his lips etc. The Latin verses describe the properties of a
good servant.

When he came to New College, he was *Terrae filius*;★ but he was so
bitterly satirical that he was expelled and put to his shifts.

★ i.e. he had to make an amusing, traditionally satirical, speech on graduation day.
Ed.

He went into Somersetshire and taught a school for about a year at Ilchester. He compiled there a Greek lexicon as far as M, which I have seen. He married (near there) a rich widow; she was a Moyle of Kent; by whom he had only one son and one daughter.

After his marriage, he admitted himself at the Middle Temple. He wore good clothes and kept good company. His excellent wit gave him letters of commendation to all ingenious persons. At his first coming to London, he got acquainted with the under-secretaries at court, where he was often useful to them in writing their Latin letters.

His great wit quickly made him be taken notice of. Ben Jonson called him 'father'. Sir Benet (Bishop Bennet of Hereford was his godfather) told me that one time desiring Mr Jonson to adopt him for his son, 'No,' said he, 'I dare not; it is honour enough for me to be your brother: I was your father's son, and it was he that polished me.' In short, his acquaintances were all the wits about the town; e.g. Sir Walter Raleigh, who was his fellow-prisoner in the Tower, where he was Sir Walter's Aristarchus to review and polish Sir Walter's style; John Donne, DD; John Owen; Marbyn, recorder of London; Sir Benjamin Rudyer, with whom it was once his fortune to have a quarrel and fought a duel with him and hurt him in the knee, but they were afterwards friends again; Sir Henry Wotton, provost of Eton College; and many others.

His conversation was exceedingly pleasant, and on the road he would make anyone good company to him. He was a great master of the Latin and Greek language; a great divine. He understood the law well, but he was worst at that.

His verses on the fart in the Parliament house are printed in some of the *Drolleries*. He had a book of poems neatly written by one of his clerks, bigger than Dr Donne's poems, which his son Benet lent to he knows not who, about 1653, and could never hear of it since. Mr Thomas Henshaw has an excellent Latin copy of the rhyme in the praise of ale of his.

He was a very strong man and active. He did the pomado* in the saddle of the horse in his armour, (which Sir John Hoskyns has still) before William, Earl of Pembroke. He was about my height.

He had a pretty ready wit, and would make verses on the road, where he was the best company in the world. In Sir H. Wotton's *Remaynes* are verses (dialogue) made on the road by him and Sir Henry. He made an anthem in English to be sung at Hereford Minster at the assizes; but Sir Robert Harley (a great Puritan) was much offended at it. He made the epitaph on Woodgate in New College

* A vault over the horse, done by placing one hand on the pommel of the saddle. *Ed.*

cloisters. He made the best Latin epitaphs of his time; amongst many others an excellent one on Finch, the Earl of Winchelsea's grandfather, who has a noble monument at Eastwell in Kent.

Besides his excellent natural memory, he acquired the artificial way of memory.

He wrote his own life (which his grandson Sir John Hoskyns, knight and baronet, has) which was to show that whereas Plutarch etc had written the lives of many generals, etc, grandees, that he, or an active man might, from a private fortune by his wit and industry attain to the dignity of a serjeant at law. But he should have said that they must have qualities like his too. This life I cannot borrow.

He was a close prisoner in the Tower, in King James's time, for speaking too boldly in the Parliament house of the king's profuse liberality to the Scots. He made a comparison of a conduit, whereunto water came, and ran out afar off. 'Now,' said he, 'this pipe reaches as far as Edinburgh.' He was kept a 'close prisoner' there, i.e. his windows were boarded up. Through a small chink he once saw a crow, and another time, a kite; the sight whereof, he said, was a great pleasure to him. He, with much ado, obtained at length the favour to have his little son Benet to be with him; and he then made a Latin distich, thus Englished by him:

> My little Ben, whil'st thou art young,
> And know'st not how to rule thy tongue,
> Make it thy slave whil'st thou art free,
> Least it, as mine, imprison thee.

I have heard that when he came out of the Tower, his crest was granted him, viz, 'a lion's head couped or, breathing fire'. The serjeant would say jocosely that it was the only lion's head in England that took tobacco.

Not many months before his death (being at the assizes sessions at Hereford) a massive country fellow trod on his toe, which caused a gangrene which was the cause of his death. One Mr Dighton★ of Gloucester (an experienced surgeon who had formerly been surgeon in the wars in Ireland) was sent for to cure him; but his skill and care could not save him. His toes were first cut off. The minister of his parish had a club foot or feet, I think his name was Hugh. Said he, 'Sir Hugh', – after his toes were cut off – 'I must be acquainted with your shoemaker.'

★ Mr Dighton would oftentimes say that he generally observed in the Irish wars that those men that went to their wenches the day before the battle either did die upon the spot or came under his hands. The finger of God!

Sir Robert Bye, attorney of the court of wards, was his neighbour, but there was no great goodwill between them – Sir Robert was haughty. He happened to die on Christmas Day: the news being brought to the serjeant, said he, 'The devil has a Christmas pie.'

He was a very strong man and valiant, and an early riser in the morning (that is at four in the morning). He was black-eyed and had black hair.

He lies buried under an altar monument on the north side of the choir of Dore Abbey in Herefordshire.

(In this abbey church of Dore are two *frustum*'s or remainders of mailed and cross-legged monuments, one said to be of a Lord Chandos, the other, the lord of Ewyas Lacy. A little before I saw them a mower had taken one of the arms to whet his scythe.)

He was wont to say that all that came to London were either carrion or crows.

Charles Howard

Near this place the honourable Charles Howard of Norfolk has very ingeniously contrived a long hope, (i.e. according to Virgil, 'a secluded valley') in the most pleasant and delightful solitude for house, gardens, orchards, boscages, etc., that I have seen in England: it deserves a poem, and was a subject worthy of Mr Cowley's muse. The true name of this hope is Dibden (almost Deep Dene).

Mr Howard has cast this hope into the form of a theatre, on the sides whereof he has made several narrow walks, like the seats of a theatre, one above another above six in number, done with a plough, which are bordered with thyme, and some cherry trees, myrtles, etc. Here was a great many orange-trees and syringas, which were then in flower. In this garden are twenty-one sorts of thyme. The pit (as I may call it) is stored full of rare flowers and choice plants. He has there two pretty lads, his gardeners, who wonderfully delight in their occupation, and this lovely solitude, and do enjoy themselves so innocently in that pleasant corner, as if they were out of this troublesome world, and seem to live as in the state of innocency.

In the hill on the left hand (being sandy ground) is a cave digged 36 paces long, 4 broad, and 5 yards high, and at about two thirds of the hill, (where the crook or bowing is) he has dug another subterranean walk or passage, to be pierced through the hill; through which (as through a tube) you have the vista over all the south part of Surrey and Sussex to the sea. The south side of this hill is converted into a vineyard of many acres of ground, which faces the south and southwest. The vaulting, or upper part of those caves, are not made semicircular, but parabolical, which is the strongest figure for bearing, and which sandy ground naturally falls into, and then stands: and thus we may see, that the conies (by instruct of nature) make their holes so. Here are caves for beer etc.

On the west side of this garden is a little building, which is (as I remember) divided into a laboratory and a neat oratory, by Mr Howard. Above the hill, on this west side is a thicket of black cherry-trees, with those walks, and the ground abounds with strawberries. The house was not made for grandeur, but retirement, (a noble hermitage) neat, elegant, and suitable to the modesty and solitude of the proprietor, a Christian philosopher, who in this iron age lives up to that of primitive times. Here Mr Newman (his steward) gave me a very civil entertainment, according to his master's order; where the pleasure of the garden, etc., were so ravishing, that I can never expect any enjoyment beyond it, but the kingdom of heaven. It is an agreeable surprise to the stranger, that neither house or garden can be discovered till you come just to it, as if it squatted down to hide itself.

Here are no ornaments of statuary or carver; but the beauty of the design and topiary speak for itself, and needs no addition out of the quarries. In short, it is an epitome of paradise, and the Garden of Eden seems well imitated here.

Edward Hyde, Earl of Clarendon

Charles II's most trusted councillor from 1651 to 1667. He was disgraced in 1667, and ended his life in exile. The History of the Rebellion *was eventually published in 1702–4.*

I think I told you that the present Earl of Clarendon told me his father was writing the history of our late times. He begins with King Charles I and brought it to the restoration of King Charles II, when, as

he was writing, the pen fell out of his hand: he took it up again to write: it fell out again. So then he perceived he was attacked by death, that is, the dead palsy [a stroke]. They say it is very well done; but his son will not print it.

Henry Isaacson
1581–1654

Mr Henry Isaacson was secretary to Lancelot Andrewes, Lord Bishop of Westminster.

Memorandum: Bourman, Doctor of Divinity, of Kingston upon Thames, did know Mr Isaacson, and told me that he was a learned man, which I easily believed when I heard he was secretary to that learned prelate, who made use of none but for merit. The doctor told me that when he presented his *Chronology* to his majesty King Charles the First, it was in the matted gallery in Whitehall.* The king presently discerned the purpose of the treatise, and turned to his own birth: said the king, 'Here's one lie to begin with.' It seems that Mr Isaacson had taken it out of a foreigner, who used the other account.† Poor Mr Isaacson was so ashamed at this unlucky encounter, that he immediately sneaked away and stayed not for praise or reward, both which perhaps he might have had, for his majesty was well pleased with it. He wrote several little books besides his *Chronology*. He was of Pembroke Hall in Cambridge. He was there about Master of Arts standing.

Dr Jaquinto

Physician to the Pope, then to King James. He went into the marshes of Essex, where they put their sheep to cure them of the rot, where he lived sometimes purposely to observe what plants the sheep did eat, of which herbs he made his medicine for the consumption, which Mr Edmund Wyld has.

George Johnson

It pleased God at Whitsuntide last to bereave me of a dear, useful and faithful friend, Mr Johnson who had the reversion of the place of Master of the Rolls;‡ who generously, for friendship and neighbour-hood sake (we were born the same week and within four miles and educated together) gave me the grant to be one of his secretaries – which place is worth £500 per annum. He was a strong lusty man and died of a malignant fever, infected by the Earl of Abingdon's brother, making of his will. It was such an opportunity that I shall never have the like again.

Mr Vere Bertie§ was his chamber-fellow (at the Inner Temple) in 1655, the wintertime, which was his rise.

---

* It was presented in an ill hour. An astrologer would give something to know *that day and hour*. He wanted a good election [i.e. choice of an astrologically favourable moment].

† i.e. the Gregorian, not the Julian calendar. The Gregorian calender was only adopted in England in 1752, by which time there was a difference of eleven days between English and Continental reckoning. *Ed.*

‡ He would have succeeded to the office on the death of the then holder. *Ed.*

§ Later Justice of the Common Pleas, and Baron of the Exchequer. *Ed.*

Inigo Jones
1573–1652

*The greatest architect of the period and designer of the sets and costumes for
many of the masques of the Stuart court.*

Inigo Jones' monument – this tomb is on the north side of the church,
but his body lies in the chancel about the middle. The inscription
mentions that he built the banqueting house and the portico at (old) St
Paul's. Mr Marshall in Fetter Lane took away the bust here to his
house, which see. Ask Mr Oliver about this.

    Mr Oliver, the city surveyor, has all his papers and designs, not
only of St Paul's Cathedral etc. and the banqueting house, but his
design of all Whitehall, in the same style as the Banqueting House; a
rare thing, which see.

    Memorandum: Mr Emanuel De Critz (sergeant painter to King
Charles I) told me in 1649, that the *catafalque* of King James at his
funeral (which is a kind of bed of state erected in Westminster Abbey,
as Robert, Earl of Essex, had, Oliver Cromwell and General Monck)

was very ingeniously designed by Mr Inigo Jones, and that he made the four heads of the caryatids (which bore up the canopy) of plaster of paris, and made the drapery of them of white calico, which was very handsome and cheap, and showed as well as if they had been cut out of white marble.

Ludolph van Keulen
1554?–1610

Ludolph van Keulen was first, by profession, a fencing-master; but becoming deaf, he betook himself to the study of the mathematics wherein he became famous.

He wrote a learned book, of the proportion of the diameter of a circle to the periphery: before which is his picture, and round about it in the compartment are swords and bucklers and halberds etc. – weapons: the reason whereof I understood not until Dr John Pell gave the aforesaid account, who had it from Sir Francis Godolphin, who had been his scholar as to fencing and boarded at his house.

Richard Knollys
1550?–1610

Knollys' General History of the Turks, *published in 1603, was very popular, and his style was praised by Dr Johnson for its clarity.*

The author of the *Battle of Lepanto* was hanged at Tyburn; he was reduced to such necessity.

The Lord Burleigh, when he read Knollys' Turkish history, was particularly extremely pleased at the description of the battle of Lepanto; sent for Knollys, who told him that an ingenious young man came to him, hearing what he was about, and desired that he might write that, having been in that action. I think he has taught in a school near Sandwich.

My lord hunted after him, and traced him from place to place, and at last to Newgate. He was hanged but a fortnight before. He unluckily lost a good opportunity of being preferred – from Mr Smyth, Magdalen College.

William Lee
d. 1610?

Mr William Lee, MA, was of Oxford (I think, Magdalen Hall). He was the first inventor of the weaving of stockings by an engine of his contrivance. He was a Sussex man born, or else lived there. He was a poor curate, and observing how much pains his wife took in knitting a pair of stockings, he bought a stocking and a half, and observed the contrivance of the stitch, which he designed in his loom, which (though some of the instruments attached to the engine be altered) keeps the same to this day. He went into France, and there died before his loom was made there. So the art was, not long since, in no part of the world but England. Oliver (Cromwell, the) Protector made an act that it should be felony to transport this engine overseas. See Stowe's Chronicle and Baker's Chronicle, if any mention of it. This information I took from a weaver (by this engine) in Pear-pool Lane, 1656. Sir John Hoskyns, Mr Stafford Tundale and I went purposely to see it.

William Lilly
1602–1681

'The last of the astrologers', Lilly's almanacs reached a wide public, though even in his lifetime his claims to be a serious scientific investigator were frequently attacked.

He was born on May Day 1601; had he lived till next May he had been full fourscore (eighty). He settled his estate at Hersham, £200 per annum, on the son of the Lord Commissioner Whitlocke (who was his great patron).

He wrote his own life very largely, which Elias Ashmole Esq., has. Memorandum: he predicted the great comet which appeared in 1680 in his almanac 1677, which was the last that he wrote himself with his own hands; for afterwards he fell blind. Memorandum: to bind up the almanac aforesaid with other octavo pamphlets, for 'tis exceeding considerable.

Sir Matthew Lister
1571?–1656

Sir Matthew Lister was born at Thornton in Craven in Yorkshire. His nephew Martin Lister, MD, FRS, from whose mouth I have this information, tells me he was of Oriel College in Oxford; he thinks he was a fellow.

He built that stately house at Ampthill in Bedfordshire (now the Earl of Aylesbury's). He sent for the architects from Italy.

He died at Burwell near Louth in Lincolnshire about 1656 or 1657, aged 92 years.

He was physician to Queen Anne (queen of King James). See the list of the names of the physicians before *The London Dispensatory*; as I remember, he was then president of the Physicians' College in London.

He printed nothing that Dr Martin Lister knows of (Sir Matthew Lister bred him up).

Mr Wyld says Sir Matthew Lister built the house (Ampthill) for Mary, Countess of Pembroke. He was her surveyor, and managed her estate. The seat at Ampthill is now in the possession of the Earl of Aylesbury, whose grandfather (the Earl of Elgin) bought it of the Countess of Pembroke. That he was president of the Physicians' College appears by the dedication of *The London Dispensatory* to him, being then president.

Sir James Long
1617–1692

A Wiltshire neighbour of Aubrey's. His career as a royalist colonel was chequered.

Sir James Long, baronet: I should now be both orator and soldier to give this honoured friend of mine 'a gentleman absolute in all numbers', his due character.

Only son of Sir W. Long; born at South Wraxhall in Wilts. Westminster scholar; of Magdalene College, Oxford; Fisher there. Went to France. Married Dorothy Leich, a most elegant beauty and wit, daughter of Sir E. Leich, aged 25. In the civil wars, colonel of horse in Sir F. Dodington's brigade. Good sword-man; horseman; admirable extempore orator for a harangue; great memory; great historian and romancer; great falconer and for horsemanship; for insects; exceeding curious and searching long since, in natural things.

Oliver, Protector, hawking at Hounslow heath, discoursing with him fell in love with his company, and commanded him to wear his sword, and to meet him a-hawking, which made the strict cavaliers look on him with an evil eye.

He wrote 'History and Causes of the Civil War' or 'Reflections' (enquire); 'Examination of witches at Malmesbury'.

¶ My honoured and faithful friend Colonel James Long of Draycot, since baronet, was wont to spend a week or two every autumn at Avebury in hawking, where several times I have had the happiness to accompany him. Our sport was very good, and in a romantic country, that is, the prospects noble and vast, the downs stocked with numerous flocks of sheep, the turf rich and fragrant with thyme and burnet. Nor are the nut-brown shepherdesses without their graces. But the flight of the falcon was but a parenthesis to the colonel's facetious discourse, who was as much the son of Mercury as of Mars; and the Muses did accompany him with his hawks and spaniels.

Henry Lyte
1529?–1607

A distant connection of Aubrey's, whose mother's father was a Lyte. His work as an antiquary was mostly on the fabulous history of Britain; he also translated an important book on plants.

I will enquire at Lyte's Cary when Henry Lyte, esq., died. He translated Dodantus' *Herbal*, and wrote a little pamphlet, which I have, called '*The Light of Britaine*, being a short summary of the old English history', dedicated to Queen Elizabeth.

He began the genealogy of King James, derived from Brute; which his eldest son Thomas Lyte, of Lyte's Cary aforesaid, finished, and presented to King James. It is most rarely done and exquisitely limned by a miniature painter – all the king's pictures etc. King James, after it had hung some time at Whitehall, ordered him to have it again and to get it engraved, which was done. Mr Humble of Pope's-Head Alley had the plates before the fire: I hope they are not lost – it is most curiously done by Hole. It is as big as the greatest map of England that ever I saw.

T. Lyte wrote the best print hand that ever yet I saw. The original, which is now in the parlour at Lyte's Cary, was written with his hand, and painted by a famous artist.

Richard Martin
1570–1618

Wit and orator, friend of several poets of the period.

Insert his picture which I sent to Mr A. Wood.

He was of the ancient family of the Martins of Athelminston in the county of Dorset, a very fair seat. The name was lost about fifty years since by a daughter and heiress, who was married to Mr Bruen, who had a daughter and heiress married to Sir Ralph Banks, who sold it to Sir Robert Long (1668). In the church are several noble monuments. Their crest is an ape; men used to say 'a Martin ape'.

'In Queen Elizabeth's time, one Penry of Wales wrote a book* called *Martin Mar-prelate*, on which there was this epigram:

> Martin the ape, the drunk and the mad,
> The three Martins are whose works we have had.
> If a fourth Martin comes after Martins so evil,
> He can be no man, he must be a devil.)

He was a very handsome man, a graceful speaker, facetious and well beloved. I think he died of a merry symposiac [drinking party].

He was recorder but [only for] a month before his death.

¶ Ben Jonson dedicates his comedy called the Poetaster to him:

'A thankful man owes a courtesy ever, the unthankful but when he needs. For whose innocence, as for the author's, you were once a noble and timely undertaker to the greatest justice of this kingdom.'

Died of a symposiac excess with his fellow wits. Was not recorder above quarter of a year: ask Sir John Hoskyns.

Nicholas Mercator
1640–87

Mathematician and expert on algebra and calculus.

Mr Nicholas Mercator: Philip Melancthon was his great-grand-mother's brother.

He is of little stature, perfect; black hair, of a delicate moist curl; dark eye, but of great vivacity of spirit. He is of a soft temper, of great

---

* He was hanged for it. He was kin to my great-grandfather.

temperance (he loves Venus a little): of a prodigious invention, and will be acquainted (familiarly) with nobody. His true German name is Nicolas Kauffman, i.e. Chapman, i.e. Mercator.

Memorandum: Mr Nicholas Mercator made and presented to King Charles II a clock ('twas of a foot diameter) which showed the inequality of the sun's motion from the apparent motion, which the king did understand by his informations, and did commend it, but he never had a penny of him for it.

Well! This curious clock was neglected, and somebody of the court happened to become master of it, who understood it not, he sold it to Mr Knibb, a watchmaker, who did not understand it neither, who sold it to Mr Fromanteel (that made it) for £5, who asks now (1683) for it £200.

In February 1682, Mr N. Mercator left London; went with his family to Paris, being invited thither by Monseigneur Colbert.

Thomas Merry
d. 1682

Thomas Merry esq., was born in Leicestershire. His father or grandfather was one of the clerks of the greencloth.

He was disciple to Sir Jonas Moore; became an excellent accountant. He had done all Euclid in a shorter and clearer manner than ever was yet done, and particularly the tenth book: I have seen it. But he never bound it; and after his death, when I came to enquire for it, it was disparted like the Sibylline books, and several of the papers lost. I got what I could find and brought them to the Royal Society, where they were committed to Mr Paget to peruse, but they were so imperfect (he said) they were not fit to be printed. What is become of them now God knows.

Sir Robert Moray
d. 1673

A founder-member of the Royal Society. His career was almost entirely abroad, until the Restoration, when he settled in London. Pepys called him 'a most excellent man of reason and learning, and understands the doctrine of music, and everything else I could discourse of, very finely.'

Sir Robert Moray, knight: he was of the ancient family of the Morays in Scotland. He was born, as I take it, in the Highlands. The Highlanders, (like the Swedes) can make their own clothes; and I have heard Sir Robert say that he could do it.

He spent most of his time in France. After his juvenile education at school and the University he betook himself to military employment in the service of Louis XIII. He was at last lieutenant-colonel. He was a great master of the Latin tongue and was very well read. They say he was an excellent soldier.

He was far from the rough humour of the camp breeding, for he was a person the most obliging about the court and the only man that would do a kindness *gratis* upon an account of friendship. A lackey could not have been more obsequious and diligent. What I do now aver I know to be true upon my own score as well as others. He was a most humble and good man, and as free from covetousness as a Carthusian. He was abstemious and abhorred women. His majesty was wont to tease at him. 'Twas pity he was a Presbyterian.

He was the chief support of his countrymen and their good angel. There had been formerly a great friendship between him and the Duke of Lauderdale, till, about a year or two before his death, he went to the duke on his return from Scotland and told him plainly he had betrayed his country.

He was one of the first contrivers and institutors of the Royal Society and was our first president, and performed his charge in the chair very well.

He was my most honoured and obliging friend, and I was more obliged to him than to all the courtiers besides. I had a great loss in his death, for had he lived, he would have got some employment or other for me before this time. He had the king's ear as much as anyone, and was indefatigable in his undertakings. I was often with him. I was with him three hours the morning he died; he seemed to be well enough. I remember he drank at least half a pint of fair water, according to his usual custom.

His lodging where he died was the leaded pavilion in the garden at Whitehall. He died suddenly July 4 about 8 pm, 1673. He had but one shilling in his pocket, i.e. in all. The king paid for his burial. He lies by Sir William Davenant in Westminster Abbey. He was a good chemist and assisted his majesty in his chemical operations.

Lancelot Morehouse
d. 1672

Mr Lancelot Morehouse, minister of Pertwood (£40 per annum), about six miles from Kilmanton, a very learned man, and a solid and profound mathematician, wrote against Mr Francis Potter's book of 666, and falls upon him, for that 25 is not the true root, but the approximate root; to which Mr Potter replied with some sharpness, and that it ought not to be the true root, for this agrees better with his purpose. The manuscript pro and con Mr Morehouse gave to Seth Ward, Bishop of Salisbury, 1668; together with a MS in folio in French of alliances between the king of England and the king of France, and a prophecy concerning England, curiously written in Latin verse, one sheet in quarto, which he rescued from the tailor's shears.

Mr Morehouse (of Cambridge) is dead and left his many excellent mathematical notes to his ingenious friend John Gaunt of Hindon.

He wrote on squaring the circle; wherein is a great deal of wit and learning; but at last Dr Davenant (his neighbour) convinced him of his paralogism. I would have it printed (for it is learnedly done) to show where and how great wits may err and be deceived.

He was a man of very searching wit, and indefatigable at solving a question, as I have heard Dr Edward Davenant oftentimes say.

He was either of Clare Hall or King's College. Westmoreland by birth, curate at Chalke to Mr Walker. He was preferred by Bishop Hinchman to Little Langford, where he died about 1672.

Cardinal Morton
1410–1500

In my last I gave you some memoirs of Cardinal Morton, and that the tradition of the country people in Dorset, when I was a schoolboy there at Blandford, was that he was a shoemaker's son of Bere in the same country: but Sir William Dugdale says 'by no means I must put in writing hearsays'.

Dr Thomas Mouffet
1553–1604

Doctor of medicine and expert on insects. He was persuaded to come to Wilton by Mary Herbert who arranged a pension for him.

Dr Mouffet lived in his later time at Bulbridge (at the west end of Wilton – it belongs to the Earl of Pembroke) at the manor-house there, which is a fair old-built house. This Bulbridge is adjoining to Wilton: the river only parts it.

At this place he died and lies buried at Wilton. The Earl of Pembroke's steward told me that he finds by the old books and accounts that a pension was paid him yearly. He was one of the learnedest physicians of that age. He wrote a book in Latin on insects which Dr John Pell told me (inquire) heretofore was first begun by a friar.

Robert Murray
1635–?1725

Murray wrote on trade and banking practice, and is said to have had the idea for a penny post in 1679.

Mr Robert Murray is a citizen of London, a milliner, of the company of clothworkers. His father a Scotchman; mother, English. Born in the Strand, 1633, December.

The penny-post was set up in 1680, our Lady day (March 25), being Friday, a most ingenious and useful project. Invented by Mr Murray first, and then Mr Dockwra joined with him. It was set up February 1680.

Mr Murray was formerly clerk to the general company for the revenue of Ireland, and afterwards clerk to the committee of the grand excise of England; and was the first that invented and introduced into this city the club of commerce consisting of one of each trade, whereof there were after very many erected and are still continued in this city. ★And also continued and set up the office or bank of credit at Devonshire house in Bishopsgate Street without, where men depositing their goods and merchandise were furnished with bills of current credit on two-thirds or three-quarters of the

---

★ What follows is not in Aubrey's hand. *Ed.*

value of the said goods answering to the intrinsic value for money, whereby the deficiency of coin might be fully supplied: and for rendering the same current, a certain or competent number of traders (viz. ten or twenty of each trade, whereof there be five hundred several trades within the city) were to be associated or formed into such a society or company of traders as might amongst them complete the whole body of commerce, whereby any possessed of the said current credit might be furnished among themselves with any kind of goods as effectually as for money could do elsewhere.

Sir William Neale
1609–1691

'Scout-master', i.e. commander of the scouts responsible for discovering the enemy's whereabouts, in Prince Rupert's army.

Sir William Neale, knight, scout-master general to King Charles the First, died on the 24th of March last, 1691, in Grays Inn Lane, being 81 years old. When he died, he was the oldest field-officer of King Charles the First.

He was not less than six foot high: very beautiful in youth. I remember him: and of great courage, but a great plunderer and cruel.

He lived in town ever since the Popish Plot (1679), and that worthy generous gentleman Edmund Wyld Esq, was much supporting to him. His mother and Sir William were cousins german. But for these five years last past his gouts etc. emaciated him extremely: so that he did often put me in mind of that of Ovid, *Metamorphoses* (xv, 229):

> Milo, grown old, weeps to see those arms hanging limp and thin, whose massive knotted muscles once rivalled those of Hercules.

He died penitent.

He was the grandson of ... Neale, Esq of Wollaston near Northampton, who married one of Sir Edmund Conquest's sisters, of Houghton Conquest, Bedfordshire. Sir Francis Clarke of Houghton Conquest aforesaid (father of Mr Edmund Wyld's mother, a daughter and heir) married another sister of Sir Edmund Conquest.

Sir William married Major-General Egerton's sister, by whom he had issue, William, a lusty stout fellow, of the guards, who died about the abdication (1688), and two daughters.

John Newton
1622–1678

Dr Newton, now parson of Ross in Herefordshire, told me that he was of St Edmund's Hall: yet living and likely to live, for when his stomach is out of order, he cures himself by eating a piece of hot roast beef off the spit.

¶ Dr J. Newton: he told me he was born in Bedfordshire, but would not tell me where.

¶ He was against learning of Latin in a mathematical school.

John Norden
1548–1625

Surveyor and topographer. He projected a series of histories of the counties of England, of which Middlesex and Hertfordshire were published, and five others completed in manuscript. The maps he made in connection with this work are of the greatest historical value; he was the first English mapmaker to include roads.

John Norden – from Mr Bagford, a good antiquary, Mr Crump's acquaintance.

He lived at Fulham, and (perhaps) died there.

He made maps of Middlesex, Herefordshire, Surrey, and Hampshire, and also Cornwall; and he did not only make the maps aforesaid but has written descriptions of them, which Mr Bagford has. The description of Cornwall (I think) was not printed; but Dr Gale of Paul's School has it in manuscript, which N.B.

Mr Morgan, the herald painter, gives us an account in his *Armorie*, that he had, in his custody, Kent, Essex, Isle of Man, Isle of Wight, and Hampshire.

In the end of Mr Gregory's posthumous works, he gives us an account of the excellency of Mr Norden's maps, and Saxton's too.

His dialogues I have, printed first, 1610; dedicated to Cecil, Earl of Salisbury, whose servant he was, (I suppose) steward or surveyor.

Sometime or other I will look into the church at Fulham; he died ('tis thought) in King James the first's reign.

Mr Wood! pray add this to the rest of the lives.

Roger North
?1585–?1652

North accompanied Raleigh on his ill-fated Guiana expedition of 1618, and in 1627 established a plantation in Guiana. He was forced to return to England for a lawsuit, and the plantation failed in his absence.

Captain Roger North was brother to Lord North. He was a great acquaintance of Sir Walter Raleigh's and accompanied him in his voyages. He was with him at Guiana, and never heard that word but he would fall into a passion for the miscarriage of that action.

He was a great algebrist, which was rare in those days; but he had the acquaintance of his fellow-traveller Mr Hariot.

He was a most accomplished gentleman.

He died in Fleet Street about 1656 or 1657.

He had excellent collections and remarks of his voyages, which were all unfortunately burnt in Fleet Street at the great conflagration of the city (1666) – from Sir Francis North, Lord Chief Justice of the Common Pleas, his nephew, and Edmund Wyld, esq., who knew him very well.

He died about the time of the fire (?); enquire again.

This family speaks not well of Sir Walter Raleigh, that Sir Walter designed to break with the Spaniard, and to make himself popular in England. When he came to (Guiana?) he could not show them where the mines of gold were. He would have then gone to the King of France (Louis XIII) but his own men brought him back.

Capt. North: enquire if of Oxford: I think of University College.

Mr Thomas North, that translated Plutarch's Lives (my lord chief justice tells me) was great-uncle to his grandfather.

Richard Norwood
?1590–1675

A teacher of mathematics and surveyor, who was involved in the early settlement of the Bermudas; he lived there at intervals from 1640 onwards.

Mr Richard Norwood: whence he was born I cannot yet learn.

Norwood is an ancient family: about three hundred years since St Low married with a daughter and heir of them and quarters the coat. They flourish still in Gloucestershire, the manor of Lakehampton belonging to them. – 'Tis probable that this learned Norwood was of that county.

He at his own charge, measured with a chain from Berwick to Christ Church (he says he came up in ten or eleven days) in order to the finding the quantity of a degree, and so the circumference of the earth and sea in our known measures – July 1 1636.

By a letter from Nicholas, Earl of Thanet, to me, concerning his purchase in the Bermudas, not dated, but written about 1674 or 1675 – thus: 'as to old Mr Norwood, to whom the Royal Society would send some queries, he is lately dead as his son informs me, who lately went captain in that ship wherein I sent my gardener and vines to the Bermudas. He was aged above 90.'

William Noy
1577–1634

Attorney-General from 1631–4

From Fabian Philips, esq.:

Mr Attorney-General Noy was a great lawyer and a great humorist. There is a world of merry stories of him.

He would play at span-counter★ with the tavern bar-boy.

A country clown asked for a good inn, and he bids him ride into Lincoln's Inn, and asked if his horse went to hay or to grass.

He caused the breeches of a bencher of Lincoln's Inn to be taken in by a tailor, and made him believe he had the dropsy.

One time he met accidentally with Butler, the famous physician of Cambridge, at the Earl of Suffolk's (Lord Treasurer). They were strangers to each other, and both walking in the gallery [waiting for audience]. Noy was wearied, and would be gone. Butler wanted to know his name. Noy had him to the Peacock Tavern in Thames Street and made him drunk all that day.

Another time Noy and Pine of Lincoln's Inn went afoot to Barnet with clubs in their hands, like country fellows. They went to the Red Lion Inn; the people of the house were afraid to trust them, fearing they might not pay.

★ 'A game in which the object of one player was to throw his counters so close to those of his opponent that the distance between them could be spanned with the hand.' (OED) Ed.

John Partridge
1644–1715

Partridge is best remembered as the subject of an attack by Swift, who published a mock-almanac similar to Partridge's own productions, in which he predicted Partridge's death on 29 March 1708. Swift then published a further pamphlet in which he announced the fulfilment of the prediction, including the following epitaph:

> *Here, five feet deep, lies on his back,*
> *A cobbler, starmonger and quack,*
> *Who to the stars in pure good will*
> *Does to his best look upward still:*
> *Weep, all you customers that use*
> *His pills, his almanacs or shoes.*

Partridge had the greatest difficulty in persuading the world at large that he was still alive.

John Partridge, astrologer, the son of (Mr) Partridge (yet living, 1680, an honest waterman at Putney in Surrey).

He was born, as by his scheme (of astrological signs) appears, January 18, 1644 in the latitude of London.

He was taught to read, and a little to write.

He was bound apprentice to a shoe-maker; where he was kept hard to his trade.

At 18 he got him a Lillie's grammar, and Goldman's dictionary, and a Latin bible, and Ovid's *Metamorphoses*.

He is of an excellent healthy constitution and great temperance, of indefatigable industry, and sleeps but (a few) hours.

In (a few) years he made himself a competent master of the Latin tongue, well enough to read any astrological book, and quickly became a master of that science. He then studied the Greek tongue, and also the Hebrew, to neither of which he is a stranger. He then studied good authors in physic, and intends to make that his profession and practice; but is yet (1680) a shoemaker in Covent Garden.

John Pell
1611–1685

Another of the Lives of the Mathematicians *projected by Aubrey; this is
an extensive example, corrected by Pell himself.*

John Pell was the son of John Pell, of Southwick in Sussex, in which
parish he was born, on St David's Day (March 1) 1610.

His father was a divine but a kind of Non-conformist; of the Pells
of Lincolnshire, an ancient family; his mother of the Hollands of
Kent. His father died when his son John was but five years old and six
weeks, and left him an excellent library.

He went to school at the free school at Steyning, a borough town in
Sussex, at the first founding of the school; an excellent schoolmaster,
John Jeffreys. At thirteen years and a quarter old he went as good a
scholar to Cambridge, to Trinity College, as most Masters of Arts in
the University (he understood Latin, Greek and Hebrew), so that he
played not much (one must imagine) with his schoolfellows, for,
when they had play-days, or after school time, he spent his time in the
library aforesaid.

He never stood at any election of fellows or scholars (of the House
at) Trinity College.

Of a person he was very handsome, and of a very strong and
excellent habit of body, melancholic, sanguine, dark brown hair with
an excellent moist curl.

Before he went first out of England he understood these languages
(besides his mother tongue), viz. Latin, Greek, Hebrew, Arabic,
Italian, French, Spanish, German and Dutch.

In 1632 he married Ithamara Reginalds, second daughter to Mr
Henry Reginalds of London. He had by her four sons and four
daughters.

Dr Pell has said to me that he did believe that he solved some
questions (not without God's help).

In 1643 he went to Amsterdam, in December; was there Professor
of Mathematics, next after Martinus Hortensius, about two years.

1646, the Prince of Orange called for him to be public professor of
philosophy and mathematics at the High School at Breda, that was
founded that year by his highness; see the doctor's inaugural oration
there.

He returned into England, 1652.

In 1654, Oliver, Lord Protector, sent him [as] envoy to the
Protestant cantons of Switzerland; he resided chiefly at Zurich. He

was sent out with the title of legate but afterwards he had order to continue there with the title of Resident.

In 1658, he returned into England and so little before the death of Oliver Cromwell that he never saw him since he was Protector.

Memorandum: when he took his leave from Zurich, June 23, 1658, he made a Latin speech, which I have seen.

Memorandum: that in his negotation he did no disservice to King Charles II, nor to the church, as may appear by his letters which are in the Secretary of State's office.

¶ Richard Cromwell, Protector, did not fully pay him for his business in Piedmont, whereby he was in some want; and so when King Charles II was restored, Dr Sanderson, Bishop of Lincoln, persuaded him to take Holy Orders. He was not adroit for preaching.

¶ When King Charles II had been at home ten months, Mr John Pell first took orders. He was made deacon upon the last of March, 1661, by Bishop Sanderson of Lincoln, by whom he was made priest in June following.

Gilbert Sheldon, Bishop of London, procured for him the parsonage of Fobbing in Essex, 1661, and two years after (1663) gave him the parsonage of Laindon with the attached chapel of Bartlesdon in the same county, which benefices are in the infamous and unhealthy feverish hundreds of Essex.

Mr Edward Waller on the death of the countess of Warwick:

> Curst be alreadie those Essexian plaines
> Where ... Death and Horrour reignes. – etc.

At Fobbing seven curates died within the first ten years; in sixteen years, six of these that had been his curates at Laindon are dead; besides these that went away from both places; and the death of his wife, servants and grandchildren.

Gilbert Sheldon being made Archbishop of Canterbury, 1663, John Pell was made one of his Cambridge★ chaplains; and complaining one day to his Grace at Lambeth of the unhealthiness of his benefice as abovesaid, said my lord, 'I do not intend that you shall live there.' 'No,' said Doctor Pell, 'I shall die there.'

Now by this time (1680) you doubt not but this great, learned man, famous both at home and abroad, has obtained some considerable dignity in the church. You ought not in modesty to guess at less than a deanery. – Why, truly, he is staked to this poor preferment still. For though the parishes are large, yet (curates, etc. paid for) he clears not above three score pound (£60) per annum (hardly fourscore) and

★ He (the archbishop) has two Oxford chaplains and two Cambridge.

lives in an obscure lodging, three stories high, in Jermyn Street, next to the sign of the ship, wanting not only books but his own MSS which are many. Many of them are at Brereton at my Lord Brereton's in Cheshire.

Memorandum: Lord Brereton was sent to Breda to receive the instruction of this worthy person by his grandfather (George Goring, the Earl of Norwich) in 1647, where he stayed for some years, where he became a good practitioner, especially in algebra to which his genius most inclined him and which he used to his dying day, which was 17 March 1680; lies buried in St Martin's church in-the-fields. I cannot but mention this noble lord but with a great deal of passion, for a more virtuous person (besides his great learning) I never knew. I have had the honour of his acquaintance since his coming from Breda into England. Never was there greater love between master and scholar than between Dr Pell and this scholar of his, whose death March 17, 1680 has deprived this worthy doctor of an ingenious companion and a useful friend.

Dr Pell has often said to me that when he solves a question he strains every nerve about him and that now in his old age it brings him to a looseness.

Dr J. Pell was the first inventor of that excellent way or method of the marginal working in algebra.

He could not cringe and sneak for preferment, though otherwise no man more humble nor more communicative. He was cast into King's Bench prison for debt September 7, 1680.

¶ In March 1682 he was very kindly invited by Daniel Whistler, MD, to live with him at the Physicians College in London, where he was very kindly entertained. About the middle of June he fell extremely sick of a cold and removed to a grandchild of his married to one Mr Hastings in St Margaret's Churchyard, Westminster, near the tower, who now (1684) lives in Browlow Street in Drury Lane, where he was almost burnt in his bed by a candle. November 26, fell into convulsion fits which had almost killed him.

¶ Gilbert Sheldon, Lord Bishop of London, gave Dr Pell the parsonage of Laindon cum Basildon in the hundreds of Essex (they call it *killpriest*, sarcastically); and King Charles the Second gave him the parsonage of Fobbing, four miles distant. Both are of the value of two hundred pounds per annum (or so accounted); but the Doctor was a most shiftless man as to worldly affairs, and his tenants and relations cheated him of the profits and kept him so indigent that he lacked necessaries, even paper and ink, and he had not sixpence in his purse when he died, and was buried by the charity of Dr Richard Busby and Dr Sharp, Rector of St Giles in the fields and Dean of

Norwich, who ordered his body to lie in a vault belonging to the rector (the price of vault-burial is £10).

I could not persuade him to make a will; so his books and MSS fell by administratorship to Captain Raven, his son-in-law.

His son (John) is a Justice of the Peace in New York and lives well. He intended to have gone over to him.

This learned person died in St Giles' parish aforesaid at the house of Mr Cothorne the reader in Dyot Street on Saturday December 12, 1685, between 4 and 5 pm. Dr Busby, schoolmaster of Westminster, bought all his books and papers of Captain Raven, among which is the last thing he wrote (which he did at my earnest request) viz. *The Tables*, which are according to his promise in the last line of his printed tables of squares and cubes (if desired) and which Sir Cyril Wych (then President of the Royal Society) did license for the press. There only wants a leaf or two for the explanation of the use of them, which his death has prevented. Sir Cyril Wych, only knows the use of them, viz. whereas some questions are capable of several answers, by the help of these tables it might be discovered how many, and no more, solutions, or answers, might be given.

I desired Mr Theodore Haake, his old acquaintance, to make some additions to this short collection of memoirs of him but he has done nothing.

He died of a broken heart.

Dr Whistler invited Dr Pell to his house in (1682), which the doctor liked and accepted of, loving good cheer and good liquor, which the other did also; where eating and drinking too much, was the cause of shortening his days.

Dr Pell had a brother, a surgeon and practitioner in physic, who purchased an estate of the natives of New York and when he died he left it to his nephew John Pell, only son of the Doctor. It is a great estate eight miles broad and – miles long (ask Capt Raven).

He had three or four daughters.

Fabian Philips
1601–1690

Fabian Philips – from himself, 1682, – born hard by Prestbury in Gloucestershire, in 1601, in September, on Michaelmas Eve. His mother's name was Bagehot (an heir to a younger brother); his father was Andrew Philips, of an ancient family in Herefordshire, seven descents [generations], who sold £600 per annum in Herefordshire, in Leominster; some of it his son Fabian (of whom I write) bought again. He was of the Middle Temple, London; a filizer [law officer] of London, Middlesex, Cambridgeshire and Huntingdonshire of great assiduity, and reading, and a great lover of antiquities. He has a great memory, which holds still well now in his eightieth year. He told me St Augustine wrote at 90; Judge Coke at 84; and Bishop Hall, of Norwich, at over 80. His house is over against the middle of Lincoln's Inn garden, in Chancery Lane. Two days before King Charles I was beheaded, he wrote 'a protestation against the intended murder of the king', and printed it, and caused it to be put upon the posts★. When all the courts in Westminster Hall were voted down by Barebones Parliament, he wrote a book to justify the right use of them, and Lenthall (the speaker) and the Keepers of the Liberty did send him thanks for saving of the courts.

He died the 17th of November 1690. His son will not pay for his father's epitaph to be set up. But I have spoken to his good daughter to set his name and date of death. His works 'will praise him in the gates'. [Proverbs xxxi, 31].

Old Fabian Philips has told me that it has cost him £800 in taking pains searching and writing to assert the king's prerogative and never got a groat. Only, when the regulation of the law was carried out, he was made one of the commissioners, which was worth £200 per annum – I think it lasted two years.

Sir William Platers
d. 1668

Sir William Platers, knight, was a Cambridgeshire (Suffolk) gentleman. He had a good estate (about £3000 per annum). He was a very well bred gentleman, as most was of these times; had travelled France, Italy, etc, and understood well these languages. He was one of the Long Parliament in the time of the late wars.

He was a great admirer and lover of handsome women, and kept several. Henry Martyn and he were great cronies, but one time (about 1644) there was some difference between them – Sir William had got away one of Henry's girls and Sir John Birkenhead inserted in the

---

★ Possibly hitching-posts in the streets. *Ed.*

Mercurius Aulicus⋆ how the saints fell out. He was temperate and thrifty as to all other things.

He had only one son, who was handsome and ingenious, and whom he cultivated with all imaginable care and education, and, knowing that he was flesh and blood, took care himself to provide sound and agreeable females for him. He allowed his son liberally, but enjoined him still temperance, and to set down his expenses.

The father was a good linguist and a good antiquary. This beloved son of his dying shortened his father's days. He built the triumphal-like arch whereon the king's arms is in the partition between church and chancel at St Margaret's Westminster.

¶ Sir William Platers, knight and baronet; about £5000 per annum. His son very ingenious, and made a very good return of his education. He was a colonel in the king's army and was killed in his service, which his father took so to heart that he enjoyed not himself afterwards.

Henry Martyn, his crony, invited him to a treat, where Sir William fell in love with one of his misses and enticed her away – which Sir John Birkenhead put in the *Mercurius Aulicus*.

¶ I do not enter him here as a worthy, but he does fill a place. He was a merry man in the reign of the Saints. *Mercurius Aulicus* made a good sport with him and Henry Martin.

Sir Robert Poyntz
1589–1665

Sir Robert Poyntz of Iron-Acton in Gloucestershire, Knight of the Bath, is the same family with Clifford (as may be seen by the pedigree), Clifford being called *de Pons* till he was lord of Clifford Castle in Herefordshire, adjoining to Breconshire.

In Henry III's reign they married with a daughter and heir of Acton, by whom they had the manor aforesaid and perhaps other lands.

Mr Player, Mr Anthony Ettrick's son-in-law, who bought this estate, June 1684, has all the old evidences and can further inform me.

¶ When I was sick of the smallpox at Trinity College, Mr Saul, who was an old servant of his, told me I think that he was of Lincoln (or, perhaps, that he lay there in the wars†).

The family have had a great estate, and were men of note at court.

⋆ The Royalist newspaper: see p. 33 above. *Ed.*
† During the Royalist occupation of Oxford. *Ed.*

¶ Sir Robert, son of Sir John, Poyntz of whom I now write, and with whom I had some small acquaintance, was a loyal, sober and a learned person. His study, law; chiefly towards the civil law. Since the king's restoration he published in print, a pamphlet, about the bigness of a good play-book, entitled, *The Right of Kings* (or to that purpose; but to my best remembrance, that is the very title.*).

As I remember he told me when I was of Trinity College, Oxford, that he was of Lincoln College. He married first Grisel, one of the daughters and co-heirs of Mr Gibbons, of Kent, by whom he had only two daughters.

After her decease he had a natural son by Cicely Smyth, who had been his lady's chambermaid, whose name was John, as I remember, who married the daughter of Mr Caesar, in Herefordshire. He died without issue about four or five years since (1684) or less. So there is an end of this ancient family.

Memorandum: Newark (now the seat of Sir Gabriel Lowe) was built by Sir Robert's grandfather to keep his whores in.

Sir Thomas Pope
?1507–1559

Privy councillor under Henry VIII; indirectly involved in the suppression of the monasteries. Trinity was established in the buildings of Durham College, which had belonged to the abbey of Durham.

Sir Thomas Pope, founder of Trinity College, Oxford, bought church lands† without money. His way was this. He contracted for them, and then at once sold long leases, for which he had great fines (premiums) and but a small rent. Those leases were expired in the reign of King James the first, and then the estate was worth £8000 per annum. He could have ridden in his own lands from Cogges (by Witney) to Banbury, about 18 miles.

I have a curious manuscript manual of Sir Thomas Pope, which if I so thought, would be chained in Trinity College library, I would give it there, but I know not how magistracy, etc. have altered somebody.‡

---

* In fact it was *A vindication of the monarchy* ... *Ed.*
† At the Dissolution of the monasteries, in the 1540s. *Ed.*
‡ A reference to Ralph Bathurst (President of Trinity), recently appointed vice-chancellor. *Ed.*

Francis Potter
1594–1678

Clergyman, inventor and Fellow of the Royal Society. He supplied Aubrey with much information on alchemy and on the supernatural, as well as with accounts of his inventions.

Mr Francis Potter's father was one of the benefactors to the organ at the cathedral church at Worcester.

Francis Potter, BD, born at Mere, a little market town in Wiltshire, 'upon Trinity Sunday eve 1594, in the evening.' 'In 1625, at 10 o'clock on December 10, the mystery of the Beast was discovered' – these words I found written in his Greek Testament. He told me the notion came into his mind as he was going up stairs into his chamber at Trinity College, which was the senior fellow's chamber then (he lay with his brother Dr Hannibal Potter): this chamber is now united to the President's lodgings.

¶ Mr Francis Potter BD was born at the vicarage house at Mere in the county of Wilts.

His father was minister there, and also of Kilmanton in Somerset about three miles distant, and was also a prebendary of the cathedral church of Worcester. He had three sons, Hannibal, Francis, and (another). His wife's name was Horsey, of the ancient and worshipful family of the Horseys of Clifton in Dorset.

He was taught his grammar learnings by Mr Bright (the famous schoolmaster of those times) of the school at Worcester.

At 15, he went to Trinity College in Oxford, where his father (who was an Oxfordshire man born) had been a fellow. His brother Hannibal was his tutor. Here he was a commoner twenty-seven years, and was senior to all the house but Dr Kettell and his brother.

His genius lay most of all to the mechanics; he had an admirable mechanical invention, but in that dark time wanted encouragement, and when his father died (which was about 1637) he succeeded him in the parsonage of Kilmanton, worth, per annum, about £140. He was from a boy given to drawing and painting. The founder's (Sir Thomas Pope's) picture in Trinity College hall is of his copying. He had excellent notions for the raising of water; I have heard him say, that he could raise the water at Worcester with less trouble, i.e. fewer [pumps?], than there are; and that he had never seen a water-house engine, but that he could invent a better. Kilmanton is on a high hill, and the parsonage well is extraordinarily deep. There is the most ingenious and useful bucket well that ever I saw. Now whereas some deep wells have wheels for men or dogs to go within them, here is a wheel with steps like stairs to walk on (outside the wheel) as if you were going up stairs, and an ordinary body's weight draws up a great bucket, which holds a barrel, and the two buckets are contrived so that their ropes always are perpendicular and consequently parallel, and so never interfere with one another. Now, this vast bucket would be too cumbersome to overturn, to pour out the water; and therefore he contrived a board with lifts about the sides, like a trough, to slide under the bucket when 'tis drawn up, and at the bottom of the bucket is a plug, the weight of the water jogging upon the sliding trough, the water pours out into the trough, and from thence runs into your pail, or other vessel. 'Tis extremely worth the seeing. I have taken heretofore a draught of it. I have heard him say that he would have undertaken to have brought up the water from the springs at the bottom of the hill to the town of Shaftesbury, which is on a waterless hill.

In 1625, going into his chamber, the notion of 25, the root of 666, for the root of the number of the Beast (in the Book of Revelation), came into his head; so he opposed 25 to 12, the root of 144.

When he took his degree of Bachelor in Divinity his question was *Whether the Pope was Anti-Christ*. He answered in the affirmative. In his younger years he was very apt to fall into a swoon, and so he did when he was disputing in the Divinity School upon that question. – I remember he told me that one time reading Aristotle, *On the Nature of Animals*, where he describes how that the lionesses, when great with young, and near time of parturition, do go between two trees that grow near together, and squeeze out their young ones out of their bellies; he had such a strong idea of this, and of the pain that the lioness was in, that he fell into a swoon.

He was of a very tender constitution, and sickly most of his younger years. His manner was, when he was beginning to be sick, to *breathe strongly* a good while together, which he said did emit the noxious vapours.

He was always much contemplative, and had an excellent philosophical head. He was no greatly read man; he had a competent knowledge in the Latin, Greek and Hebrew tongues, but not a critical. Greek he learned by Montanus' Interlineary Testament, after he was a man, without a grammar, and then he read Homer. He understood only common arithmetic, and never went farther in geometry than the first six books of Euclid; but he had such an inventive head, that with this foundation he was able to do great matters in the mechanics, and to solve phenomena in natural philosophy. He had but few books, which when he died were sold for fifty-six shillings, and surely no great bargain. He published nothing but his *Interpretation of the number 666*, printed at Oxford in 1642, which has been twice translated into Latin, into French, and other languages. He made that fine sun-dial with its furniture, on the north wall of the quadrangle at Trinity College, which he did by Samminitatus's book of sun-dialling (it has been gone since about 1670, and another is there put). He lived and died a bachelor. He was very hospitable, virtuous and temperate; and as I said before, very contemplative. He looked the most like a monk, or one of the pastors of the old time, that I ever saw one. He was pretty long visaged and pale clear skin, grey eye. His discourse was admirable, and all new and unvulgar. His house was as undecked as a monk's cell; yet he had there so many ingenious inventions that it was very delightful. He had a pretty contrived garden there, where are the finest box hedges that ever I saw. The garden is a good large square; the middle is a good high mount, all fortified (as you may say) and adorned with these hedges, which at the interstices have a high pillar (square cut) of box that shows very stately both summer and winter.

On the buttery-door in his parlour he drew his father's picture at length, with his book (foreshortened), and on the spectacles in his hand is the reflection of the Gothic south window. I mention this picture the rather, because in process of time it may be mistaken by translation for his son Francis's picture, author of the book aforesaid.

I never have enjoyed so much pleasure, nor ever been so much pleased with such philosophical and hearty entertainment as from him. His book was in the press at Oxford, and he there, when I was admitted of the College, but I had not the honour and happiness to be acquainted with him till 1649 (Epiphany), since which time I had close friendship with him to his death, and corresponded frequently with him. I have all his letters by me, which are very good, and I believe near 200, and most of them philosophical.

I have many good notes from him as to mechanics, etc., and I never was with him but I learned, and always took notes; but now indeed the Royal Society has outdone most of his things, as having a better apparatus, and more spare money. I have a curious design of his to draw a landscape or perspective (1656), but Sir Christopher Wren has fallen on the same principle, and the device is better worked. He was smith and carpenter enough to serve his turn, but he did not pretend to skill in each. He gave me a quadrant in copper, and made me another in silver, of his own projection, which serves for all latitudes. He showed me 1649, the best way of making an arch was a parabola with a chain; so he took off his girdle from his cassock, and applied it to the wall to demonstrate.

He invented and made with his own hands a pair of beam compasses, which will divide an inch into a hundred or a thousand parts. At one end of the beam is a roundel, which is divided into a hundred parts, with a centre bar to turn about it with a handle: this handle turns a screw of a very fine thread, and on the back of the sail or beam is a graduation. With these compasses he made the quadrants aforesaid. He gave me a pair of these compasses, which I showed to the Royal Society at their first institution, which they well liked, and I presented them as a rarity to my honoured friend, Edmund Wyld Esq.; there are but two of them in the world.

Memorandum: that at the Epiphany, 1649, when I was at his house, he then told me his notion of curing diseases, etc., by transfusion of blood* out of one man into another, and that the hint came into his head reflecting on Ovid's story of Medea and Jason,† and that this was a matter of ten years before that time. About a year after, he and I went to try the experiment, but 'twas on a hen, and the creature too little and our tools not good; I then sent him a surgeon's lancet. I received a letter from him concerning this subject, which many years since I showed, and was read and entered in the books of the Royal Society, for Dr Lower would have arrogated the invention to himself, and now one Griffith, doctor of physic, of Richmond, is publishing a book of the transfusion of the blood, and desires to insert Mr Potter's letter.

In 166– he was chosen fellow of the Royal Society, and was there admitted and received with much respect.

As he was never a strong man, so in his later times had his health best, only about four or five years before his death his eyesight was bad, and before he died quite lost.

Memorandum: he played at chess as well as most men. Col. Bishop, his contemporary at Trinity College, is accounted the best of England. I have heard Mr Potter say that they two have played at Trinity College (I think two days together) and neither got the mastery. Memorandum: he would say that he looked upon the play at chess as very fit to be learned and practised by young men, because it would make them to have a foresight and be of use to them (by consequence) in their ordering of human affairs. Which NB.

He has told me that he had oftentimes dreamt that he was at Rome,

---

* Memorandum: Mr Meredith Lloyd tells me that Libacius speaks of transfusion of blood, which I dare swear Mr F. Potter never saw in his life.

† In which Medea rejuvenates Jason's aged father Aeson by draining his blood and filling his veins with a magic potion (*Metamorphoses*, VII, 250 ff) *Ed.*

and being in fright that he should be seized on and brought before the Pope, did wake with the fear.★

'Twas pity that such a delicate inventive wit should be staked to a private preferment in an obscure corner (where he lacked ingenious conversation) from whence men rarely emerge to higher preferment, but contract a moss on them like an old fence in an orchard for want of ingenious conversation, which is a great want even to the deepest thinking men (as Mr Hobbes has often said to me).

The last time I saw this honoured friend of mine, October 1674. I had not seen him in three years before, and his shortsightedness then was come even to blindness, which did much grieve me to behold. He had let his beard be uncut, which was wont to be but little. I asked him why he did not get some kinswoman or kinsman of his to live with him, and look to him now in his great age? He answered me that he had tried that way, and found it not so well; for they did begrudge what he spent that was too much and went from them, whereas his servants (strangers) were kind to him and took care of him.

In the troublesome times 'twas his happiness never to be sequestered. He was once maliciously informed against to the Committee at Wells (a thing very common in those times). When he came before them, one of them, (I have forgotten his name) gave him a pint of wine, and gave him great praise, and bade him go home, and fear nothing.

Robert Pugh
1609–1679

Roman Catholic writer and pamphleteer

Captain Pugh, my acquaintance, a writer and a poet. Bred as a Jesuit; but turned out because he was a captain, viz. in the late wars.

He has a Latin poem, printed, which will be augmented; and printed a book against Dr Bates' *Review of recent motions.*

He was born of a good family in Penrhyn in North Wales. He was educated at St Omer. When his study was searched, his orders were there found, and also a letter from the queen-mother, whose

★ Pope . . . (against whom Robert Grosseteste, Bishop of Lincoln, wrote) dreamt that the bishop of Lincoln came to him, and gave him a great blow over the face with his staff.

confessor he had sometimes been, to the king, that, if he should fall into any danger of the law, upon sight of that letter, he should obtain his majesty's pardon.

My honoured friend, Captain Robert Pugh, died in Newgate on, January 22, 1679, Wednesday night, 12 o'clock.

He wrote a book, which is almost finished, 'Of the several states and governments which have been here since the troubles,' in the Earl of Castlemaine's hands.

All his books were seized on; amongst others his almanac, wherein he entered all the vices of Charles II, which was carried to the council board [the king's council of state]: but, as I have said, the Earl of Castlemaine has got the former-mentioned treatise.

William Radford
1623–1673

(*From a letter to Anthony Wood*) William Radford, my good friend and old acquaintance and fellow colleger, ended his days at Richmond, where he taught school, fourteen days since. I was with him when he first took [to] his bed.

And when I was sick of the smallpox at Trinity College, Oxford, he was so kind as to come to me everyday and spend several hours, or I think melancholy would have spoiled a scurvy antiquary. He was recounting not many days before he died your brother Ned's voyage and Mr Marriett's to London on foot.

Thomas Randolph
1605–1635

Poet and dramatist, protégé of Ben Jonson

Thomas Randolph, the poet, Cambridge: I have sent to A. Wood his nativity etc. which I had from his brother John, an attorney, viz. Thomas Randolph was the eldest son of William Randolph by his wife Elizabeth Smythe; he was born at Newnham near Daventry in Northamptonshire, June 15, 1605.

At the age of nine years, he wrote the history of our Saviour's incarnation in English verse, which his brother John has to show under his own handwriting – never printed, kept as a rarity.

From Mr Needler: his hair was of a very light flaxen (colour), almost white (like J. Scroope's). It was flaggy, as by his picture before his book appears. He was of a pale ill complexion and pock-pitten – from Mr Thomas Fludd, his schoolfellow at Westminster, who says he was of about my stature or scarce so tall.

His father was steward to Sir George Goring in Sussex. He had been very wild in his youth; and his father (i.e. grandfather to Thomas Randolph) left him but a groat or threepence in his will, which when he received he nailed to the post of the door. His father was a surveyor of land, i.e. a land measurer.

In 1623 he was elected to Trinity College in Cambridge.

He (once) encountered captain Stafford (an ingenious gentleman and the chief of his family, and out of which the great Duke of Buckingham branched [was descended]) on the road. He gave him a pension of I think £100 per annum, and he was tutor to his son and heir.

He was very precocious, and had he lived but a little longer would have outlived his fame.

He died in the twenty-eighth year of his age at Mr Stafford's, Blatherwycke, aforesaid.

Eleanor Radcliffe, Countess of Sussex
d. 1666

Countess of Sussex: a great and sad example of the power of lust and slavery of it. She was as great a beauty as any in England and had a good wit. After her lord's death (he was jealous) she sends for one formerly her footman, and makes him groom of the chamber. He had the pox and she knew it; a damnable sot. He was not very handsome, but his body of an exquisite shape (*hence the arrows [of love]*). His nostrils were stuffed and borne out with corks in which were quills to breath through. About 1666 this countess died of the pox.

Edmund Rich
?1170–1240

Edmund Rich was a teacher at Oxford and preacher before becoming Archbishop of Canterbury in 1234. His time as archbishop was troubled, and he died in exile in France. He was canonised in 1248, largely at the insistence of Louis IX of France.

Seth Ward, Lord Bishop of Salisbury, tells me that he finds Saint Edmund was born at Abingdon. He was Archbishop of Canterbury. He built the college at Salisbury, by St Edmund's church; it is now Judge Wyndham's son's house. He resigned his archbishopric and came and retired hither. In St Edmund's church here were windows of great value. Gondomar (the Spanish ambassador) offered a good sum for them; I have forgotten what. In one of them was the picture of God the Father, like an old man (as the fashion was) which much offended Mr Shervill, the recorder, who in zeal (but without knowledge) clambered up on the pews to break the window, and fell down and broke his leg (about 1629); but that did not excuse him for being questioned in the Star Chamber for it. Mr Attorney Noy was his great friend, and showed his friendship there. But what Mr Shervill left undone, the soldiers since have gone through with, that there is not a piece of glass-painting left.

Sir John Rocklington

Concerning furzecutters: Bryanston by Blandford in Dorset was, in Henry VIII's time, belonging to (Sir John, I think) Rocklington. He had a fair estate, and no child, and there was a poor cottager whose name was Rogers that had a pretty wife whom this knight did visit and had a mind to have a child by her. As he did suppose, he afterwards had; and in consideration of affection, etc, settled his whole estate on this young Rogers. William, Lord Marquis Hartford (Duke of Somerset), was son of the granddaughter of this Rogers.

This present Lord Roberts of Truro (now Earl of Radnor) his grandfather (or great-grandfather) was a furze cutter in Cornwall – which I have heard old parson Wodenote of Linkinhorne in Cornwall say many times.

Henry Rolle
?1589–1656

Lord Chief Justice under the Commonwealth from 1549 to 1556.

I remember about 1646 (or 1647) that Mr John Maynard (now Sir John, and serjeant) came into the Middle Temple hall, from Westminster Hall, weary with business, and hungry, when we had newly dined. He sat down by Mr Bennett Hoskyns (the only son of Serjeant Hoskyns the poet), since baronet, and some others; who having made an end of their commons, fell into various discourse, and what was the meaning of the text (Romans 5.7) 'For a just man one would dare to die; but for a good man one would willingly die.' They asked Mr Maynard what was the difference between a just man and a good man. He was beginning to eat, and cried: 'Ho! you have eaten your dinners and now have leisure to discourse; I have not.' He had eaten but a bite or two when he replied: 'I'll tell you the difference presently [at once]: Serjeant Rolle is a *just man*, and Matthew Hale is a *good man*'; and so fell to make an end of his dinner. And there could not be a better interpretation of this test. For Serjeant Rolle was just, but by nature penurious; and his wife made him worse: Matthew Hale was not only just, but wonderfully charitable and open-handed, and did not sound a trumpet neither, as the hypocrites do.

Laurence Rooke
1622–1662?

Founder-member of the Royal Society; professor of astronomy at Gresham College, London.

Laurence Rooke, born in Kent, was of (King's) College in Cambridge, a good mathematician and a very good man, an intimate friend of Dr Seth Ward (now lord bishop of Salisbury).

I have heard him read at Gresham College on the sixth chapter of Oughtred's *Key to Mathematics*, an excellent lecture: ask for his papers which the bishop of Salisbury hath.

He was a temperate man and of strong constitution, but took his sickness of which he died by sitting up often for astronomical observations. He lies buried in the church of St Benet Fink in London, near the Old Exchange.

His dear friend the bishop (then of Exeter) gave to the Royal Society a very fair pendulum clock, dedicated to Mr Rooke's memory.

Walter Rumsey
1584–1660

A successful barrister and later judge on the Welsh circuit until 1647, when he was dismissed by parliament. He was reappointed in 1660, but died the same year.

Walter Rumsey, of Lanover in Monmouthshire, esquire (born there) was of Oxford; afterwards of the society of Gray's Inn, where he was a bencher.

He was one of the judges in South Wales, viz. Caermarthen, Pembrokeshire, and Cardigan circuit. He was so excellent a lawyer, that he was called 'the picklock of the law'.

He was an ingenious man, and had a philosophical head; he was most curious for grafting, inoculating, and planting, and ponds. If he had any old dead plum tree, or apple-tree, he let them stand, and planted vines at the bottom, and let them climb up, and they would bear very well.

He was one of my counsel in my law-suits in Breconshire about the entail. He had a kindness for me and invited me to his house, and told me a great many fine things, both natural and antiquarian.

He was very polished, and a good musician, played on the organ and lute. He could compose.

He was much troubled with phlegm, and being so one winter at the court at Ludlow, (where he was one of the counsel), sitting by the fire, spitting and spawling, he took a fine tender sprig, and tied a rag at the end, and imagined he might put it down his throat, and fetch up the phlegm, and he did so. Afterwards he made this instrument of whalebone. I have oftentimes seen him use it. I could never make it go down my throat, but for those that can 'tis a most incomparable engine. If troubled with the wind it cures you immediately. It makes you vomit without any pain, and besides, the vomits of apothecaries have some poison in them. He wrote a little octavo book, of this way of medicine, called *The Compendium of Health*. I had a young fellow (Mark Collins), that was my servant, that used it incomparably, more easily than the judge; he made the instruments. In Wiltshire, among my things, are some of his making still. The judge said he never saw anyone use it so dexterously in his life. It is no pain, when down your throat; he would touch the bottom of his stomach with it.

John Rushworth
?1612–1690

Rushworth's Collections, *a history of parliamentary proceedings and the general events of the political history of England from the early seventeenth century until 1648, are a valuable if erratic source for the history of the Civil War. Rushworth was clerk-assistant to the House of Commons, and was closely associated with Sir Thomas Fairfax, but played little part in politics after the rise of Cromwell.*

'I was born in Northumberland, but my parents were both born in the county of York. The title of the books I wrote went by the name of *Historical Collections*; except *The Earl of Strafford's trial*, which I took with my own pen in characters at the time of his trial, which I have impartially published in folio. And I gave the first precedent of my method in writing and declaring only matter of fact in order of time, without observation or reflection: but Dr Nalson, a learned man, finds fault with me, but I leave it to posterity to judge.

'I being near of kin to Sir Thomas Fairfax, the parliament's general, he made choice of me to be his secretary in the wars, by which means I am better enabled to give account of military affairs, both in the first wars and in the second which happened in the year 1648 – all which I am now upon the perfecting the same, but the times favours not the coming forth of it.

'There is another thing which enables me the better to proceed with the work I am now upon, my intimacy with all the debates and passages in the house of Commons: for that house made choice of me to be assistant at the table to Mr Ellsing, clerk of that parliament to the house of Commons, by which means I was privy to all circumstances in their proceedings.

'I might particularly demonstrate more concernments of my own, as being with the King Charles the First at the camp at Berwick, at the great council at York, at Newborne near Newcastle upon the Scots invading of England, et cetera.

'Both the houses of parliament had the confidence in me that they sent by me their addresses to the king after he left the parliament and went to York. And so it fell out that I rode several times, with that expedition between London and York (being 150 miles) in 24 hours at a time.

'Sir, pardon my boy's ignorance in writing.

Jo. Rushworth

Southwark, July 21, 1687.'

Mr Rushworth tells me he is superannuated [out of date, i.e. out of touch with current affairs]. He has forgotten to put down the name of the place where [he was] born: as also that he was secretary to Sir Orlando Bridgeman, when Lord Keeper of the great seal, which was a considerable place.

(*From a letter to Anthony Wood*) Yesterday I saw Mr Rushworth: which was a great mortification. He has quite lost his memory with drinking brandy. Remembered nothing of you etc. His landlady wiped his nose like a child.

¶ John Rushworth, of Lincoln's Inn, esq., historian, died in the Rules Court Alley in Southwark, at the widow Bayley's house, a good woman and who was very careful and tendful of him, on Monday the twelfth day of May 1690. He was about 83, onwards to 84. He had no son, but three or four daughters, virtuous women: one is married to Sir Francis Vane in the north. He had forgotten his children before he died.

Richard Sackville, 3rd Earl of Dorset
1589–1624

Richard, Earl of Dorset (eldest son and heir to the Lord Treasurer): he lived in the greatest grandeur of any nobleman of his time in England. He had thirty gentlemen, and gave to each £50 per annum, besides keeping his horse. George Villiers (after, Duke of Buckingham) was a petitioner to have had a gentleman's place under him, and missed it, and within a twelvemonth was a greater man himself; but the duke ever after bore a grudge to the Earl of Dorset – from the Countess of Thanet.

Richard Sackville, 5th Earl of Dorset
1622–1677

Richard Sackville, Earl of Dorset, father of the present earl (Richard) – 'twas he that translated *The Cid*, a French comedy, into English, about 1640. It was Sam Butler told me that my lord of Dorset translated it.

Sam Butler (Hudibras) one time at the tavern said that 'twas *this* Earl of Dorset's father that translated the comedy called *The Cid*, written by Corneille. Methinks he should not be mistaken; but the world is mighty apt to it, you see.

He died in 1677. He was a fellow of the Royal Society. He married Frances Cranfield, daughter of the Earl of Middlesex, by whom he had several sons and daughters.

His eldest son is Richard, Earl of Dorset and Middlesex, a most noble lord and my most kind friend.

Robert Sanderson
1587–1663

Bishop of Lincoln and Regius Professor of Divinity at Oxford 1642–8 and 1660–3.

Dr Robert Sanderson, lord bishop of Lincoln, would confess to his intimate friends, that 'he studied and mastered only Tully's *Offices,*★ Thomas Aquinas's *Secunda Secundie*, and Aristotle's *Rhetoric*, and that all other books he read but cursorily': but he had forgotten, by his favour, to speak of Aristotle's Organon etc. [logic books], else he could never have compiled his own excellent *Logic*. – From Seth Ward, Bishop of Salisbury, and Pierson, Bishop of Chester. And Bishop Ward said that he would do the like were he to begin the world again.

He was a lover of music, and was wont to play on his bass viol, and also to sing to it. He was a lover of heraldry, and gave it in charge in his articles of enquiry; but the clergymen made him such a lamentable imperfect return that it signified nothing. The very parliamentarians reverenced him for his learning and his virtue, so that he always kept his living, which NB.

★ Harsenet, Archbishop of York, always carried it in his bosom.

He had no great memory, I am certain not a sure one; when I was a freshman and heard him read his first lecture, he made a mistake in the Lord's Prayer. He always read his sermons and lectures. Had his memory been greater, his judgement had been less: they are like two well-buckets.

In his *Logic*, he recommends disputation to young men, as the best exercise for young wits.

Sir William Saunderson
?1586–1676

Sir W. Saunderson: he did read and write to his dying day. Sir Christopher Wren said that as he wrote not well, so he wrote not ill. He died at Whitehall (I was then there): went out like a spent candle – died before Dr Holder could come to him with the sacrament.

Sylvanus Scory
c. 1540–1617

Sylvanus Scory (enquire if he was not knighted?) was the son and heir of Scory, Bishop of Hereford.

His father, John Scory, in the reign of Edward the Sixth, was bishop of Rochester, and translated from thence to Chichester, and afterwards to Hereford.

He was a very handsome gentleman, and had an excellent wit, and his father gave him the best education, both at home and beyond the seas, that that age would afford, and loved him so dearly that he fleeced the church of Hereford to leave him a good estate, and he did let such long, and so many leases, that, as Mrs Masters (daughter of Herbert Westphaling esq., eldest son and heir to Bishop Westphaling, of Hereford) told me, they were not out till about these 60 years. To my remembrance, she told me the estate left him was £1500 per annum, which he reduced to nothing (allowing himself the liberty to enjoy all the pleasures of this world), and left his son so poor, that when he came among gentlemen, they would fancy a crown or ten shillings for him.

I have heard Sir John Denham say (at Chalke, 1652) that he had been well informed that he was the most accomplished gentleman of his time. 'Tis a good testimonial of his worth, that Mr Benjamin Jonson (who ever scorned an unworthy patron) dedicated his ... to him. I have heard Sir John Denham also say that he was the greatest confidant and intimate favourite of Monsieur of France (brother to the French king), who was a suitor to Queen Elizabeth, and whom her majesty entirely loved (and as a signal of it one time at St Paul's Church, London, openly kissed him in time of divine service) and would have had him for her husband, but only for reasons of state. When her majesty dismissed him, 'twas done with all passion and respect imaginable. She gave him royal presents; he was attended to Dover by the flower of the courtiers; among others, by this spark of whom I now write. When Monsieur took his leave of him he told him that though 'twas so that her majesty could not marry him (as aforesaid), yet he knew that she so much loved him that she would not deny him any request, whereby he might honour and benefit a friend; and accordingly writes his love-letter to his mistress, the Queen of England, and in it only begs that single boon, to look upon Mr Scory, (the bearer) with a particular and extraordinary grace, for his sake; delivered him the letter (and as I take it, gave him a jewel). As Sylvanus returned to London, through Canterbury, the mayor there (a shoemaker), a pragmatical fellow, examined him, who and whence, etc. and what his business was, and if he had a pass? 'Yes,' quoth he, 'I have a pass,' and produces Monsieur's letter, superscribed to her majesty, which, one would have thought, had been enough to have shown. The mayor very fairly breaks open the love-letter, and reads it. I know not how, this action happened to take wind, and 'twas brought to court, and became so ridiculous that Sylvanus Scory was so laughed at and jeered that he never delivered the letter to the queen, which had been the easiest and most honourable step to preferment that mortal man could have desired.

Dorothy Selby

Most of the epitaphs quoted by Aubrey are verbose Latin affairs: this is a delightful exception.

From Mr Marshall, the stone-cutter:
Dedicated to the pious memory of Dame Dorothy Selby (etc).

She was a Dorcas
Whose curious needle turn'd the abused stage
Of this lewd world into a golden age:
Whose pen of steel, and silken ink, enroll'd
The acts of Jona in records of gold;
Whose art disclos'd that plott, which had it taken,
Rome had triumph't and Britaine's walls had shaken.
                    Shee was
In heart a Lydia, and in tongue a Hanna,
In seale a Ruth, in wedlock a Susanna.
Prudently simple, providently wary,
To the world a Martha, and to heaven a Mary.

June Smyth
b. 1649

Mrs June Smyth born the 15th of April 1649, between four and five o'clock in the morning. – She was told on Venus's Day, i.e. Friday: if not so 'twas on a Tuesday. It was the April after the beheading King Charles the First. It thundered and lightened and the house was on fire then.

My almanac, 1676, says the birthday was the 14th April – which NB: but Mrs J.S. tells me again 'twas the fifteenth.

About seven years old she lived in Sussex, Redhill, near which Mr Bradshaw, schoolmaster, lived – cousins-german.

She came the second time to London half a year before the great plague in 1665.

She was sick of a fever 1665; she said not in London.

She was like to die of St Anthony's fire about Michaelmas 1675. Mrs Smyth fell sick dangerously of a pleurisy about the first week of October 1675. About the latter end of March 1676 she had a terrible chronic disease (*Lues venerea*), under which she laboured a twelve-month or so. The first week in August 1683, in extreme danger of death by a suppression of urine, the ureters being stopped.

(*From a letter to Anthony Wood*) Now I conclude with an earnest request that you would please to enquire for a college lease, as you did for Edward Sherbourne (whom nobody can find). It is for that obliging body, Mrs Smyth, that lives with Mr Wyld. They cohabit, like Mary, Countess of Pembroke, with Sir Martin Lister. I owe most of Mr Wyld's civility from her goodness. And herein you will do me the greatest kindness that you could imagine, for I am more obliged to her than to anybody. I beseech you, for God's sake, to mind this humble request of mine.

Richard Stokes
d. 1681

Richard Stokes, MD – his father was fellow of Eton College (enquire if not prebend of Windsor, and if not schoolmaster of Eton? ask Christopher Wase about these things).

He was bred there and at King's College. Scholar to Mr W. Oughtred for mathematics (algebra). He made himself mad with it, but became sober again, but I fear like a cracked glass: see my *Lives*, and Surrey notes. He edited Mr Oughtred's Trigonometry. He became a Roman Catholic; married unhappily at Liège, dog and cat etc. Became a sot. Died in Newgate, prisoner for debt, 1681.

Thomas Street
1621–1689

Mr Thomas Street,* astronomer, was born in Ireland, his widow thinks, Castle Lyons, March the 5th, 1621.

He had the true motion of the moon by which he could discover how to find true longitude – (he hath finished the tables of the moon and also of Mercury, which was never made perfect before) – but two of his familiar acquaintance tell me that he did not commit this discovery to paper: so it is dead with him. He made attempts to be introduced to King Charles II and also to King James II, but courtiers would not do it without a good gratuity.

He was of a rough and choleric humour. Discoursing with Prince Rupert, his highness affirmed something that was not according to art; said Mr Street, 'Whoever affirms that is no mathematician.' So they would point at him afterwards at court and say, 'There's the man that huffed Prince Rupert.'

* His astronomical tables are the best that ever were yet made.

He was one of Mr Ashmole's clerks in the Excise Office, which was his chiefest livelihood.

He has left with his widow (who lives at Warwick Lane) an absolute piece of Trigonometry, plain and spherical, in manuscript, more perfect than ever was yet done, and more clear and demonstrated.

He died in Cannon Row (vulgarly Channel Row) at Westminster, the 17th of August 1689. He made this following epitaph himself:

> Here lies the earth of one that thought some good,
> Although too few him rightly understood:
> Above the starres his heightned mind did flye,
> His hapier spirit into Eternity.

His acquaintance talk of subscribing towards an inscription. No man living has deserved so well of astronomy.

Captain Thomas Stump, of Malmesbury

'Tis pity the strange adventures of him should be forgotten. He was the eldest son of Mr William Stump, rector of Yatton Keynell; was a boy of a most daring spirit; he would climb towers and trees most dangerously; nay, he would walk on the battlements of the tower there. He had too much spirit to be a scholar, and about sixteen went in a voyage with his uncle, since Sir Thomas Ivy, to Guyana, in the year 1633, or 1632. When the ship put in somewhere there, four or five of them straggled into the country too far, and in the interim the wind served, and the sails were hoist, and the stragglers left behind. It was not long before the wild people seized on them and stripped them, and those that had beards they knocked their brains out, and (as I remember) did eat them; but the queen saved T. Stump, and the other boy. Stump threw himself into the river Oronoco to have drowned himself, but could not sink; he is very full chested. The other youth shortly died. He lived with them till 1636 or 1637. His narrations are very strange and pleasant; but so many years since have made me almost forget all. He says there is incomparable fruit there, and that it may be termed the paradise of the world. He says that the spondyles of the back-bones of the huge serpents there are used to sit on, as our women sit upon butts. He taught them to build hovels, and to thatch and wattle. I wish I had a good account of his abode there; he is 'worthy of belief'. I never heard of any man that lived so long among those savages. A ship then sailing by, a Portuguese, he swam to it; and they took him up and made use of him for a seaboy. As he was sailing near Cornwall he stole out of a port-hole and swam to shore; and so begged to his father's in Wiltshire. When he came home nobody knew him, and they would not own him: only Jo. Harris the carpenter knew him. At last he recounted so many circumstances that he was owned, and in 1642 had a commission for a Captain of Foot in King Charles I's army.

John Taylor
1580–1653

Taylor was a 'drop-out' from the grammar-school at Gloucester, who could not master Latin and became apprentice to a London waterman. He was press-ganged and served at the siege of Cadiz in 1596 and on the Azores voyage in 1597. His descriptive tours in verse still make excellent reading, and he earned his living from verse after about 1630 until 1645. He kept a pub in Long Acre from 1645 until his death.

John Taylor, the water-poet: his works are a fair folio, printed, London, 1630.

He was born in the city of Gloucester: . . . Taylor, a painter, was his brother, who told me thus 23 years since (he lives yet at Oxford): and his picture hung in the Schools [Bodleian] gallery.

He came to London and bound [apprenticed] himself to a waterman, in which capacity he wrote his poems. I have heard Josias Howe, MA, say that he will choose out six verses (ask which) there as good as you will find in any other.

He was very facetious and diverting company; and for stories and lively telling them, few could outdo him.

In 1643, at the Act time, I saw him at Oxford. I guess he was then near 50. I remember he was of middle stature, had a good quick look, a black velvet plush-gippe [tunic] and silver shoulder-belt; was much made of by the scholars, and was often with Josias Howe at Trinity College.

He had heretofore in the long peace several vagaries [voyages] e.g. he came from London to Salisbury in his sculler. He went so to Calais.

He went to Scotland (I think round Great Britain) hugging the shore in his sculler.

Ever since the beginning of the civil wars he lived in Turnstile Alley in Long Acre, about the middle on the east side over against the Goat (as it is now), where he sold ale. His conversation was incomparable for three or four mornings' draughts. But afterwards you were entertained with old stories warmed over. His sign was his own head, and very like him, which about 22 years since was removed to the alehouse, the corner house opposite to Clarendon House. Under his picture are these verses; on one side:

> There's many a head stands for a signe.
> Then, gentle reader, why not mine?

on the other:

> Though I deserve not, I desire
> The laurel wreath, the poet's hire.

This picture is now almost worn out.

Silas Taylor
1624–1678

Antiquary and musician. Pepys, who was MP for Harwich, knew him, and said he was 'a good scholar and a great antiquary', but had mixed feelings about his musical talent, saying on one occasion that he 'composed bravely', but elsewhere that an anthem of his was dull and old-fashioned: 'the Duke of York, when he came out, told me that he was a better store-keeper than anthem-maker, and that was bad enough too.'

He was a captain in the Parliament army, under Col. Massey. He was a sequestrator, in Herefordshire, and had, in those times, great power, which power he used civilly and obligingly, that he was beloved by all the king's party.

He was very musical, and has composed many things, and I have heard anthems of his sung before his majesty, in his chapel, and the king told him he liked them. He had a very fine chamber organ in those unmusical days. There was a great friendship between Matthew Locke, since organist of the queen's chapel, and him.★

★ Mr Lock married Mr Garnon's daughter in Herefordshire.

His father left him a pretty good estate, but he bought church lands (during the Commonwealth) and had half of the bishop's palace at Hereford, where he laid out much money in building and altering. Col. John Burch had the other half.

The times turning, he was fain to disgorge all he had got, and was ruined, but Sir Paul Neile got for him the keeper of the king's stores at Harwich, worth about £100 per annum.

He was a great lover of antiquities, and ransacked the MSS of the church of Hereford (there were a great many that lay uncouth and unkiss [in disorder]).

He also ransacked the library of the church of Worcester, and evidences, where he had the original grant of King Edgar – (rule of the sea), whence the Kings of England derive the right to the sovereignty of the sea. 'Tis printed in Mr Selden's *Mare Clausum*. I have seen it many times and it is as legible as but lately written (Roman character). He offered it to the king for £120, but his majesty would not give so much. Since his death, I acquainted the Secretary of State that he died in debt, and his creditors seized on his goods and papers. He told me that it did of right belong to Worcester Church. I told one of their prebends, and they cared not for such things. I believe it has wrapped herrings by this time.

He had several MSS by him of great antiquity: one thin quarto of the Philosopher's Stone, in hieroglyphics, with some few Latin verses underneath; the most curiously drawn that ever I saw. His majesty offered him £100 for it, and he would not accept it. Tell Dr Crowder (one of the Worcester prebendaries) of the deed of King Edgar.

Memorandum: Captain Taylor searched the records in the Tower etc., and retrieved some privileges that the borough [of Harwich] had lost, for which the borough ought ever to have his remembrance in esteem: and though he died above £100 in their debt, yet the town lost not by him, for the reason aforesaid.

The history or collection of this ancient borough he pawned a little before his death to Mr Baker, the printseller by the old Exchange, for £4 15s. I acquainted Sir Philip Parker, whom the borough usually chooses for their burgess [MP], to buy it for his borough. He would not lay out so much money, which would do them more service than all his roast beef, wine and ale at an election.

The finger of God.* All that family came to unfortunate ends. His eldest son, wife and children, were all burnt in their beds, near Lothbury; another son (a dragoon), a churchyard wall fell on him and killed him.

---

* Because Taylor had bought church lands. *Ed.*

He surveyed very ingeniously and carefully the antiquities of Herefordshire, that is about three-quarters of the county, before the restoration of his majesty. He then left the country, and went to his friend, Sir Edward Harley, then governor of Dunkirk, who gave him some command. These papers are in the hands of Sir Edward Harley at Brampton Brian castle.

John Tombes
?1603–1676

One of the first Baptist clergy.

Mr John Tombes, BD was born at Bewdley in Worcestershire.

In (1618) he was admitted at Magdalen Hall in Oxford. He read to pupils and was tutor there to John Wilkins, afterwards Bishop of Chester. He was a great master of the Greek tongue, and the Hebrew he understood well. He always carried a little Greek Testament about with him; he had it almost by heart. He was an admirable disputant; 'tis requisite for one to be a good grammarian, as well as logician. I have forgotten if he was pupil to the learned Mr Pemble; but his favourite he was. He was soon taken notice of for his curious searching, piercing wit: he preached somewhere eastwards from Oxford, and had a company following him; and 'twas predicted he would do a great deal of mischief to the Church of England, that the greatest wits have done the most mischief to the church, introducing new opinions, etc. He was vicar of a market-town in Herefordshire, where he was very well beloved by his parish, and Sir . . . Croftes, eldest brother to the now Bishop of Hereford, built a house in Leominster, to live there, to hear him preach. In 1645, 1646, he was master of the Temple at London, i.e. minister. In 1647 he was supplanted there by parson Johnson. Then he went into his own country, to Bewdley (a market-town), at which time Mr Baxter (his antagonist) preached at Kidderminster, the next market town, two miles distant. They preached against one another's doctrines, and printed against each other. Mr Tombes was the chorus-leader of the Anabaptists: both had great audience; they went several miles on foot to each doctor. Once (I think oftener) they disputed face to face, and the followers were like two armies, about 1500 of a party; and truly, at last they fell by the ears, hurt was done, and the civil magistrate had much ado to quiet them. About 1664 he came to the Act at Oxford (query), and did there at evening service set up a challenge to maintain against all comers the Anabaptistical doctrine; but not a man would grapple with him. Now though *prima facie* this might seem very bold to challenge a whole university, 'twas not so very strange neither, for he came thoroughly prepared, after thirty years' study and thoughts, and most of them surprised.

Dr Sanderson, Lord Bishop of Lincoln, and he, had a great esteem for each other, so also had Dr Barlow (now bishop there). Putting aside his Anabaptistical positions, he was comfortable enough to the Church of England. About 1658 or 9, he married the widow of Wolston Abbott, of Salisbury, and went to hear the Common Prayer there, and received the sacraments; and sometimes waited on Bishop Ward, who respected him for his learning. He was thought to be as great a divine as most we had after Bishop Sanderson died. I remember he never, or seldom, was wont to say 'our saviour Christ', but 'my lord Christ'. He seemed to be a very pious and zealous Christian. I have heard him say (though he was much opposite to the Romish religion) that truly, for his part, should he see a poor zealous friar going to preach, he should pay him respect. He was but a little man, neat limbed, a little quick searching eye, sad, grey.

Ezreel Tong
1621–1680

Notorious for his involvement with Titus Oates in the fabrication of the 'Popish Plot' of 1680.

Ezreel Tong, DD, was born at Tickell, in Yorkshire, between Bawtry and Doncaster. He was buried on 23 December (1680) in the vault of the church-yard of St Mary Stayning, London; where, before the conflagration (1666), was a church, of which he was the parson; but I have heard his brother, Captain Tong (of the King's Guards) say 'twas worth but £18 per annum, for he had gathered it.

Mr Jones (who preached his funeral sermon: printed) says that he has left two tomes in folio of alchemy. His excellency lay *there*.

About 1658 or 1659, the then power (Cromwell) made an academy of the Bishop's Palace at Durham, for the benefit of the north. Dr Tong was the governor, or one of the professors. Ned Bagshawe was proposed to have been another. This Dr had an excellent school there, and followed precisely the Jesuits' method of teaching; and boys did profit wonderfully, as needs they must, by that method.

He afterwards taught at Islington, at Sir Thomas Fisher's house, where was a long gallery, and he had several printed heads of Caesars, etc., verbs under such a head, governed a dative case; under another, an ablative. The boys had it as ready as could be. I have been there.

Ezreel Tong, DD, invented, among other things, the way of teaching children to write a good hand in twenty days' time, by writing over, with black ink, copies printed from copper-plate in red ink: viz., the children (that is, aged about 8 or 9) were to do it four hours in the day: i.e. two hours or two half-hours in the morning at a time (as the boy's temper could endure it, without tiring him); and then to play as long; and then to it again, to keep up the idea in the child fresh. Since his death, Mr Robert Moray (projector of the Penny Post) has engraved several plates printed off in red letters, by which means boys learn (to admiration) as aforesaid – which NB.

His funeral sermon was preached in the church of St Michael, Wood Street; the church of St Mary Staining being burned, and never to be re-edified, but both parishes put together.

Thomas Triplett
1603–1670

He went to school to Dr Gill, as appears by his ballad, which will last longer than any sermon that ever he made.

After his sequestration* he kept a school at Dublin (when the king was beheaded); afterwards at Hayes, Surrey, twelve miles from London. 'Twas here our common friend George Ent went to school to him, who told me that he had not forgotten the smart of his old master, Gill; he was very severe.

I'll tell you a story of our old friend [i.e. George Ent]. His master Triplett was a great lover of honey, and one of his schoolfellow's mother having sent a pot of honey to the doctor, G. Ent put his schoolfellow to beg a little of his master, and he had got a small loaf and so they would have a feast. The doctor was in his study; and the boy takes the confidence to approach, with his, 'Quaeso, preceptor, da mihi mel [Please, teacher, give me some honey].' G. Ent was sneaking behind. Said the disturbed doctor, 'You audacious rascal,'

* Dismissal from his living by the Puritans. *Ed.*

and gave him a good cuff on the ear, 'how dare you be thus impudent? Sirrah, who put you on?' The boy answered (whiningly) 'G. Ent.' The enraged doctor flies out of his study (he was a very strong man), gives poor George a kick in the breech, and made him fly down a flight of seven or eight stairs to the landing place, where his head first came to. He was stunned, but 'twas well his neck was not broken. 'Twas a most cruel and inhumane act to use a poor child so. It so happened that a day or two before G.E. has lost a tooth. He writes a letter to his father (now Sir George Ent) and encloses the tooth in it; relates the story and that he lost the tooth by that means. The next the grave and learned Dr Ent comes to Hayes (the fame of whose learning and testimony did give great credit and reputation to this school); expostulates with the doctor about his son. To be short, took him away, and placed him with Mr William Radford at Richmond (an honest sequestered fellow of Trinity College, Oxford, and an excellent schoolmaster, having been bred at Thame under Dr Birt, and afterwards sent to Winchester). This accident well-nigh did break Dr Triplett's school. But shortly after this time, happened the restoration of his majesty, and then he was also restored to his former preferments.

Thomas Tyndale
1588–1672

These notes were collected by Aubrey when he was working on his comedy The Country Revel; *Tyndale, who was a Wiltshire neighbour of Aubrey's, was the model for an old gentleman, 'an old courtier of the Queen's.'*

In those days (Queen Elizabeth) the great men prospered, and when a senator went to the Parliament House a-foot, or a-horseback with his footcloth, he had at his heels half a dozen or ten tall fellows with blue coats and badges and long basket-hilt swords. Now forsooth only a lackey and a little spit-pig (short sword).

T.T. – The advantage that King Charles I had: gentlemen then kept good horses, and many horses for a man-at-arms, and men that could ride them; hunting horses. Now we are come all to our coaches forsooth! (Sir Philip Sidney). Now young men are so far from managing good horses, they know not how to ride a hunting nag nor handle their weapons. So God help the king if, etc.

In Sir Philip Sidney's time 'twas as much disgrace for a cavalier to be seen in London riding in a coach in the street as now 'twould be to be seen in a petticoat and waistcoat. They rode in the streets then with their rich foot-clothes (horse-clothes), and servants waiting on them blue coats and badge, six, eight, twelve or more.

T.T., an old gentleman that remembers Queen Elizabeth's reign and court, one of true gravity and prudence, not one that depends upon the grave cut of his beard to be thought so. He has seen much in his time both at home and abroad; and with much choler inveighs against things now: 'Alas! O'God's will! Nowadays everyone, forsooth! must have coaches, forsooth! In those days gentlemen kept horses for a man at arms besides their hackney and hunting horses. This made the gentry robust and hardy and fit for service; were able to be their own guides in case of a rout or so, when occasion should so require.★ Our gentry forsooth in these days are so effeminated that they know not how to ride on horseback. – Then when the gentry met, it was not at a poor blind sordid ale-house, to drink up a barrel of drink and lie drunk there two or three days together; fall together by the ears. They met then in the fields, well-appointed, with their hounds or their hawks; kept up good hospitality; and kept a good retinue, that would venture that blood and spirit that filled their veins which their masters' tables nourished; kept their tenants in due respect of them. We had no depopulation in those days.'

'You see in me the ruins of time. The day is almost at end with me, and truly I am glad of it: I desire not to live in this corrupt age. I foresaw and foretold the late changes, and now easily foresee what will follow after. Alas! O'God's will! It was not so in Queen Elizabeth's time: then youth had respect to old age.'

'Revels – then the elders and better sort of the parish sat and beheld the pastimes of the young men, as wrestling, shooting at butts, bowling and dancing. All this is now lost; and pride, whoring, wantonnesses, and drunkennesses. Then the charity of the feast, St Peter's box, maintained the old impotent poor.'

★ See Machiavelli's *Prince*.

James Ussher
1581–1656

Archbishop of Armagh 1625–1656; 'learned to a miracle' according to Selden, his published works run to twenty-seven books.

Memorandum: Ussher, Lord Primate (of Ireland) was at Llantrithed★ for several months, and directed himself much to talk with the poor people to understand Welsh, for that 'it had', he said, 'a great affinity with the Irish.' He said the Old Testament was translated by the Universities, but the New Testament was translated by the bishops; but the Old is much better done.†

★ Home of Sir John Aubrey, Aubrey's cousin. *Ed.*
† i.e. in the 'King James' Bible of 1611, the Authorised Version. *Ed.*

Henry Vaughan
1622–1695

Vaughan's poems, published between 1647 and 1650 under the title Silex
Scintillans, *were only recognised as masterpieces in the nineteenth century.*

[*From a letter to Anthony Wood*] There are two Vaughans, twins, both
very ingenious and writers. One wrote a poem called *Olor Iscanus*
(*The Swan of Usk*) [Henry Vaughan, the first-born], and another
book of divine meditations. His brother wrote several treatises,
whose names I have now forgotten, but names himself *Eugenius
Philalethes*.

They were born at Llansanfraid in Brecknockshire by the river Usk
(Isca). Their grandmother was an Aubrey: their father, a coxcomb
and no honester than he should be – he cosened me of 50s. once.

'Eugenius Philalethes' was of Jesus College. Whither Henry was I
have forgotten; but he was a clerk sometime to Judge Sir Marmaduke
Lloyd.

Henry Vaughan, 'Silurist': you know Silures [the ancient British
tribe] contained Brecknockshire, Herefordshire, etc.

[*A letter from Henry Vaughan to Aubrey*] 'My brother and I were
born at Nauton, in Brecknockshire, in the parish of St Bridget's, in
the year 1621.

'I stayed not at Oxford to take my degree, but was sent to London,
being then designed by my father for the study of the law, which the
sudden eruption of our late civil wars wholly frustrated.

'My brother continued there for ten to twelve years, and I think he
could be no less than Master of Arts. He died upon an employment
for his majesty, within five or six miles of Oxford, in the year that the
last great plague visited London (1665). He was buried by Sir Robert
Moray, his great friend (and then secretary of state for the kingdom of
Scotland); to whom he gave his books and MSS.

'My profession also is physic, which I have practised now for many
years with good success (I thank God) and a repute big enough for a
person of greater parts than myself.'

Francis Villiers
1629–1648

Posthumous son of Charles I's favourite, George Villiers, Duke of Buckingham.

In this parish (Kingston) in the lane between Kingston and Sathbyton Common, was slain the beautiful Francis Villiers, at an elm in the hedge in the east side of the lane, where, his horse being killed under him he turned his back to the elm and fought most valiantly with half a dozen. This elm was cut down, 1680. The enemy coming on the other side of the hedge, pushed off his helmet and killed him, July 7, 1648, about six or seven o'clock in the afternoon. On this elm was cut an ill-shaped V for Villiers, in memory of him.

William de Visscher
1595–1668

From Mr Bovey: – William de Visscher, merchant in London, born at Emden in East Friesland in Germany, a Hanse town – now under the Dutch. At two years old, was brought into England by his father, an eminent merchant; lived 55 years in one house at St Mary Hill, and died in the 74th year of his age. He lived there till the fire of London; he died about three years after – he did not enjoy himself afterwards.

In the last great dearth of corn in England*, when there was a great complaint and cry of the poor, he bade them be of good comfort for they should not starve, for he would give them his labour and the use of his estate for that year. He being a man of vast credit, gave his factors order that what corn they could buy at such and such rates beyond sea, to hire fly-boats and send them over to the port of London, of which he bought in one year two thousand five hundred sail. The corn that cost him 12s per bushel beyond sea, he sold here for 14s; and some of the places from whence he had corn (they selling it by reason of the greatness of the price) afterwards wanted it themselves and were fain to pay half value more than the first cost, or else must have starved.

* About thirty years since. I believe it was 1647, or 1648 – enquire.

Many disasters happened to many of the ships that were bound for London (some that never arrived were destroyed by foul weather; some wind-bound so long till their corn fired for want of airing, and was fain to be thrown overboard) that in the whole matter, after all the adventures run, he did not gain five and twenty hundred pounds. The fly-boats carried 800 tons, and some more.

He left two sons and a daughter behind him, named Isabella (who was married to Mr James Bovey, by which he has one son and one daughter).

He was a very eminent merchant, as most was of his time; and was valued by common reputation (when he married his daughter) to be worth £120,000.

He stayed in London during the whole time of the plague, and had not all that time one sick in his family. He was a temperate man, and had his house very cleanly kept.

Sir Isaac Wake
?1580–1632

Diplomat and writer.

Sir Isaac Wake: he had a fine seat at Hampstead in Middlesex, which looks over London and Surrey, where he made those delicate walks of pines and firs, also corme-trees [sorb-apple trees] etc. – The Lord Chief Baron Wild had it afterwards. His study was mighty pleasant.

The Lord de la Ware, who married the daughter and heir of the chief baron, sold this seat about 1683 to a citizen of London, who pulled it down to build a house (1686).

The chief baron told his cousin Edmund Wyld Esq that Sir Isaac Wake was the first that planted pines and firs in England. E.W. might have had the study for £8 per annum.

John Wallis
1616–1703

Mathematician and founder-member of the Royal Society.

John Wallis, DD, was born at Ashford, in the county of Kent, in (1616). His father was minister there. He went to school there.

He was admitted at Emmanuel College in Cambridge; 'where he was a pupil, then a fellow of King's College at the same place' (Mr Oughtred's preface to his *Key to Mathematics*). He was a good student, but fell not to the study of mathematics until he was above twenty.

A remarkable passage of his life was, that he was a witness of W. Laud's (archbishop of Canterbury) trial, for his introducing popish innovations into the University of Cambridge. The first remarkable passage of his life was his deciphering the letters of King Charles I taken at Naseby, which book is called the *King's Cabinet Opened*. He was scholar to Mr W. Oughtred.

In 1649 after the visitation by the parliament*, he came to Oxford, and was made Savilian Professor of Geometry. He was a Fellow of the Royal Society. Great contests between him and Mr Thomas Hobbes, of Malmesbury: sure their Mercuries are in square or opposition. In 1657, he got himself to be chosen by unjust means to be keeper of the

* Commissioners were sent to remove Royalist or high church sympathisers from the Universities. *Ed.*

archives of the University of Oxford, at which time Dr Zouch had the majority of voices, but because Dr Zouch was a malignant (as Dr Wallis openly protested, and that he had talked against Oliver), he was put aside. Now for the Savilian Professor to hold another place besides, is so downright against Sir Henry Savile's statutes, that nothing can be imagined more; and if he does, he is downright perjured. Yet the Dr is allowed to keep the other place still.

In (1654) he took his degree of Doctor, at the Act, at Oxford, and went out grand compounder★ (which costs £200), only that he might take precedence over Dr Seth Ward, who was about a year his senior. In 1661 Dr Ward was made dean of Exeter, and the next year bishop of the same place; and so Dr Wallis's £200 was merely cast away. The bishop protested he was troubled for the loss of his brother Wallis's two hundred pounds.

He has written several treatises, and well; and to give him his due praise, has exceedingly well deserved of the commonwealth of learning, perhaps no mathematical writer so much.

'Tis certain that he is a person of real worth, and may stand with much glory upon his own basis, needing not [to] be beholding to any man for fame, of which he is so extremely greedy, that he steals flowers from others to adorn his own cap, – e.g. he lies at watch, at Sir Christopher Wren's discourse, Mr Robert Hooke's, Dr William Holder, etc; puts down their notions in his note book, and then prints it, without owning the authors. This frequently, of which they complain.

But though he does an injury to the inventors, he does good to learning, in publishing such curious notions, which the author (especially Sir Christopher Wren) might never have the leisure to publish himself.

When Mr Oughtred's *Key to Mathematics* was printed at Oxford (third edition, with additions) Mr W.O. in his preface, gives worthy characters of several young mathematicians that he informed, and, amongst others, of John Wallis, who would be so kind to Mr Oughtred, as to take the pains to correct the press (proofs), which the old gentleman does with respect there acknowledge, after he has enumerated his titles and preferments: 'an ingenious, pious, industrious man, deeply versed in all recondite literature; most perspicacious in things mathematical, and in the unravelling and explanation of ciphered writings most intricately concealed (which is an argument of very subtle ingenuity) miraculously successful.' This last, on the cyphers, was added by Dr Wallis himself; which when, the book

★ Candidates for degrees with estates of over £300 p.a. paid this extra fee, and took precedence over ordinary degree-holders. *Ed.*

being printed, the old gentleman saw, he was much vexed at it; and said, he had thought he had given him sufficient praise, with which he might have rested content.

He has a good temporal estate in Kent. He has only two daughters, handsome young gentlewomen; one married to Mr Blencowe of Middleton Cheyney.

He lives at a well-built house, near New College in Oxford; is a Justice of the Peace there, and has been 167–, 1679, 1680.

Walter Warner
d. 1640

Mathematician

From Dr John Pell: – Mr Walter Warner: his youngest brother was High Sheriff of Leicestershire, about 1642. He and his brother died both bachelors. Dr Pell has seen him that was sheriff; but was well acquainted with Walter. The estate came to a middle brother, a lame man.

Walter had but one hand (born so), he thinks a right hand; his mother was frightened, which caused this deformity, so that instead of a left hand, he had only a stump with five warts upon it, instead of a hand and fingers. He wore a cuff on it like a pocket. The Doctor never saw his stump, but Mr Warner's man has told him so.

This Walter Warner was both mathematician and philosopher, and 'twas he that put out Thomas Hariot's *Algebra*, though he mentions it not.

Mr Warner did tell Dr Pell, that when Dr Harvey came out with his circulation of the blood, he did wonder whence Dr Harvey had it; but coming one day to the earl of Leicester, he found Dr Harvey in the hall, talking very familiarly with Mr Prothero (in Welsh, ap Roderic), to whom Mr Warner had discoursed concerning this exercitation of his *On the Circulation of the Blood,* and made no question but Dr Harvey had his *hint* from Prothero. Memorandum: Dr Pell says that Mr Warner reasoned demonstratively by beats of the pulses that there must be a circulation of the blood.

When Mr Hariot died, he made Sir Thomas Alesbury and Mr Prothero his executors, by which means his papers came to be divided into two hands. Those which fell to Sir Thomas Alesbury, fell, after his death, to his son–in–law, Edward, Earl of Clarendon, Lord

Chancellor, and in his son's hands (this present, 1680, Earl of Clarendon) 'tis believed are these that are yet left; none of them were printed, save that *The Practice of the art of analysis*, which was printed by Mr Warner upon this occasion, viz. Sir Thomas Alesbury obtained of Algernon, Earl of Northumberland (son to that Earl, prisoner in the Tower), a continuation of the annuity, during Warner's life, upon condition that he should, out of Mr Hariot's papers, draw out some piece fit to be published, which he did, under the title aforesaid: but did not set his name to it, and accordingly Warner had his money as long as he lived. The other part of Mr Hariot's papers, which were in Mr Prothero's keeping, came to the hands of the Lord John Vaughan, eldest son to the Earl of Carbery, lately governor of Jamaica.

Mr Warner's younger brother was a good husband and an industrious man, and would say that he had so much money, he could improve it to very great advantage; whereupon his eldest brother (Walter) did let him sell his land, by which means he did so improve his estate by grazing etc. that he became High Sheriff as aforesaid (ask of the attorneys when). Dr Pell has seen him, and spoke with him.

Mr Walter Warner made an inverted logarithmical table, i.e. whereas Briggs' table fills his margin with numbers increasing by units, and over against them sets their logarithms, which because of incommensurability must needs be either too great or deficient, Mr Warner (like a dictionary of the Latin before the English) fills the margin with logarithms increasing by units and sets to every one of them so many continual proportions between 1 and 10, and they for the same reason must also have the last figure incomplete. These, after the death of Mr Warner, came to the hands of Mr Herbert Thorndike, prebendary of Westminster, and by him left the hands of Dr Richard Busby, schoolmaster and prebendary of Westminster, which, before Mr John Pell grew acquainted with Mr Warner, were ten thousand, and at Mr Warner's request were by Mr Pell's hands, or direction, made a hundred thousand. The difference of the hands will show the workman's in the originals which Dr Busby has.

Mr Tovey, of Leicestershire, was his kinsman: he could tell when and where he died: – from Seth, bishop of Salisbury.

The bishop thinks he was of Cambridge University, but is not certain. Dr Pell believes that he was of no university.

Ask Dr Pell, what is the use of those inverted logarithms? For W. Warner would not do such a thing in vain. Mr Tovey was fellow of Christ's College in Cambridge; was beneficed in Leicestershire; and married a niece of Mr Warner's; and from Mr Tovey they (the tables) came to Mr Thorndike.

George Webb
1581–1642

Protestant bishop of Limerick 1634–1642

Dr Webb, one of King Charles I's chaplains, afterwards bishop of Limerick in Ireland, has some sermons, or divinity, in print; and a translation of Terence, English and Latin.

He died and was buried in Limerick, about two or three days before the town was taken by the Irish, who dug up the body again – it was about 1642.

He was of Corpus Christi College, Oxford: born at Brumhum in Wiltshire.

I confess I do not like that super-zeal in the Canon Law, not to let alone there the bodies of heretics. It is too inhumane. – This, as to the bishop's body being dug up again, which I fear was so: for his nephew who was his archdeacon, was with him when he died and the town taken, and I remember, being then a freshman. I heard him tell the story. He was minister in the next parish to Mr Hine.

James Whitney
1593–166?

[*From letters to Anthony Wood*] Parson Whitney was a great rememberer of names of Oxford men, being an old fellow there; and were he alive now he would be 81.

¶ My old cousin, parson Whitney, told me that in the Visitation of Oxford in Edward VI's time they burned mathematical books for conjuring books, and if the Greek professor had not accidentally come along, the Greek testament had been thrown in the fire for a conjuring book, too.

Thomas Willis
1622–1675

A Wiltshire doctor and neighbour of Aubrey's.

Thomas Willis, MD – from himself – born at Great Bedwyn in the county of Wilts., January 27th, 1621. His father was steward to Sir Walter Smyth there, and had been sometime a scholar at St John's College in Oxford.

1647 and 1648 (enquire, if not longer) frequented Abingdon market (in hope of finding patients), and Dr Lydall and he had a horse between them: this was before he was a doctor. He grew more and more into good practice. He studied chemistry in Peckwater Inn chamber. He was in those days very mathematical, and I have heard him say his genius lay more to mathematics than to chemistry. His father was steward to Sir John (I think) Smyth, and had a little estate at Hinksey, where my Lady Smyth (widow) died.

He went to school to Mr Sylvester in Oxford, over the meadows, where he aired his muse, and made good exercise: from William Hawes, his schoolfellow. In about 1657 (enquire there) riding towards Brackley to a patient, his way led him through Astrop, where he observed the stones in the little rill (stream) were discoloured and of a kind of [saffron] colour; thought he, this may be an indication of iron; he gets galls, and puts some of the powder into the water, and immediately it turned blackish; then said he, 'I'll not send my patients now so far as Tunbridge', and so he in a short time brought these waters into vogue, and has enriched a poor obscure village. He was middle statured: dark red hair (like a red pig): stammered much.

He was first servitor to Dr Iles, one of the canons of Christ Church, whose wife was a knowing woman in physic and surgery, and did many cures. Tom Willis then wore a blue livery-cloak, and studied at the lower end of the hall, by the hall-door; was pretty handy, and his mistress would oftentimes have him to assist her in the making of medicines. This did him no hurt, and allured him on.

John Wilmot, Earl of Rochester
1647–1680

Famous as one of the most dissolute members of Charles II's court. His pornographic verse is redeemed by his sense of style, and his lyrics and satires at their best rank with those of Marvell and Dryden.

John, Earl of Rochester: – he went to school at (Burford); was of Wadham College, Oxford: I suppose, had been in France.

About 18, he stole his lady, (Elizabeth) Malet, a daughter and heir, a great fortune; for which I remember I saw him a prisoner in the Tower about 1662.

His youthly spirit and opulent fortune did sometimes make him do extravagant actions, but in the country he was generally civil enough. He was wont to say that when he came to Brentford the devil entered into him and never left him till he came into the country again at Alderbury or Woodstock.

He was ranger of Woodstock park and lived often at the lodge at the west end, a very delightful place and noble prospect westwards. Here his lordship had several lascivious pictures drawn.

His lordship read all manner of books. Mr Andrew Marvell, who was a good judge of wit, was wont to say that he was the best English satirist and had the right vein. 'Twas pity death took him off so soon.

In his last sickness he was exceedingly penitent and wrote a letter of his repentance to Dr Burnet, which is printed.

He sent for all his servants, even the pigherd boy, to come and hear his palinode. He died at Woodstock Park, 26 July, 1680.

George Wither
1588–1677

A minor poet and writer of Puritan pamphlets.

Mr George Wither was born at Bentworth, near Alton, in Hampshire, on the eleventh of June, 1588.

He married Elizabeth, eldest daughter of H. Emerson, of South Lambeth, in the county of Surrey, esquire, whose ancestors he entombed in the choir of St Saviour's, Southwark, near the monument of Bishop Andrews, with a statue of white marble. She was a great wit, and would write in verse too.

He was of Oxford. He would make verses as fast as he could write them. And though he was an easy rhymer, and no good poet, he was a good prophet. He had a strange sagacity and foresight into mundane affairs.

He was an early observator of *Quicquid agunt homines* (whatever men do); his wit was satirical. I think the first thing he wrote was 'Abuses whipped and stripped', for which he was committed prisoner to, I believe, Newgate. I believe 'twas in King James's time. He was

captain in the Parliamentary army, and the Parliament gave him for his service Mr John Denham's estate at Egham, in Surrey. The motto of his colours was, *For king, law and company.*

After the restoration of his majesty he was imprisoned in the Tower about three quarters of a year. He died the second of May, 1667. He was pupil to Bishop Warner of Rochester.

Edward Wright
?1558–1615

Mathematician and expert on navigation; he redrew existing charts on the basis discovered by Mercator (and still in use today), which Mercator had not been able to develop to the full.

Amongst Mr Laurence Rooke's papers (left with Seth, Lord Bishop of Salisbury) I found: *A hypothesis of fixed stars* by Edward Wright, three sheets, of his own handwriting. I deposited it in the Royal Society, but Mr R. Hooke says that it is printed in a book by itself.

It appears by his preface that his worth was attended by a great deal of envy.

He was in the voyage of the right honourable the Earl of Cumberland in the year 1589.

John Collins says that he happened upon the logarithms and did not know it, as may be seen in his *Errors:* and Mr Robert Norwood says to the reader in his Trigonometry 'neither is Mr Edward Wright to be forgotten though his endeavours were soonest prevented', speaking of the logarithms.

Mr Edward Wright was of Caius College, in Cambridge. He was one of the best mathematicians of his time; and the *then* new way of sailing, which yet goes by the name of 'sailing by Mr Mercator's chart', was purely his invention, as plainly Mr Mercator brought this invention in fashion beyond seas.

He did read mathematics to Prince Henry, and caused to be made, for his highness' more easy understanding of astronomy, a sphere of wood, about three-quarters of a yard diameter, which lay neglected and out of order in the Tower in London, and Sir James More begged it of his present majesty who showed it to me.

Edmund Wyld
1614–1696

Fellow of the Royal Society and one of Aubrey's chief patrons.

Edmund Wyld esq., born at Houghton Conquest in Bedfordshire, 3 p.m. on a Saturday, October 10th, 1616.

He had the misfortune to kill a man in London, upon a great provocation, about 1644. He had the plague in the Inner Temple, 1647, and had a grievous quartan ague in September 1656.

Memorandum: Mr Wyld says that the doctors told him that in 1656 there died in London of the quartan ague fifteen hundred; NB In 1658 Oliver Cromwell, Protector, died of a quartan ague.

Sir Edward Zouche

Knight-marshal of the household in 1618.

Mr Philips also tells me that Robson was the first that brought into England the art of making Venice glasses, but Sir Edward Zouche (a courtier and drolling favourite of King James) oppressed this poor man Robson, and forced it from him, by these four verses to King James, which made his majesty laugh so that he was ready to beshit his breeches. The verses are these:

> Severn, Humber, Trent and Thames,
> And the great Ocean and her streames
> Must putt down Robson and his fires
> Or down goes Zouche and his desires.

The king granted this ingenious manufacture to Zouche, being tickled as aforesaid with these rhymes; and so poor Robson was oppressed and utterly undone, and came to that low degree of poverty that Mr Philips told me that he swept the yard at Whitehall and that he himself saw him do it.

Sir Robert Mansell had the glassworks afterwards, and employed Mr James Howell (author of *The Vocal Forest*) at Venice as a factor to furnish him with materials for his work.

Aubrey as antiquary:

Monumenta Britannica and other writings

The contents page of Aubrey's Monumenta Britannica *evolved over a number of years, and only achieved its final form just before it left Aubrey's hands for the bookseller, Awnsham Churchill, who hoped to publish it. It runs as follows:*

PART I
1. Templa Druidum
2. (crossed out) The Religion and Manners of the Druids
3. A Review of Stonehenge. Religio Druidum. Dr Gaden's letter of the bards
4. (crossed out) Of the Bards

PART II
1. Camps
2. Castles
3. Military Architecture
4. Roman Towns
5. Pits
6. Horns

PART III
1. Barrows
2. Urns
3. Sepulchres
4. Ditches
5. Highways
6. Roman pavements
7. Coins
8. Embanking and Draining
9. Chronologia Architectonica ★
10. Chronologia Aspidologica
11. Chronologia Graphica
12. Chronologia Vestiaria
13. Weights and measures
14. Prices of corn
15. Diversity of standards, and the value of moneys

The last part is the 'Στρώματα sive Miscellanea', discussed in the Introduction. Much of the manuscript is taken up either with brief observations and notes, or with material copied from other writers — it is not always immediately obvious when Aubrey is quoting or when he is expressing his own views, though almost any passage of more than a page

★ 9–15 are crossed through, with the note 'This more properly to be annexed to the Antiquities of Wiltshire.' *Ed.*

proves to be a quotation or the work of one of his many informants! What follows is a selection of the more extended original passages of the work: it has never been printed, except in a curious facsimile privately published in Dorset in 1980–2, which neither reproduces the original as it stands nor edits it in the modern sense – one feels that Aubrey would have approved, but it is an impossible book to use. So the reader who wants a closer acquaintance with Aubrey's greatest work is likely to be disappointed both by the facsimile, and by what follows, which is in a sense a distorted view, since extracts will inevitably make it seem more coherent than it really is.

1. Aubrey discovers Avebury for the first time, January 7 1649.

I was inclined by my genius, from my childhood, to the love of antiquities; and my fate dropped me in a country most suitable for such enquiries.

Salisbury plains and Stonehenge I had known from eight years old: but I never saw the country about Marlborough till Christmas 1648; being then invited to the Lord Francis Seymour's, by the honourable Mr Charles Seymour, with whom I had the honour to be intimately acquainted, and whose friendship I ought to mention with a profound respect to his memory.

The morrow after Twelfth Day [7 January] Mr Charles Seymour and Sir William Button met with their packs of hounds at the Grey Wethers. These downs look as if they were sown with grey stones, very thick , and in a dusky evening, they look like a flock of sheep: from whence it takes its name – one might fancy it to have been the scene where the giants fought with huge stones against the gods.

'Twas here that our game began, and the chase led us at length through the village of Avebury, into the closes there: where I was wonderfully surprised at the sight of those vast stones of which I had never heard before; as also at the mighty bank and graffe [ditch] about it. I observed in the enclosures some segments of rude circles, made with those stones, whence I concluded they had been in the old time complete. I left my company a while, entertaining myself with a more delightful indagation [investigation]: and then (steered by the cry of the hounds) overtook the company, and went with them to Kennet, where was a good hunting dinner provided. Our repast was cheerful; which, being ended, we remounted and beat over the downs with our greyhounds. In this afternoon's diversion I happened to see Wansdyke and another camp and two or three sepulchres.

The evening put a period to our sport, and we returned to the Castle [Inn] at Marlborough, where we were nobly entertained – 'it is cheerful to remember these things.' I think I am now the only surviving gentleman of that company.

In the year 1655 was published by Mr Webb a book entitled *Stonehenge Restored* (but written by Mr Inigo Jones) which I read with great delight: there is a great deal of learning in it. But, having compared his scheme with the monument itself, I found he had not dealt fairly, but had made a rule, which is conformed to the stone: that is, he framed the monument to his own hypothesis, which is much differing from the thing itself. This gave me an edge to make more researches: and a further opportunity was that my honoured and faithful friend Colonel James Long of Draycot was wont to spend a week or two every autumn at Avebury in hawking, where several times I have had the happiness to accompany him. Our sport was very good, and in a romantic country; the prospects were noble and vast, the downs stocked with numerous flocks of sheep: the turf rich and fragrant with thyme and burnet: '. . . The tired shepherd, lying by his crook or sitting on a rock soothes his sheep with a tune on his pipe.'

Nor are the nut-brown shepherdesses without their graces. But the flight of the falcon was but a parenthesis in the colonel's facetious discourses, who was 'as much of Mars as of Mercury' and the muses did accompany him with his hawks and his spaniels.

Drawing by Aubrey of Stonehenge

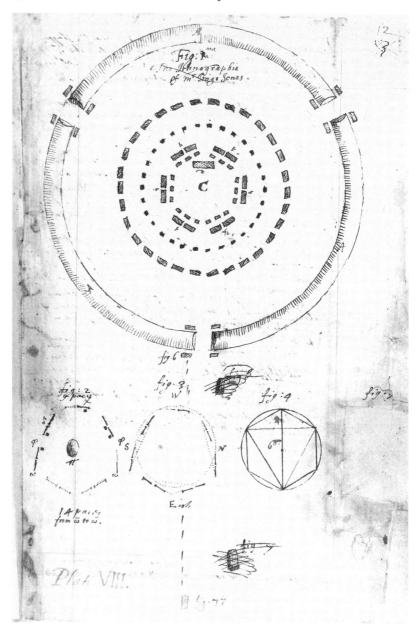

Aubrey's drawing of Inigo Jones' 'iconographie' of Stonehenge

2. Aubrey's visits to the stone circle at Stanton Drew, known as 'The Wedding'

'Twas a strange chance, you may say, that I should come to know this old monument, which lies so very obscure in a place far from any great roads. But it came to pass that Rachel Danvers, the relict [widow] of my grandfather John Aubrey married to (his fourth wife) John Whitson Alderman of Bristol (who was my godfather) who was a great benefactor to the city of Bristol; having no child living, he gave the manors of Dundry and Burnett in the county of Somerset and several houses in Bristol to the hospital in Bristol for the maintaining of blue coat boys yearly. Burnett was my grandmother's jointure by him; where I was often in my youthhood; and is about four miles from Stanton Drew. He died about 1629. She died 1638. So, methinks, I seem to have been designed by nature for this inquisition.

At Stanton Drew in Somersetshire (about a mile from Pensford) behind the manor house is the ancient monument which the vulgar do call the Wedding. All the account they can give is this tradition, namely that a bride going to be married, she and the rest of the company were metamorphosed into these stones: but whether it were true or no they told me they could not tell. I know that some will nauseate these old fables: but I do profess to regard them as the most considerable pieces of antiquity I collect, and that they are to be registered for posterity, to let them understand the encroachment of ignorance on mankind: and I see what strange absurdities man can by custom and education be brought to believe.

Homer in the Travels of Ulysses tells a story of a place seated 'twixt day and night; upon which Mr Thomas Hobbes animadverts that Homer knew well that there could not be a town at one end whereof was day, at the other night, at the same time: but had a mind to tell the learned how much the unlearned can believe. But to return again to these stones: they call them the Bride, the Parson's stone, the Cook's stone. They are about 5 or 6 feet high and as hard as marble. They seem to be of the very same stone with St Vincent's rocks near Bristol about 6 miles hence. They are of several tons: in some of them is iron ore, as likewise appears at St Vincent's rocks. As hard as these stones are, they do make a shift to break them with sledges, because they so encumber the good land: and they told me (1664) they are much diminished within these few years.

This monument is much bigger than Stonehenge: the diameter is ninety paces. I could not perceive any trench about it as at Stonehenge: it is in ploughed land and consequently easily worn out.

When I last saw this, it was in harvest-time, and the barley being then ripe, I could not come to survey the stones so exactly as I would otherwise have done: but this scheme (as it is) resembleth it.

The stones a a a a etc. [on the plan] seem to be the remainder of the avenue as at Kennet and Avebury, the length of the avenue is about half a quarter of a mile: and the stones d d d d might be a leading to another temple; as from West Kennet to the temple on the top of the hill.

I do presume that the like approaches (or avenues) were at Stonehenge and at Rollright, as are here, though now decayed by time. Northeastward from Stonehenge is a stone a good distance off, which seems to me to be the remains of it: and the stone called the King's stone at Rollright seems to be so there.

About a quarter of a mile from this monument of the Wedding is a stone called Hakewell's Quoit, which is a great roundish stone of the shape of a quoit; and lies flat and seems to have been left: it is of the same sort of stone with those at the Wedding. This is not erect as they of Stonehenge etc. The common people tell this incredible story that Hakewell stood upon the top of Norton Hill, about half a mile off, where the quoit now lies, and quoited it down to this place: for which having the manor of Norton given him and thinking it too little, did give it the name of Norton Malreward, which they pronounce 'Small reward'.

That in these parts anciently was one Hakewell, a person of great estate and strength of body, is manifest by the figure in his monument in Chew church.

3. Notes on other prehistoric monuments

Oxfordshire: The Rollright Stones

Ralph Sheldon of Beoley Esq, my honoured friend, told me he was at some charge to dig (in 167–) within this circle to try if he find any bones: but he was sure that nobody was buried there. But had he digged without the circle, and near to it, it is not unlikely he might have found bones there, as at the Temple above Kennet aforesaid.

Cornwall: Boscawen-Un stone circle

Camden: 'In Cornwall, at Biscaw-woun, stand nineteen stones in a circle, twelve feet distant each from other. In the centre is pitched one far higher than the rest.' This Mr Camden believes was a trophy of King Athelstan, but it agreeing in its architecture with the temples aforesaid, I presume this also to have been a temple. I have not (yet) seen this antiquity but it must give such a representation as this.

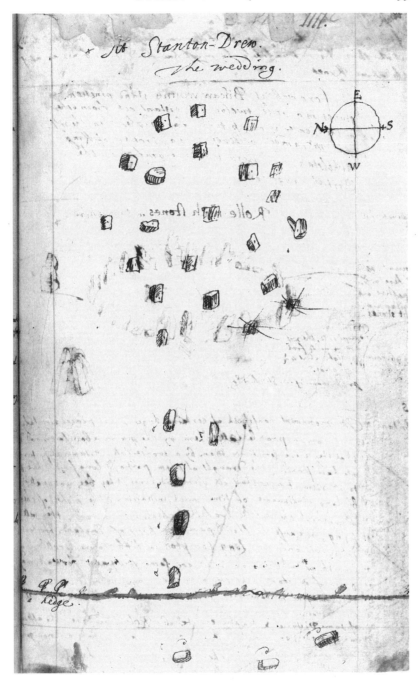

Drawing by Aubrey of 'The Wedding' at Stanton Drew

Yorkshire: Aldborough near Boroughbridge (The Devil's Arrows)
Aldborough, a Roman town enclosed within a wall of free stone a
mile in compass, upon a gentle ascent from the river. On the south is
an hill with a rampart, but much diminished. The Roman way runs
through the town of old and the bridge was under the town, lower
than now, $\frac{3}{4}$ of a mile. Grounds and closes are named as abutting
on the bridge. Formerly, they say, there were five of these pillars
(arrows): now they speak but of 4 and of these 4 one was converted
into a bridge. Coins, aqueducts, urns, bricks, polished stones are here
found without number.

Near Boroughbridge, on the west of the Fosse Way about quarter
of a mile (in the lordship of Aldborough), stand three pyramidish
stones called 'The Devil's Arrows'. The arrow standing towards the
south is seven yards and a half in height: the compass of it five yards
and a half. The middle arrow seven and a half yards, in compass six
yards. The arrow towards the north is in height five yards and a half,
in compass seven yards. Here was another stone that stood in a
straight line, that was taken down, and a bridge made of it. They are
a hard kind of ragstone, and not much weatherbeaten ... Those
stones seem to be remains of a temple of the like nature with the
former.

I did not perceive any sign of a circular trench, as at other monuments before mentioned: the fields here are ploughed with deep
furrows and so worn out.

The three stones that remain, their sides do stand parallel to one
another: and so (they tell me) did the side of that stone which was
converted to a bridge. In Plate XI I give the ichnography of the
Arrows where sides are placed parallel to one another: and I have
drawn two imaginary circles in which it may be supposed that the
stones were placed, as at Avebury, Stonehenge, etc. Perhaps there
might be more stones in each circle than I have here fancied. I had not
a right idea of this antiquity till I saw it myself, September 1687. The
stones do stand almost in a direct line except that near the Three
Greyhounds which wants about two yards and a half of being in a
right line.

The Arrows are striated from the top down about two foot plus, as
if those furrows had been worn by droppings of rain. They are entire
stones grown hard by the weather. I should be inclined to believe
these strias were artificial, for a kind of ornament.

The cross in Boroughbridge (as also the crosses in the villages
thereabout) are the highest that ever I saw of one entire stone: and
they are of the same sort of stone with these arrows. I have a conceit
that when Christianity was established in these parts, and it became in

fashion then to set up crosses (as a sign of their conversion) that to save themselves the trouble of drawing huge stones out of the quarries to make their crosses, they made use of these Arrows, which they found near to their land: and by that means the number of them became lessened.

4. Introduction to 'The Religion of the Druids' (*Religio Druidum*)

The Welsh call starlings Derrin Y Derwyddon, the druids' birds, and sturnas Addar y Derwyddon. They are talkative birds; and Pliny tells of a starling in his time that could speak Greek, as Drexelius tells us of a parrot that could rehearse the credo.

I thought on the 'druids' birds' when I saw the starlings breed in the holes of the stones at Stonehenge: but that perhaps is but an accidental thing.

In the Irish testament (which I saw at the College at Dublin, 'tis in the Saxon character), the word Magi is expressed drurite (druids).

I am apt to believe, that in most counties of England are, or have been, ruins of these kind of temples. But where they were made of free-stone, there remains nothing left of them as at Yatton Keynell in Wiltshire, on the west side of the road where it makes a Y, is a little close called Stone-edge: where by the name one would suspect such a kind of monument to have been: but time hath defaced it and the tradition. Near this place is a great quarry of freestone fit for that purpose. Who knows but that Staines in Middlesex had its denomination from such stones?

I have heard persons of quality, and worthy of belief, aver that in the kingdom of Ireland, (especially in Ulster) are several monuments of the like nature. Mr Thomas Henshaw, RSS, tells me that at Dun Lary, about two miles south from Dublin, do stand three stones together, eleven foot high. Mr Gethin of the Middle Temple, London, tells me that at Killian Hill (or a name like it) in Ireland is a monument like that at Stonehenge; and from whence the old tradition is that Merlin brought them to Stonehenge by conjuration.

The right honourable John Lord Yester and Sir Robert Moray* do assure me (as also several other learned gentlemen of Scotland) that in

---

* Broadchalk 1665: Sir Robert Moray promised me, to send me an account of some of these temples, and how the vulgar called them: but sudden death prevented him. He was a courtier, that would do courtesies for friendship sake.

that kingdom are several monuments of the fashion before shown: nay, in the middle and most northern parts of that country where the Romans had no domain. Sir George Mackenzie in his *History of Scotland*, affirmeth that Scotland was never conquered by the Romans.

Archbishop Spottiswood saith (out of Hector Boethius and G. Buchanan) that the power of Druids in those days was so great that it did a long time give a stop to the propagation of the Christian religion.

Now to wind up this discourse: the Romans had no dominion in Ireland or in Scotland (at least not far): therefore these temples are not to be supposed to be built by them: nor had the Danes dominion in Wales; and therefore we cannot presume the two last mentioned temples to have been works of them. But all these monuments are of the same fashion, and antique rudeness; wherefore I conclude that they were erected by the Britons: and were temples of the Druids.

5. Of camps (excerpts)

The Lord Chancellor Bacon says that the 'writings of speculative men upon active matter, seem to men of experience to be but dreams and dotage: and that it were to be wished, that active men would or could become writers.'

My frequent journeyings between south and north Wiltshire and the south part of Wales have given me more opportunities than most men to make remarks on this country, and particularly on Salisbury plains. Passing therefore so often by those monuments of ancient time, I could not but make somewhat a deeper inspection into them than one of the vulgar. Methought the venerableness of them did require a stop and respect. The prodigious graffs [dykes] and ramparts of the old encampings seemed justly to claim admiration in the beholder. The greatness and numerousness of the barrows (the beds of honour where now so many heroes lie buried in oblivion) do speak plainly to us, that death and slaughter once raged here, and that here were the scenes where terrible battles were fought: wherein fell so many thousands, mentioned by historians. By the burying places it might be presumed whereabout the engagement began and which way the victor made his pursuit: and by vestigia of the imperial camps (whereupon now sheep feed, and the plough goes) one may trace out the way, the which way the victorious Roman eagle took her course.

Certainly it were no difficult matter for the Kentish gentlemen that use field-sports between the Downs and London to find out the encampings and places of fights so clearly described by J. Caesar in his Commentaries: for by such means are the best discoveries of this kind made, many of them being now overgrown with woods and brakes.

In Colonel Archer's lands at Tamworth in Warwickshire are two entrenchments or camps – I have not seen them – which were (it seems) the entrenchments of Vortigern and Hengist, concerning which see Holinshed's chronicle. I shall add to this paragraph a most remarkable story, which I have well attested by the colonel's eldest son and Thomas Marriott and his eldest son, viz. one Mr Smyth of Tamworth (an empiric), a good understanding sober person, reading Holinshed's chronicle, found an account there of a great fight between Vortigern and Hengist about these parts at a place called Colemore. Shortly after, as he lay in his bed, awake, he heard a voice that said to him, 'You shall shortly see some of the bones of the men and horses slain, that you read of.' He was surprised at the voice and asked in the name of God, who 'twas that spoke to him. Answer was made, that he should not trouble himself about that; but what was told him should come to pass. Shortly after as he went to visit Colonel Archer, whose men then happened to be digging for marl, he saw a great many bones of men and horses and potsherds (I suppose to boil their meals in) and upon the view it appeared according to the description, and to be the place where the fight was, which is now called Blackmore. There was a brass key found, and spears' heads: which are kept in the colonel's closet. This discovery was about 1685.

Eruolevis Napolitana, smooth bank cresses of Naples, after the fire, [of London] over all the ruins, in so much that they thatched their sheds and cellars with it. Before the fire 'twas very rarely to be found, viz. in the back of Old Street, beyond Gray's Inn towards Battle Bridge; but since the fire on the top of the wall of Paul's Church in abundance. It never flourished so much as in the ruins. From Thomas Willisell.

6. Castles and towns (excerpts)

Mr Inigo Jones (architect to King James I and to King Charles I) was wont to wait upon their Majesties when they went their progress. He designed admirably well: and in these progresses he drew a great many prospects of the old Gothick, or ancient castles, in sheets of paper. He bought the manor of Butleigh near Glastonbury (once belonging to it but very unfortunate to its late possessors) where in a large parlour, I saw these draughts of the castles: they did furnish the room: one of them was down, and in a child's hands, which I rescued

(1656) and hung it up myself. I have often intimated this to our engravers to make them publish: but I cannot persuade them to it. But had the ingenious Mr Wenceslaus Hollar lived, he would have done it, upon my request. Of these once stately castles, there is not now a stone left upon a stone.

Of Roman towns
Force in this here (though it be foreign as is the country) to preserve it from being lost and forgotten.

A description of St Giles's Token
St Giles's church stood without the gate of the city of Hereford: it was built much in the fashion of the Temple church at London. On the turret of it was a fane exactly like this figure, which resembled a woodcock's bill, and was some metal commonly thought to be iron. It was accounted an infallible token of the change of weather, for it did certainly shut against dry weather, and open against wet weather. This turret was not very high and the bars a – a were to sight about the bigness of a tobacco pipe, and near a foot long. This church, standing in the suburbs, was demolished when the Scots besieged Hereford AD 1643. It gaped about an inch wide, or scarce so much. That this fane did foretell the change of weather I have been satisfied by several serious and discreet persons in and near this city; but this more exact relation and description I had from Mr Cook of the Nag's Head in Hereford, who went to school in the church. Sir W. Gregory also testifies this.

7. Aubrey's notes on King Arthur

Queen Guinevere's tomb was in the wall of the abbey at Amesbury: the inscription on it were in golden letters, which were sold at a mark apiece. The officers of Edward Earl of Hertford made rings of them: one of whom I knew well, who gave me this relation: it was in King James's time. The letters were RGAC 600 – RG as much to say Regina Guinevera AC Anno Christi but I much doubt whether the figures were of this Saracenical [Arabic] kind. Mr Seymour Bowman affirms that the inscription was Regina Guinevera, in gold letters.

Memorandum: Sir John Denham told me that King Arthur would be as good a subject for a romance as can be. 'Tis a great pity that so famous and great a worthy should ever have been abused, either by monkish verses, or vile painting in an alehouse.

At the foot of the rocks near St Michael's Mount, in the memory of our fathers, were digged up spears' heads, axes and swords of brass, wrapped in linen, the weapons that the Cimbrians and ancient Britons used.

At Camelford likewise pieces of armours both for horse and man are many times found in digging of the ground, computed to be the signs of the fight wherein Mordred was slain, and wherein great Arthur receives his death's wound.

King Arthur having taken York and the British gentry and nobility lodging there gave themselves to all luxury and voluptuousness as in triumph of their glorious victories. It is reported that the celebration of the nativity of our Lord for 13 days together with immoderate feasting and gluttony used at this day by the English and Scots was begun at this time by King Arthur, and that it is nowhere else in use beyond the seas.

Chronologia Vestiaria

Enquire how long, and in what king's reign hoods were in fashion.

What the Roman habits were, we may see by the old statues and bas-reliefs, which is the same (or very near) with that the Moors do still use (except their little turbans). Elias Ashmole and I observed, when the Morocco ambassador was in London, we were walking in the priory garden at Whitehall, and looking on the old senatorian habits of the statues there, we found the fashion of those to be almost the same with these, and the Highlands plaid is something like it. But as the incursion of the Goths made an alteration in the architecture, it did so likewise also in habits, as also in the saddlers' and upholsterers' trades.

Elias Ashmole, founder of the Ashmolean Museum

CROWNS

The original of crowns was a diadem (to compare royal ornaments with vile) like the leatherstrap the shoemakers wear on their heads at their work.

Constantine the Great and several of the Roman emperors on their coins have only a diadem (or chaplet) on their heads. The first crowns were but with the addition of pointed spikes to the diadem: which points in after time they adorned or topped with pearls and after adorned the interstices with trefoils. But as the Gothic building deviated from the Roman, so did their habits, and their crown is as is to be seen in the crowns of our Saxon kings.

The City of London being at that time governed by bailiffs, could get no man to be their catchpole. At last a couple of Flemings, which fled by reason that their country was drowned by the sea, accepted, and according to order, had garments given them of two colours, blue and red, their coats, breeches and stockings, whereby they were known and discerned from other men.

GIRDLES

In old time when men wore their gowns close girt (as the Romans did, and of latter days our countrymen) bankrupts were forbidden wearing of girdles, that the decay of their estate being notorious, their deceitful fetches might be prevented. And even in these times, if a man want a girdle, some will merrily demand, if he be not a bankrupt.

Old fashions of clothes

CAPS

Caps or bonnets were the general fashion till about the middle of Queen Elizabeth's reign. King Edward the Sixth and his father were always drawn with caps (like those worn by the doctors of law) and so all the aldermen of London, done pretty late in the queen's (Elizabeth) time. I have heard my honoured and learned friend Dr Edward Davenant say, that his father (a London merchant), eldest brother to J. Davenant (bishop of Salisbury) was the first citizen of London that wore a hat*, and brought them into use among the citizens; as also

* Bishops and grave divines often covered their hats with taffeta all over, with an hatband like a cable. The gentry wore velvet caps with brooches and horn tops higher than the cap.

coloured clothes; before, the citizens wore tawny, or puke-coloured clothes and short rockets.

CODPIECES

Codpieces were like the penis of a man erected: it was stuffed with bombast; and they did stick pins in them. When this fashion began, I know not*; but I have seen it in armour, before Henry the Eighth, but it lasted down to about 1585, as I have heard my grandfather Mr Isaac Lyte say. (Memorandum: Sir Thomas Gresham's statue and pictures have a codpiece.)

COATS

Parti-coloured coats (as the knaves in the cards) were in fashion in the time of Richard II, Henry IV, and Henry V, and not much longer. Only the serjeants at law continued the use of them: and beadles yet wear them: and till the beginning of King James the first (or since) the bailiffs i.e. catchpoles, wore them, whence came the saying, 'Sirrah, I'll make you go in a parti-coloured coat, that we may know you from an honest man.'

The abbots' servants wore tawny coats as we may see in Ben Jonson's masque, and so do our bishop's footmen etc.

Old Mr Ambrose Brown of Winterborn Basset, Wilts, wore his coat gathered at the girdleplace (the same fashion that the Yeoman of the Guard do wear) as long as he lived: he died 1660, aged one hundred and three: it was anciently the general fashion: as may appear by the pictures of King Henry VIII etc of that time. But before this, men wore gowns, as appears by Sir Geoffrey Chaucer's picture and in his tale of the plowman, that Jenkins should have a new gown for his invention of the equal dividend of the feast to the friars: also in old windows, e.g. Dominus Thomas Nye in the chancel window of Kingston St Michael. 'Twas a loose coat down in the calves of the leg, with wide sleeves. No bands then.

CHAPLETS

John Gower Esq the poet has a worshipful monument at St Saviour's church in Southwark (to which he was a great benefactor); he lies in effigy in his scarlet gown, his silver collar of SS, on his head a chaplet,

---

* From the Swiss: Francis I, to curry favour of them, put himself into that fashion.

Geoffrey Chaucer. Almost certainly the portrait to which Aubrey refers

viz. a diadem of gold adorned with four red roses placed at equal
distances. He flourished in the times of Edward III and Richard II. See
in my book *Antiquities of Wiltshire* of the garland at Newton given by
a maid every Easter Monday.

Memorandum: When Doctors of Divinity in Oxford take their
degrees they are to wear boots.

BANDS AND CUFFS

King Edward the first wore no band, a little of the collar of his shirt
appeared above the collar of his doublet; shortly after his time was
invented a little ruff and ruff-cuffs; the ruff in not many years grew to
be a monster (like cartages) a fist long: which was occasioned by a
Spanish queen or duchess that had a great wen in her neck. I

remember 'tis mentioned in the History of the Netherlands, I think by James Howell. The common lawyers wore falling ruffs, half a dozen bands one upon another and looked very venerably: this lasted till the Civil Wars. The Lord Keeper Finch was the first judge that wore a band.

In King Charles I or later end of King James I the bands came to be like women's veils, from shoulder to shoulder, and the cuffs reached to the elbows: this lasted till 1639. There was a play made, and I think printed: amongst other of the *personae* there was Cuffy Ruff and Falling-band.

> *Enters* Falling-band: Cuff, where are you?
> Cuff: Here, up to the elbows

Bands and cuffs are the shirt ends. The Romans wore none, and at first it was honour to have a shirt and they let the ends appear, as the Jesuits and Theatines do still: and they made them separate to have clean oftener.

HIGH SHOES

Were the common wearing for husbandmen in Wilts etc, in 1633 and after, and it was a very useful fashion to preserve them from wet and from the stinging of venomous creatures. It was a kind of half-boot laced: it came up to the upper part of the small of the leg. The monks of the Benedictine order wore boots, I believe something like these. In 1642 the war brake out and then both citizens and ploughmen wore boots altogether, which was very uncommodious and ridiculous.

Jingling spurs: the rowels as broad as a crownpiece, standing out as a crane's neck, and might hear one walk at a great distance.

TRUNK-HOSE

Alderman Wellington of the city of Hereford, a venerable magistrate and of a good presence, was the only person that I have seen (1634) that wore trunk-hose. The Knights of the Garter use it at installations as a part of their habit. Sir Lionel Ducket (Lord Mayor in the fourteenth year of Queen Elizabeth) did endeavour to make some reformation among the apprentices of London in relation to their hose, that they should not waste so much cloth: but it made a kind of mutiny among them: and they made this distich on him, viz.

> Good Sir Lionel with your long nose
> What have you to do with the prentices' hose?

TABARDS

In the times of King Henry IV and Henry V of England, noblemen and gentlemen did wear tabards, that is, short coats without sleeves, as the heralds do still, wherein was embroidered their arms★; whence comes that expression of a coat of arms. In Queen's College in Oxford there is a certain number of alumni called vulgarly tabbiters: but the meaning is tabarders: before the civil wars the scholars of New College in Oxford were not to stir out of the gates without their habit and ruff; for so they termed it, which was a black tabard of some stuff, e.g. serge. And Dr Ralph Bathurst, Dean of Wells, affirms to me that when he was presented Bachelor of arts (1639) he was presented in such a habit and this custom was then generally used. In the Heralds' office is the picture of the famous John the first Earl of Shrewsbury, in the time of Henry VI, in his tabard, with his arms and quarterings. Also Sutton, one of the founders of Brasenose College in Oxford, is painted with his coat of arms as aforesaid, and this fashion was common in those days as appears by the old glass windows then made.

Tabards are for pilgrims, as the poor man's *garde de pluie*; the coat having the crest in profile was the sleeve or side coat.

SHOES

And on their heads did yellow bonnets wear
Of a wolf skin, with their left foot they did
March naked, a raw brogue the other hid.
(Virgil, *Aeneid* book VII)

The first armature or defence for the feet were raw skins, as the wild Irish use, i.e. leather sewed on the top of the foot, which they call brogues. The sabots or wooden shoes used by the French are more modern: necessity compelling them to be so thrifty. Till 1633 or 1634 I remember when I was a little boy that generally in North Wiltshire husbandmen did wear high shoes which were very useful for them: not only to keep out the wet and dirt: but to preserve them from the stinging of serpents. They were, suppose a boot cut off a little below the calf of the leg, and slit down to the foot, and laced with a thong. They were generally used over all England by the countrymen, till a little before the Scottish wars, at which time they grew proud and everybody in city as well as country wore boots, even the ploughboys. Dr Donne in his *Satyris*.

★ A duke of Savoy lately had his cloak embroidered with the pictures of all his chief cities and towns.

The six foot high, high-shoed, iron-bound serving man. See the fashions of shoes in the Lord Hungerford's chapel at the cathedral church of Salisbury, in Hungerford's chapel, on the north side of the church in my book, as also [another] window in book A where the shoes turn up pricked at the toe. In the years 1647, 1648, 'twas the fashion to wear their shoes two inches longer than their feet: the end of the shoe was lined with latten, and the extremity was like a half-moon; it was a very troublesome and ridiculous fashion. A Cavalier captain being pursued, having quitted his horse, the tin did so gall his foot and lamed him so, that he was taken and hanged.

Some wore shoes so pointed and so long that they were fain to tie the point with a ribbon or small chain to their knees. They were made almost in the shape of a skate (the Dutch sliding shoe).

BEARDS

The bishops before the Reformation all shaved close: as is to be seen in their monuments and pictures. When the Protestant religion came in, the bishops did wear great (brush) beards, as is to be seen in their pictures before their works, e.g. Bishop Babington of Worcester etc, which fashion continued till the time of King Charles I. William Laud, Archbishop of Canterbury and Bishop Andrews were the two that left off that besom fashion. The clergy then wore poked ruffs.

Perruques [wigs] counted scandalous till Charles II: then universal, and bands left off for cravats for a while. Surcoats and easy wastcoats with them or girdles again and buckled garters etc., a comely mode too soon quitted.

Mr William Shakespeare (poet) on his monument in the church at Stratford upon Avon: his figure is thus, viz. a tawny satin doublet, I think pinked, and over that a black gown, like an undergraduate's at Oxford, namely the sleeves of the gown do not cover the arms, but hang loose behind. When I learnt to read (1638) of John Browne the parish clarke of Kington St Michael, his old father (above eighty) who had been clerk there before, daily wore such a gown with the sleeves pinned behind. I do believe that about the latter end of Queen Elizabeth's time 'twas the fashion for grave people to wear such gowns.

WROUGHT NIGHT-CAPS

In the times of Queen Elizabeth and King James I and Charles the First, the privy councillors did wear wrought night-caps. Likewise the divines did wear them, e.g. the picture of Mr John Dod, black and white. The Doctors of Physick's caps were wrought with gold and silk, as the privy councillors. The Puritans in the time of Charles I wore black satin caps tipped with a white one under, to appear weak and sickly, to move pity in their hearers:

> He railed much against the man of sin,
> His cap looked like a black pot tipped with tin.

Sir Henry Spelman's picture in Sir Robert Cotton's library is drawn so: and so is old Dr Napier at Mr Ashmole's. Aldermen wore such before the late wars: the last wrought night-cap that I saw was on Sir Thomas Allen's head, who carried the sword before King Charles II.

Heretofore the shoes were all black: hence the proverb 'As honest a man as ever wore black shoes of leather.' The gentry did wear punched shoes: 'like Pauly's windowes [the windows of St Paul's] carved were her shoen'. This fashion held till 1640; I wore them; and rich roses were in fashion to wear on them for shoe-ties. Now buckles take their place: which one may find by the old proverb to be ancient, sc. 'I would not do such and such for shoe-buckles'. The little children's shoes were printed with silver figures, as the backside of the horn books, with St George on horseback on red leather: and they wore yellow shoes, which I think they do still. The ladies had (and yet have) a sharp heel reduced almost to a point.

The commode or tiara, a very incommode fashion worn by the ladies: King James II.

HOODS

See Apollo with a hood to fall back in a Greek coin.

Plutarch was a priest and is drawn with a hood like a monk's hood.

King Henry IV of England is always painted with a hood, as the livery hoods are in London: and I have seen the like about that king's time in old glass windows at Newcourt in Herefordshire.

The ladies had great bosses on their arms, made stiff with whalebone and bent in such a manner as they could hardly bend their arm.

Also broad plumes for fans in enamelled handles till the French introduced the Chinese fan.

They wore points at the knees with tags dangling about their boot-tops making a rattling noise as they walked with the jingling also of their spurs. Also points about the waist and to their girdles.

Skirts cut into several quarters; some had six, eight, twelve, others but four, and sometimes almost every seam of a suit was powdered and set with rows of buttons.

They wore trunk-hose, cloakbag hose and some so very close and pinched towards the knee as if put on with a shoeing horn, and could hardly stoop in them.*

They also sliced their doublets in slashes richly laid and an half-shirt under, which peeped out 'twixt every slash: some only opened the sleeve of the arms at the bending place or cubit, and some also behind the shoulder: some a slash on the middle of the back, which were cool and handsome enough.

Memorandum: the gowns of our old country-women were gathered and plaited in the back, as the benchers gowns are, or as the panels of wainscot in the time of Henry VII and VIII till the late civil wars, 1642. The Spanish fashion of broad wings to the doublet with a jerkin or surcoat over it with hanging sleeves, and the pocadillo, brought in by Gondomar. The women's head tires in Queen Elizabeth, a French hood. Bibs, the gorget till Queen Mary, wife of King Charles I.

White apron: a comely fashion, was worn by the greatest countesses abroad as well as at home.

For several sorts of fashions and garments see the excellent painting of Holbein in Whitehall [that] describes the triumphs and tournaments at Turvere in Flanders.

HAIR

Before the late civil wars, in the time of Charles I, if a barrister had come to the bar with long hair, the judge would have sent him to the barbers before he would have heard him: the like if he appeared in court in a band. In those days the common lawyers wore ruffs, that is, falling ruffs, not poked. The divines wore them like cartages:

> With a set ruff of musket bore which wears
> Like cartages or linen bandoleros.

King Charles I wore a long lock on the left side, which was much imitated. Some tied ribbons etc. Also men wore earrings and pearls pendant in their ears; falconers generally.

---

* Breeches that came down almost to the shoes, and so their belts. 1650.

Nouvelles (Novelties)

APOTHECARIES

They were not very ancient in England, for that in the 32nd year of King Edward III, John Falconti of Lucca in Italy was the first apothecary in England, as appeareth in my Lord Coke's 8th report, in the case of the City of London, fol. 126 b.

Old Jacquez, who lived at Kington St Michael, near the priory (which from his house was but a little way) I have heard was wont to say that he had seen fifty nuns (i.e. sisters) in the ground called the 'Nymph-hay', in a morning spinning with their rocks and spinning-wheels. Now rocks are utterly unknown in these parts. I never saw any but in Staffordshire, where the poor women spin with them in the streets: they are certainly of the elder house to the spinning wheel.

The paper-mill at Bemarton, near Salisbury, is 112 years standing (now 1682): 'twas the second in England.

A Bristol man, living in Castile, learned their art of making soap, now (1681) eighty or more years since. Upon this *nouvelle* of Castile-soap: one Richard Rogers took up the trade of soap-boiling: and left a fair estate (I think at least a thousand pounds per annum). He was knighted before he died and 'twas he built the elegant house in Ratcliff Street where King Charles II and his queen and court were royally treated by the city of Bristol in 1663. 'Twas when the king and queen went to Bath. He was a plain dull man and understood nothing beyond his trade, but became the richest man in the city. His neighbours did believe that he found a barrel or barrels of money from Spain, instead of commodities: but I have a conceit this estate was obtained by his great industry and his skill in turning the penny.

Mr Broughton (father of Bess Broughton) living at that time at Bristol, and the haven being like to be choked up with the soap-ashes, for which several complaints and indictments, considering that grounds were improved by compost, made the experiment of improving by soap-ashes, having land near the city: and mightily improved it. This I had from himself.

Jessamines came in with Mary Queen of Scots – enquire whence?

Laurel by Alathea Countess of Arundel.

Phidynia by John Evelyn, FRS. (*samatii angustifolii*)

COFFEE

Mr James Howell in his epistle to Judge Rumsey's *Organum Salutis, or an instrument to cleanse the stomach*:

> Therefore that worthy gentleman Mr Mundiford, who introduced the practise of coffee first to London, deserves much respect of the whole nation. This was about 1650.

The way of gilding now so universally used, by a varnish made of amber, aloes, spirits of wine etc. upon leaf-silver, was first brought into England by John Evelyn out of France and communicated to several gentlemen. But I think the Howards procured a patent.

Chocolate first brought out of Spain by Sir Arthur Hopton, ambassador there about 1647. My Lady Browne, wife to Sir Richard Browne, his majesty Charles I's resident with the French king, in whose house Sir Arthur lived, being recalled from Spaine, was the first English lady who brought it into common use.

Marble paper was not truly made till Mr Evelyn brought home the right receipt.

SPOONS

In the old time, they did suppe their pottage, e.g. King Henry I's son said to Symon of Southampton: 'Sup, Symon, 'tis good broath', and at the Temple yet, on rice milk days, they go to the kitchen and sup or lap out of a dish.

They had only the bottom of the loaf for a trencher. Plates came in after trenchers in the time of Charles I or a little after: nor till then used they forks: 'twas counted affected. And then they more used of glasses, before they drank in bowls and beakers and instead of flagons and pots, black jacks, especially in the halls.

LIMEING OF LAND

Limeing of grounds first used in Devonshire, something after the coming-in of tobacco, that is, it was first used about the year 1595. From Sir Edward Ford of Devon. Mr Clark of the Hill in Herefordshire found the fruitfulness of ground where a load of lime fell and slaked in the dirt, and so made use of it for improvement in that country.

Mr Lort in Pembrokeshire got his estate by being the Earl of Pembroke's steward and brought lime from Devonshire.

TOBACCO

Riders Almanack 1682: since tobacco was brought into England by Sir Walter Raleigh, 99 years.

The custom hereof is now the greatest of all others, and amounts now (1688) to four hundred thousand pounds per annum, from Mr Michael Weekes of the Custom House. Sir Richard Baker's *Chronicle* says tobacco was first brought into England by Ralph Lane in the eight and twentieth year of Queen Elizabeth. They first used silver pipes, which they washed, before the earthen were invented – Mr J. Evelyn.

The taking of tobacco in snuff brought out of Italy and Spain into France; then by King Charles II into England – J. Evelyn.

GUNPOWDER

Not far from Wolton in Surrey (the seat of John Evelyn Esq) upon the streams and ponds since filled up and drained, stood formerly many powder-mills, created by his ancestors, who were the first who brought this invention into England: before which we had all our powder out of Flanders. The grandfather of John Evelyn Esq aforesaid transferred his patent to the later Sir John Evelyn's grandfather of Godstone in the same county in whose family it continued till the late civil wars. By this *nouvelle* he got a great estate that would be worth now above eight thousand pounds per annum honestly and ingeniously which his posterity enjoys and hath much augmented.

CLOVER GRASS

Mr Randall of Chiswick in Surrey and Mr Anthony Thomas do affirm that Sir Richard Weston of Surrey was the first that brought clover grass into England, which was about the year 1643.

CATS

W. Laud, Archbishop of Canterbury, was a great lover of cats. He was presented with some Cyprus cats, i.e. our tabby cats, which were sold at first for £5 a piece: this was about 1637 or 1638. I do well remember that the common English cat was white with some bluish piedness, that is a gallipot blue: the race and breed of them are now almost lost.

CANE-CHAIRS

One Hedband (of Holstein) invented the cane chairs in the time of Oliver the Protector. The first that were sold by him were bought by Sir Daniel Harvey of Comb in Surrey: this information I had from one that was apprentice to Hedband.

The fashion brought out of the East Indies.

SEDANS (OR CHAIRS)

George Duke of Buckingham (the father) first used sedans in England. First brought in by Sir Sanders Duncomb, who obtained a patent.

SLITTING MILLS

Mr Foley (a nailer of Staffordshire) had the curiosity to take a journey into Cologne to see how they did slit their iron or steel: he thought it a shameful thing that we that have so much iron should be ignorant in that trick. He returns and sets up the slitting mills (by the assistance of some that he procured to assist him) and left an estate of six thousand pounds per annum. This was I believe in King Charles I's reign.

(Foley carried nails: then hired nailers; then went to Cologne and pretended to buy coney-skins, so saw the mill.)

FLAX AND LINEN

About the second year of King William and Queen Mary; Queen Mary encouraged the establishing of the flax and linen manufacture at the Salisbury exchange in the Strand.

CABBAGES

The mother of John Ash (the famous clothier) was born at Weymouth in Dorset: who remembered when all the cabbages were brought out of Holland: she was 80 years old when she died about 1659. This I had from her son Samuel Ash.

Memorandum: Sir Anthony Ashley of Wimborne St Giles in Dorset had great plantations of cabbages: he was one of the first planters of them in England. He had a command in the voyage to Cadiz, where he got a great deal of riches by rapine, and particularly from a great lady there, who entrusted him with all her jewels upon his honour, which his avarice made him forfeit. Whereupon there goes a jest in Dorsetshire made upon him, viz. that 'Sir Anthony got more by Cadiz, than ever he did by cabbage.' In Dorset the worts they call colewort cale. The Hon. Charles Howard of Dorking hath brought in scores of plants now common; but he values it not.

Aubrey as local historian

The Wiltshire Antiquities and Natural History of Wiltshire

Note: The *Wiltshire Antiquities* were edited by J. E. Jackson in 1862 as *Wiltshire. The Topographical Collections of John Aubrey*. Excerpts from the *Natural History of Wiltshire* were printed under that title by John Britton in 1847: I have used the original manuscripts in the Bodleian Library (MSS Aubrey 1 and 2) for the *Chorographia* of which Britton only printed a small selection.

1. The preface to Aubrey's *Wiltshire Antiquities*

At a meeting of gentlemen at Devizes for choosing of knights for the shire in March 1659, it was wished by some that this county, wherein are many observable antiquities, were surveyed in imitation of Mr Dugdale's Illustration of Warwickshire: but it being too great a task for one man, Mr William Yorke (counsellor at law and a lover of this kind of learning) advised to have the labour divided. He himself would undertake the middle division. I would undertake the north. T. Gore, Esq. Jeffrey Daniel, Esq. and Sir John Erneley would be assistants. Judge Nicholas was the greatest antiquary as to evidences that this county hath had in memory of man: and had taken notes in his *Adversaria*, of all the ancient deeds that came to his hands. Mr Yorke had taken some memorandums in this kind too. Both now dead. 'Tis pity that those papers should fall into the merciless hands of women, and be put under pies.

But this good design vanished 'over their tobacco pipes', and was never thought of since. I have, since that, occasionally made this following collection which perhaps may some time or other fall into some antiquary's hands to make a handsome work of it. I hope my worthy friend Mr Anthony Wood of Oxford will be the man. I am heartily sorry I did not set down the antiquities of these parts sooner, for since the time aforesaid many things are irrevocably lost.

In former days the churches and great houses hereabouts did so abound with monuments and things remarkable that it would have deterred an antiquary from undertaking it. But as Pythagoras did guess at the vastness of Hercules' stature by the length of his foot, so among these ruins are remains enough left for a man to give a guess what noble buildings, etc were made by the piety, charity, and magnanimity of our forefathers.

> And as in prospects we are there pleased most,
> Where something keeps the eye from being lost,
> And leaves us roome to guess;
> > [Sir John Suckling]

so here, the eye and mind is no less affected with these stately ruins than they would have been when standing and entire. They breed in generous minds a kind of pity; and set the thoughts to work to make out their magnificence as they were when in perfection. These remains are (like fragments of a shipwreck) that after the revolution of so many years and governments have escaped the teeth of time and

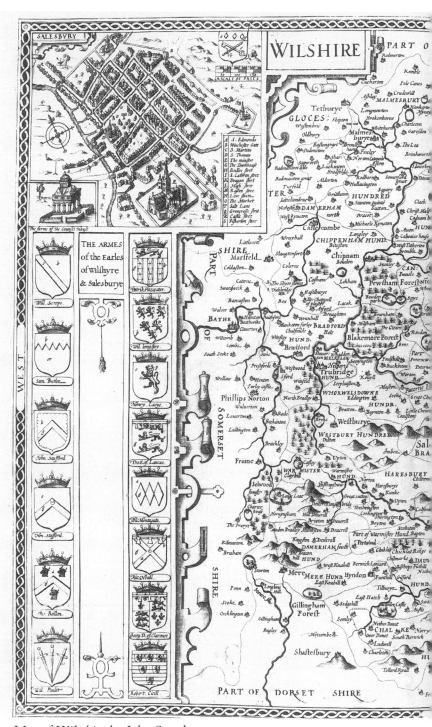

Map of Wiltshire by John Speed

(which is more dangerous) the hands of mistaken zeal. So that the retrieving of these forgotten things from oblivion in some sort resembles the art of a conjuror who makes those walk and appear that have lain in their graves many hundreds of years: and represents as it were to the eye, the places, customs, and fashions, that were of old time. It is said of antiquaries, they wipe off the mouldiness they dig, and remove the rubbish.

Let us imagine then what kind of country this was in the time of the ancient Britons. By nature of the soil, which is a sour woodsere land, very natural for the production of oaks especially, one may conclude that this north division was shady dismal wood: and the inhabitants almost as savage as the beasts whose skins were their only raiment. The language British, which for the honour of it was in those days spoken from the Orcades to Italy and Spain. The boats on the Avon (which signifies river) were baskets of twigs covered with an ox skin: which the poor people in Wales use to this day. They call them curricles. Within this shire I believe that there were several petty kings which often made war one upon another: and the great ditches which run on the plains and elsewhere so many miles were (not unlikely) their boundaries: and withal served for defence against the incursions of their enemies, as the Pict's Wall, Offa's Ditch: and that in China, to compare things small to great. Their religion is at large described by Caesar. Their priests were the Druids: some of their temples I pretend to have restored, as Avebury, Stonehenge, etc, as also British sepulchres. Their way of fighting is lively set down by Caesar. Their camps with their way of meeting their antagonists I have set down in another place. They knew the use of iron; and about Hedington fields, Bromham, Bowden, etc, are still ploughed up cinders, the scoria of melted iron. (In Herefordshire, towards Monmouthshire, are many Roman cinders found; which they use in their bloomeries now to make their ore run the better). They were two or three degrees I suppose less savage than the Americans. Till King John's time wolves were in this island: and in our grandfather's days more foxes than now, and martens (a beast of brown rich fur) at Stanton park etc: the race now extinct thereabout.

The Romans subdued and civilized them. At Lackham, Mr Camden saith was a colony of them, as appears by the Roman coin found there. About 1654 in Weekfield in the parish of Heddington digging up the ground deeper than the plough went, they found for a great way together, foundations of houses, hearths, coals, and a great deal of Roman coin, silver and brass; whereof I had a pint: some little copper pieces no bigger than silver halfpence – query if they were not the Roman *denarii*. The pot in which a good deal was found, I had. I presented it to the Royal Society's repository: it resembles an apprentice's earthen Christmas box. At Sherston hath several times been found Roman money in ploughing. I have one silver piece found there not long since (1653), of Constantine the Great. Among other arts, that of architecture was introduced by them, and no doubt but here as well as in other parts were then good building, here being so good stone. I know not any vestige now left in this county, except the fragment of the castle of Salisbury: which takes its name from Caesar: Caesaris burghus, from whence Sarisburgh, whence Salisbury: R being often changed into L. At Bath are several Roman inscriptions, which Mr Camden hath set down, and by the west gate a piece of a delicate Corinthian frieze which he calls 'wreathed leaves', not understanding architecture; and by, a bas-relief of an Ophiouchus. At Bathford about 1663 was found a grotto paved with mosaic work.

(Memorandum: we find in England, never an elm to grow naturally in a wood, as oaks, ashes, etc. This consideration made me reflect that they were exotic: but by whom brought into England? By the Saxons they could not: for upon enquiry they tell me none there, nor in Denmark, nor yet in France: therefore neither by the Danes, nor French. But in Italy they are naturally, e.g. Lombardy, etc. Therefore they were brought by the Romans, who were great improvers, and had great skill in husbandry, as we see by Columella.)

The Britons received the knowledge of husbandry from the Romans: the foot and the acre which we yet use is the nearest to them. In our west country (and I believe so in the north) they give no wages to the shepherd, but he has the keeping so many sheep with his master's flock. Plautus hints at this in his *Asinaria*, Act iii, scene i, 1.36.

The herdsman, too, who, like a mother, pastures strangers' sheep
Has some of his own too, who are his chiefest hope.

The Saxons succeeded them, and driving them away to Ireland, Cornwall, etc, these Roman Britons left here: (for they used the best of them in their wars, being their best soldiers). Here was a mist of ignorance for 600 years. They were so far from knowing arts that they could not build wall with stone. The church of Glastonbury was thatched.

They lived sluttishly in poor houses, where they ate a great deal of beef and mutton, and drank good ale in a brown mazer: and their very kings were but a sort of farmers. After the Christian religion was planted here it gave a great shoot; and the kings and great men gave vast revenues to the church, who were ignorant enough in those days. The Normans then came and taught them civility and buildings;

which though it was gothic as also their policy (feudal law) yet they were magnificent. For the government, till the time of Henry VIII, it was like a nest of boxes: for copy-holders, (who till then, were villeins) held of the lords of the manor, who held of a superior lord, who held perhaps of another superior lord or duke, who held of the king. Upon any occasion of bustling in those days, one of the great lords sounded his trumpet (all lords then kept trumpeters, even to King James) and summoned those that held under them: those again sounded their trumpets, and so on downwards to the copyholders. Old Sir Walter Long, grandfather to Colonel Long, kept a trumpeter: and rode with thirty servants and retainers to Marlborough and so for others of his rank in his time.

The Court of Wards was a great bridle in those days.

A great part of this Division held of the honour of Trowbridge, where is a ruinated castle of the dukes of Lancaster. No younger brothers then were by the custom and constitution of the realm to betake themselves to trade: but were churchmen, or retainers and servants to great men: rode good horses, (now and then took a purse) and their blood that was bred of the good tables of their masters, was upon every occasion freely let out in their quarrels. It was then too common amongst their masters to have feuds with one another, and their servants, at market, or where they met (in that slashing age) did commonly bang one another's bucklers. Then an esquire when he rode to town, was attended by eight or ten men in blue coats with badges. The lords (then lords in deed as well as in title) lived in their countries like petty kings, had *jura regalia* belonging to their seignories, had their castles and boroughs, and sent burgesses to the lower house [of parliament]: had gallows within their liberties where they could try, condemn, hang, and draw.

(At Combe, a gallows were standing within these 50 years. At Tormarton in Gloucestershire anciently the seat of Rivers [then St. Loe by match] is a dungeon about thirteen or fourteen foot deep of good ashlar work. About 4 foot high are iron rings fastened into the wall, which was probably to tie offending villeins, as anciently all lords of manors had this power over their villeins, and had all of them no doubt sure places for their punishment. To ascend higher to seignories; all castles have dungeons: and I believe so had monasteries, for they have within themselves power of life and death; witness the poor monk in France that upon complaint of his friends to the bishop, had him plucked out, but his feet and hands rotten, and shortly after died, 1663.) The lords of manors never went to London but in parliament time, or once a year to do their homage and duty to the king. They kept good houses in their countries, did eat in their great gothic halls, at the high table, or oriel, the folk at the side tables. The meat was served up by watchwords. Jacks are but an invention of the other age. The poor boys did turn the spits, and licked the dripping pan, and grew to be huge lusty knaves. The beds of the servants and retainers were in the great halls, as now in the guard chamber, privy chamber, etc.

> A neat built chapel and a spacious hall
> Were all the rooms of note: the rest were small.

The hearth was commonly in the middle, as at most colleges, whence the saying 'round about our coal fire'. Anciently, till about the reformation, ordinary men's houses had no chimneys, but flues, like louvre holes; some of them were in being when I was a boy. Here in the Halls were the mummings, cob-leaf stealing, and great number of old Christmas plays performed. Every baron and gentleman of estate kept great horses for a man-at-arms: lords had their armouries to furnish some hundreds of men. The halls of justices of the peace were dreadful to behold. The screens were garnished with corselets and helmets gaping with open mouth: with coats of mail, lances, pikes, halberds, brown bills, batterdashers, bucklers, and the modern culvers and petronels, (in King Charles the first's time) turned into muskets and pistols. Then were entails in fashion (a good prop for monarchy). Destroying of petty manors began in Henry VII's reign to be now common: whereby the mean people lived lawless, nobody to govern them, they cared for nobody, having on nobody any dependence; and thus, and by the selling the church lands, is the balance of the government quite altered, and put into the hands of the common people. No ale house nor yet inns then, unless upon great roads. When they had a mind to drink, they went to the friaries: and when they travelled they had entertainment at the religious houses for three days, if occasion so long required. The meeting of the gentry was not held at tippling houses; but in the fields or forests with their horses and hounds, with their bugle horns in silken baldrics. This part very much abounded with forests and parks. Thus were good spirits kept up: and good horses and good riders made. Whereas now, the gentry of the nation is so effeminated by coaches, they are so far from managing great horses that they know not how to ride hunting horses; besides the spoiling of several trades dependent. In the last age, every gentlemanlike man (yeoman) kept a sparrow-hawk. A priest, I think, kept a hobby. And it was a divertisement for young gentlewomen to man sparrow-hawks and merlins. In Henry VI's time, one Dame Juliana Berners wrote *The Art of Hawking*, in English verse: it is in Wilton library. This country was then a lovely *campania*, as that about Sherton and Cotswold. Very few enclosures, unless near houses. My grandfather Lyte did remember when all between Cromhall's (Easton) and Castle Combe was so, when Easton, Yatton, and Combe did intercommon together. In my remembrance much hath been enclosed, and every year more and more is taken in. Anciently the leas (now corruptly called sleights), i.e., pastures, were noble large grounds as yet the demesne lands at Castle Combe are. So likewise in his remembrance was all between Kington St Michael and Draycot Cerne common field. Then were a world of labouring people maintained by the plough as yet in Northamptonshire, etc. There were no rates for the poor even in my grandfather's days: but for Kington St Michael (no small parish) the church ale at Whitsuntide did their business. In every parish is, or was, a church house, to which belonged spits, crocks, etc, utensils for dressing provision. Here the housekeepers met, and were merry and gave their charity: the young people came there too, and had dancing, bowling, shooting at butts, etc, the ancients sitting gravely by, looking on. All things were civil and without scandal. This church ale is doubtless derived from the Agapae or love feast mentioned in the New Testament. Mr A. Wood assures me that there were scarcely any almshouses before the Reformation. That over against Christchurch, Oxford, is one of the ancientest. In every church was a poor man's box; but I never remembered the use of it. Nay, there was one at great inns. I remember it before the wars. Before the Reformation, at their vigils or revels they sat up all night fasting and praying the night before the dedication of the church: certain officers were chosen for gathering the money for charitable uses. Old John Wastefield of Langley near Chippenham was peterman at St Peter's Chapel there: at which time is yet one of the greatest revels in these parts: but the chapel converted into a dwelling house. Such joy and merriment was every holiday: which days were kept with great solemnity and reverence. These were the days when England was famous for the grey goose quill. The clerk's ale was in the Easter holidays, for his benefit, and the solace of the neighbourhood.

Since the Reformation and enclosures aforesaid, these parts have swarmed with poor people. The parish of Calne pays to the poor (1663) £500 per annum: and the parish of Chippenham little less, as appears by the poor's books there. Enclosures are for the private, not for the public good. For a shepherd and his dog, or a milk maid, can manage that land, that upon arable employed the hands of several scores of labourers.

In those times (besides the jollities already mentioned) they had their pilgrimages to Walsingham, Canterbury, and several shrines hereabout; to St Joseph of Arimathea at his chapel in Glastonbury Abbey. In the roads thither were several houses of entertainment built purposely for them. Among others was the house called the Chapel of Plaister near Box: and a great house without Lafford's gate near Bristol. Then the crusades to the Holy War were most magnificent and glorious, and the rise, I believe, of the adventures of knights errant and romances. The solemnities of procession in and about the churches and the perambulation in the fields, besides their convenience, were fine diversions. The priests went before in their formalities singing the Latin service, and the people came after making their good-meaning responses. The reverence given to holy men was very great. Then were the churches open all day long, men and women going in and out leisurely to and from their devotions. Then were the consciences of the people kept in so great awe, by confession, that just dealing and virtue were habitual. Sir Edwyn Sandys did observe in his travels in the Catholic Countries so great use of confession as aforesaid, that though a severe enemy to the Church of Rome, he doth heartily wish it had never been left out by the Church of England: perceiving the great good it does beyond sea. In the halls, parlours, etc, there were written texts of scripture: and good sentences on the painted cloths, which does something evidence the piety of those days more than now.

The tablecloth was on the board all day long ready for what was to be set thereon for strangers, travellers, friars, pilgrims, etc: And so it was, I have heard my grandfather say, in his grandmother's time called Old Joan of Easton; and my honoured grandmother Mrs Israel Lyte was also of this hospitable nature. At the parish priest's houses in France, especially in Languedoc, is the like.

Lent was a dismal time: strictly observed by fasting, prayer, and confessing against Easter. During the forty days the friars preached every day. Before the Reformation pulpits were generally stone. Several were in my boyhood altered. This country was very full of religious houses: a man could not have travelled but he must have met monks, friars, *bonshommes*, etc, in their several habits, black, white, and gray, etc: and the tingle-tangle of their convent bells I fancy made very pretty music, like the College bells at Oxford. 'The monks were good chemists, and invented many good recipes, which they imparted to their penitents; and so are handed down to their great grandchildren a great many rarities.' There were no free schools. The boys were educated at the monasteries. Mr M. Lloyd says that in Wales before the Reformation every man almost, of any fashion, could speak Latin. They learned it at the monasteries, where they spake it of duty. I believe the same might be said of England. The young maids were brought up not at Hackney, Sarum schools, etc to learn pride and wantonness, but at the nunneries, where they had examples of piety, and humility and modesty and obedience, to imitate and to practise. Here they learned needlework, the art of confectionery, surgery, (anciently no apothecaries or Surgeons – the gentlewomen did cure their poor neighbours: their hands are now too fine – *vide* Sir Courtly Nice in comedy, epilogue) physic, writing, drawing, etc. Old Jacques, (who lived where Charles Hadnam did) could see from his house the nuns of the Priory, (St Mary's near Kington St Michael) came forth into the Nymph-hay with their rocks and wheels to spin: and with their sewing work. He would say that he hath told threescore and ten: but of nuns there were not so many, but in all, with lay sisters, as widows, old maids, and young girls, there might be such a number. This was a fine way of breeding up young women, who are led more by example than precept; and a good retirement for widows and grave single women to a civil, virtuous, and holy life.

Plato says that the foundation of government is the education of youth. By this means it is most probable that then was a golden age. I have heard Judge Jenkins, Mr J. Latchmere and other lawyers say that before the reformation one shall hardly in a year find an action of the case as for slander, etc. It was the result of a good government. It is a sarcasm more malicious than true commonly thrown at the churchmen, that they had too much land for their constitution, being in truth considered that they were rather administrators of these great revenues to pious and public uses, than usufructuaries. As for themselves, they had only their habit and competent diet, every order according to the prescribed rule, from which they were not to vary. Then for their tenants, their leases were almost as good to them as fee simple, and perchance might longer last in their families. Sir William Button (the father) hath often told me, that Alton farm (£400 a year), had been held by his ancestors from the abbey of Winchester about four hundred years. The Powers of Stanton Quintin held that farm, of the abbey of Cirencester, in lease three hundred years and my ancestors the Danverses held West Tokenham for many generations of the abbey of Broadstock, where one of them was a prior. (Memorandum: that in the abbeys, were several corrodies granted for poor old shiftless men, which Fitzherbert speaks of amongst his writs.) In France to every parish church is more than one priest; because of the several masses to be said; which fashion Mr Dugdale tells me was used here.

In many chancels are to be seen three seats with niches in the wall (most commonly on the south side) rising by degrees, and sometimes only three seats; the first being for the bishop, second for the priest: and third for the deacon, whenever the bishops visited their churches in person. This from Mr Dugdale; as also that in many churches where stalls are, as at cathedrals, (which I mistook for chantries) were collegiate churches. The architecture of the churches of the west is much better than the east of England. Mr Dugdale told Dr Wren and me that about Henry III's time, a pope gave a bull or patent to a company of Italian architects to travel up and down to build churches.

Heretofore (before Henry VIII's reign) glass windows were very rare, only used in churches and best rooms of gentlemen's houses. Even in my remembrance, before the civil wars, copyholders, and ordinary poor people had none. Now, the poorest people that are upon alms, have it. In Herefordshire, Monmouth, Salop, etc, it is so still; but now [1671] are going up no less than three glass-houses between Gloucester and about Worcester. So that glass will be common over all England.

When I came to Oxford crucifixes were common in the glass in the study windows; and in the chamber windows were canonized saints: (e.g. in my chamber window, St Gregory the Great, and another broken) and scutcheons, with the pillars, the whip, the dice, and the cock. But after 1647 they were all broken: down went Dagon. Now no religion to be found. Without doubt before the Reformation there was no county in England but had several glass-painters. I only remember one poor one, an old man, Harding at Blandford.

Memorandum: anciently no bands worn about their necks, but fur, as in old glass pictures.

Memorandum: till Queen Elizabeth's time, no hats, but caps – i.e. bonnets. Trunk hose in fashion till the latter end of King James I's reign.

By reason of fasting days, all gentlemen's houses had anciently fishponds, and fish in the moats about the house.

About ninety years ago (about 1580) noblemen's and gentlemen's coats were of the fashion of the beadles and yeomen of the guard – i.e. gathered at the girdle place. Our bencher's gowns retain yet that fashion of gathering.

All old bailiff's accounts with numeral letters. Even in my remembrance when I was a boy, in the country bailiffs commonly used no other. The shopkeepers anciently counted with counters: which is the best way and still used by the French.

I remember that before the late wars the Ministers in Herefordshire and counties that way had the title of 'Sir'; as the bachelors of arts have at Oxford, as 'Sir Richard of Stratford', 'Sir William of Monkland', and so it was in Wilts when my grandfather Lyte was a

boy: and anciently everywhere. An example of this appears in the
excellent comedy of *The Scornful Ladie* where 'Sir Roger', the
chaplain, has a great part. It was made by Mr T. Fletcher about the
beginning of King James's times: but in old wills before the
Reformation it is upon record. When I was a child (and so before the
civil wars) the fashion was for old women and maids to tell fabulous
stories night-times, of sprites and walking of ghosts, etc. This was
derived down from mother to daughter, etc, from the monkish
balance which upheld holy church, for the divines say, 'Deny spirits,
you are an atheist.' When the wars came, and with them liberty of
conscience and liberty of inquisition, the phantoms vanished. Now
children fear no such things, having heard not of them; and are not
checked with such fears.

Sir John Danvers told me that when he was a young man the
principal reason of sending their sons to travels, was to wean them
from their acquaintance and familiarity with the servingmen: for
then parents were so austere and grave, that the sons must not be
company for their father; and some company man must have – so,
contracted a familiarity with servingmen who got a hank upon them
they could hardly claw off. Nay: parents would suffer their servants to
domineer over their children, and some, in what they found their
children to take delight, in that would be sure to cross them.

The use of 'your humble servant' came into England by the
marriage of Queen Mary, daughter of Henry IV of France (Henrietta
Maria) derived from 'vostre tres humble serviteur'; and never heard
of before; but 'God keep you', 'God be wi' ye', 'How dost do?' with a
thump on the shoulder.

Till this time the court itself was unpolished and unmannered.
King James's court was so far from being civil to women, that the
ladies, nay the queen herself, could hardly pass by the king's
apartment without receiving some affront.

Before the late civil wars, in gentlemen's houses at Christmas time,
the first dish that was brought to table was a boar's head with a lemon
in his mouth. At Queen's College in Oxford they still retain this
custom: the bearer of it brings it into the hall, singing to an old tune,
an old Latin rhyme 'Caput apri defero', etc.

Heretofore noblemen and gentlemen of fair estates had their
heralds who wore their coat of arms at Christmas and at other solemn
times and cried 'Largesse' thrice.

The first dish that was brought up to the table on Easter Day was a
red herring riding away a-horseback; i.e., a herring ordered by the
cook something after the likeness of a man a-horseback, set in a corner
sallett.

From the time of Erasmus till about twenty years past [1536–1650], the learning was downright pedantry. The conversation and habits of those times were as starch as their bands and square beards: and gravity was then taken for wisdom. The doctors in those days were but old boys, when quibbles passed for wit, even in their sermons. The gentry and citizens had little learning of any kind, and their way of breeding of their children was suitable to the rest. They were as severe to their children as their schoolmasters; and their schoolmasters, as masters of the house of correction. The child perfectly loathed the sight of his parents as the slave his torture. Gentlemen of thirty and forty years old were to stand like mutes and fools bareheaded before their parents; and the daughters (grown women) were to stand at the cupboard-side during the whole time of the proud mother's visit, unless (as the fashion was) leave was desired, forsooth, that a cushion should be given them to kneel upon, brought them by the serving man, after they had done sufficient penance in standing. The boys, (I mean the young fellows), had their foreheads turned up, and stiffened with spittle: they were to stand mannerly forsooth thus: the foretop ordered as before, with one hand at the bandstring: the other behind them. The gentlewomen had prodigious fans, as is to be seen in old pictures, like that instrument which is used to drive feathers: and in it had a handle at least half a yard long: with these the daughters were oftentimes corrected. (Sir Edward Coke, Lord Chief Justice, rode the circuit with such a fan. Sir William Dugdale told me he was an eyewitness of it. The Earl of Manchester also used such a fan.) But fathers and mothers slashed their daughters in the time of their besom discipline when they were perfect women. At Oxford, (and I believe at Cambridge) the rod was frequently used by the tutors and deans. And Dr Potter, of Trinity College, I knew right well, whipped his pupil with his sword by his side, when he came to take his leave of him to go to the Inns of Court.

This searching after antiquities is a wearisome taske. I wish I had gone through all the Church monuments. The records at London I can search gratis. Though of all studies I take the least delight in this, yet methinks I am carried on with a kind of divine oestrum: for nobody else hereabout hardly cares for it, but rather makes a scorn of it. But methinks it shows a kind of gratitude and good nature to revise the memories and memorials of the pious and charitable benefactors since dead and gone.

Easton Piers   *John Aubrey*
April 28, 1670

2. Two typical entries from the topographical collections for Wiltshire

COLERNE

Here is a most noble prospect, a stately high well built tower, which, when the bells, which are new cast, ring, shakes much. A very fair church, but nothing of antiquity left, unless the three seats in the chancel for the bishop, and others; an old niche of a monument, but figure and inscription gone.

This coat, a plain cross, is on the west side, of the outside of the tower of the church.

In Burywood is a camp, double works; ergo, not Roman but British: very large, and the graffes [ditches] are very deep, notwithstanding the rock. It hath an aperture, west, towards Colerne down. It stands on a kind of promontory, and every other side is well secured by the precipice. A pretty clear little stream runs on the rock, and gravel in each bottom.

At Colerne Park, above Slaughtenford, they tell me there is a single works camp: i.e. Roman, which see.

Memorandum: at Ford-hill is a rampart with graffe eastward, but no camp; it was to obstruct the enemy's coming; the like whereof is to.be seen in several other places. – Q. If the trench aforementioned, at Colerne Park, is not of the same nature?

Ask Dominie Matravers about this: as also what old things he can remember. He is almost one hundred years of age.

Colerne down is the place so famous and frequented for stool-ball playing. The turf is very fine, and the rock is within an inch and a half of the surface, which gives the ball so quick a rebound.

They smite the ball with a staff, commonly made of withy about three feet and a half long. A stool-ball is of about four inches diameter, stuffed very hard with quills, sewed into sole leather, and as hard as a stone. I do not hear it is used but hereabout and in Gloucestershire adjacent.

Hall Farm
Q. If this was not anciently the [property of the] Halls? Sutton bought this manor of King James to give it to Charterhouse, at London.

Thickwood
In this manor wills are proved and recorded in the court rolls.

SEEND

This village is about a mile from the spring at Poulshot before-mentioned. It is on a red-sandy hill, from whence it has its name, Sand in the Old English being called Send; as Send, a village in Surrey, on a sandy soil. In this hill underneath the sand is iron ore, and the richest that I have seen, for the smith can make the ore he takes up in the street melt in his forge, which the ore in the Forest of Dean will not do. In the street, where the sand has been worn and washed away, the ore appears after a shower, and it glisters when the sun shines. Melksham Forest reached to the foot of this hill. It was full of good oaks, which were cut down about 1634, and sold, and nobody then ever took notice of this iron ore, which every sunshiny day, after a shower, glistered in their eyes; now there are very few oaks left in this parish, or thereabout, and so this rich mine cannot be melted. Finding this plenty of ore, I presently concluded that I should find here some water impregnated with it, and tried some wells with powder of galls, with which infusion the wells of the South side did turn; the North side not. The principal well is that belonging to Mr John Sumner, which upon infusion with galls, immediately became as black as ink, so that I could write with it to read it. Neither Tunbridge water, nor any other iron water I ever could meet with, would do the like.

Memorandum: Mr Francis Lodwyck told me that mention is made in some of our histories, that Henry VII was in exile some time, and lived at the Duke of Burgundy's court. The staple for our wool was then at Calais, and 'twas manufactured by the Walloons. When he came to the Crown he sent for a number of them to come into England, to set up the clothing trade there, and Mr Lodwyck says the history says, that they were settled in Wiltshire, and that there are still several of their descendants with Dutch and French names. I remember one Mr Goupy, and I had to do with a merchant of his name at Tours. I remember I heard them say, that heretofore this was a great place of clothing, namely about ninety and more years since. I have now forgot the reason of their removal hence to Trowbridge. The good houses here were built by the clothiers; I know not any small country village that has so many well built houses.

In The Natural History of Wiltshire, *Aubrey expands the above notes on the well at Seend, and adds:*

In June 1667, I sent for three bottles of this well water to London, and experimented it before the Royal Society at Gresham College, at which time there was a frequent assembly, and many of the Physicians of the College of London. Now, whereas the water of Tunbridge, and others of that kind, being carried but few miles lose

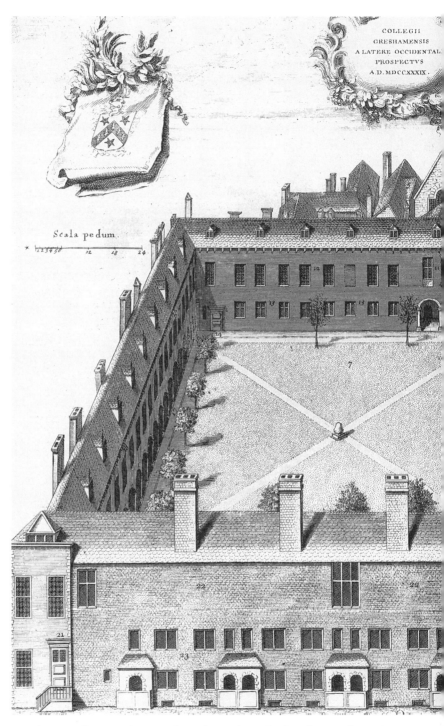

COLLEGII
GRESHAMENSIS
A LATERE OCCIDENTAL.
PROSPECTVS
A.D. MDCCXXXIX.

Scala pedum.

*Gresham College, in the city of London, where the founder members of
The Royal Society regularly met*

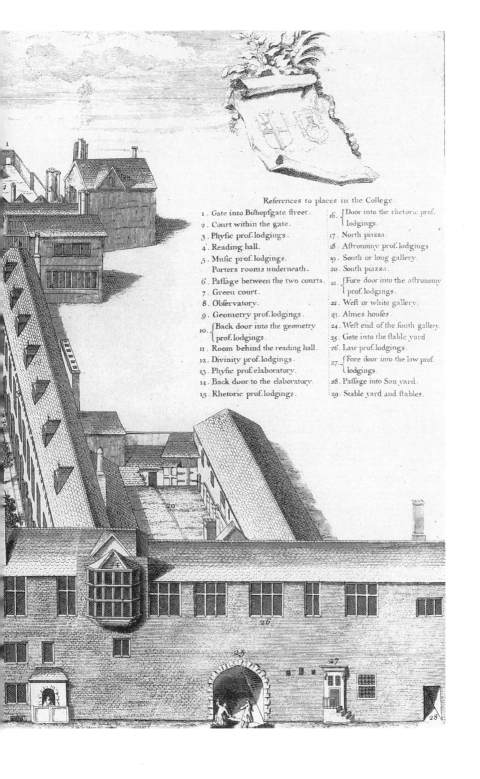

References to places in the College.

1. Gate into Bishopsgate street.
2. Court within the gate.
3. Physic prof. lodgings.
4. Reading hall.
5. Music prof. lodgings. Porters rooms underneath.
6. Passage between the two courts.
7. Green court.
8. Observatory.
9. Geometry prof. lodgings.
10. { Back door into the geometry prof. lodgings.
11. Room behind the reading hall.
12. Divinity prof. lodgings.
13. Physic prof. elaboratory.
14. Back door to the elaboratory.
15. Rhetoric prof. lodgings.
16. { Door into the rhetoric prof. lodgings.
17. North piazza.
18. Astronomy prof. lodgings
19. South or long gallery.
20. South piazza.
21. { Fore door into the astronomy prof. lodgings.
22. West or white gallery.
23. Almes houses.
24. West end of the south gallery.
25. Gate into the stable yard
26. Law prof. lodgings.
27. { Fore door into the law prof. lodgings.
28. Passage into Sun yard.
29. Stable yard and stables.

their spirits, and do not alter their colour at all with powder of galls, these bottles, being brought by the carrier eighty odd miles, and in so hot weather, did turn, upon the infusion of the powder, as deep as the deepest claret; to the admiration of the physicians then present, who unanimously declared that this water might do much good; and Dr Piers said that in some cases such waters were good to begin with, and to end with the Bath; and in some the contrary. This place is but 9 or 10 miles from Bath.

The doctors then spake to me, to write to some physicians at Bath, and to recommend it to them, whom I knew; which I did. But my endeavours were without effect till August 1684. But they do so much good that they now speak aloud their own praises. They were satisfied (I understood at last) of the goodness and usefulness of these waters, but they did not desire to have patients to be drawn from the Bath. Now, whereas one person is grieved with aches, or bruises, or dead palsies, for which diseases the Bath is chiefly proper, ten or more are ill of chronical diseases and obstructions, for the curing whereof these chalybeate waters are the most sovereign remedy.

This advertisement I desired Dr Richard Blackburn to word. He is one of the College of Physicians, and practiseth yearly at Tunbridge-wells. It was printed in an Almanack of Hen. Coley about 1681, but it took no effect.

'Advertisement. – At Seend (near Devizes in Wiltshire) are springs discovered to be of the nature and virtue of those at Tunbridge, and altogether as good. They are approved of by several of the physicians of the College in London, and have done great cures, viz. particularly in the spleen, the reins, and bladder, affected with heat, stone, or gravel; or restoring hectic persons to health and strength, and wonderfully conducing in all cases of obstructions.'

I proceeded and tried other wells, but my ingenious faithful servant Robert Wiseman tried all the wells in the village, and found that all the wells of the south side do turn with galls more or less, but the wells of the north side turn not with them at all. This hill lies eastward and westward; quod NB.

The water of John Sumner's well was so bad for household use that they could not brew nor boil with it, and used it only to wash the house, etc; so that they were necessitated to sink a well in the common, which is walled, about a bowshot or more from his dwelling house, where is fresh and wholesome water.

Memorandum: Dr Greer in his (catalogue) of the Royal Society has mistaken this well in the common for the medieval well of J. Sumner. But, memorandum, there is another well that turns, I think, as deep as J. Sumner's.

The Natural History of Wiltshire

PREFACE

Till about the year 1649,* 'twas held a strange presumption for a man
to attempt an innovation in learning; and not to be good manners to
be more knowing than his neighbours and forefathers. Even to
attempt an improvement in husbandry, thought it succeeded with
profit, was looked upon with an ill eye. Their neighbours did scorn to
follow it, though not to do it was to their own detriment. 'Twas held
a sin to make a scrutiny into the ways of nature; whereas Solomon
saith, 'The world is betrayed by the arguments of men' and it is
certainly a profound part of religion to glorify God in his works.

In those times to have had an inventive and enquiring wit was
accounted affectation, which censure the famous Dr William Harvey
could not escape for his admirable discovery of the circulation of the
blood. He told me himself that upon his publishing that book he fell
in his practice extremely.

Foreigners say of us that we are 'lynxes abroad, moles at home'.
There is no nation abounds with greater variety of soils, plants, and
minerals than ours; and therefore it very well deserves to be surveyed.
Certainly there is no hunting to be compared with 'the hunting of
threads'; and to take no notice at all of what is daily offered before our
eyes is gross stupidity.

I was from my childhood affected with the view of things rare;
which is the beginning of philosophy: and though I have not had
leisure to make any considerable proficiency in it, yet I was carried on
with a secret impulse to undertake this task: I knew not why, unless
for my own private pleasure. Credit there was none; for it gets the
contempt of a man's neighbours. But I could not be quiet till I had
obeyed this secret call. Mr Camden, Dr Plott, and Mr Wood confess
the like.

I am the first that ever made an essay of this kind for Wiltshire, and,
for ought I know, in the nation; having begun it in the year 1656. In
the year 1675 I became acquainted with Dr Robert Plott, who had
then his 'Natural History of Oxfordshire' upon the loom, which I
seeing he did perform so excellently well, desired him to undertake
Wiltshire, and I would give him all my papers: as I did also my papers
of Surrey as to the natural things, and offered him my further
assistance. But he was then invited into Staffordshire to illustrate that
county; which having finished in December 1684, I importuned him

---

* Experimental Philosophy was then first cultivated by a club at Oxford.

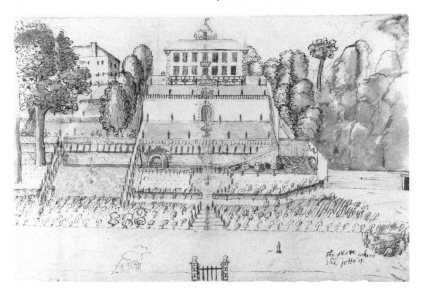

Two watercolours by Aubrey of Easton Piers, or Percy, his family home, after its rebuilding. The sketches show his plans for the garden

again to undertake this county: but he replied he was so taken up in arranging of the Ashmolean Museum that he should meddle no more in that kind, unless it were for his native county of Kent: and therefore wished me to finish and publish what I had begun. Considering therefore that if I should not do this myself, my papers might either perish, or be sold in an auction, and somebody else, as is not uncommon, put his name to my pains; and not knowing any one that would undertake this design while I live, I have tumultuarily stitched up what I have many years since collected; being chiefly but the observations of my frequent road between South and North Wilts; that is, between Broad Chalk and Easton Piers. If I had had then leisure, I would willingly have searched the naturals of the whole county. It is now fifteen years since I left this country, and have at this distance inserted such additions as I can call to mind, so that methinks this description is like a picture that Mr Bathurst, BD of Trinity College, Oxon, drew of Dr Kettle some years after his death, by strength of memory only, he had so strong an idea of him: and it did well resemble him. I hope hereafter it will be an incitement to some ingenious and public-spirited young Wiltshire man to polish and complete what I have here delivered rough-hewn; for I have not leisure to heighten my style. And it may seem nauseous to some that I have raked up so many western vulgar proverbs, which I confess I do not disdain to quote, for proverbs are drawn from the experience and observations of many ages; and are the ancient natural philosophy of the vulgar, preserved in old English in bad rhythms, handed down to us.

But before I fly at the mark to make a description of this county, I will take the boldness to cancelleer, and give a general description of what parts of England I have seen, as to the soils: which I call *Chorographia Super and Subterranea* (or think upon a more fitting name).

Chorographia super, et subterranea

East from Bridgeport in Dorsetshire to Dover in Kent runs a vein of chalk: and the like south and north from Merton in South Wilts, near to Calne in North Wiltshire, namely over Salisbury plain about twenty miles distance: except the vale to Cherhill, no chalk farther northward.

About the middle of Salisbury plains are two villages called

Chiltern (*vulgo* Chittern). Chilt in the Saxon language signifies chalk.

The Isle of Wight is chalk: the Needles at the west end are peaked rocks of chalk. In the rocks here is jet found.

From Merton aforesaid (*vulgo* Martin) over the New Forest to the sea, is red gravel. Between Merton and Downton on the hills are woods of yew trees and underground stratums of thunderstones, i.e. copperas stones. From Roundway Down (which is like a promontory pointing at Devizes) to Newmarket in Cambridgeshire do run a ridge of hills of chalk, viz. from Roundway Down to White Horse hills, thence to Wathington Hills, Bucks, Bedfordshire, Hertfordshire and so to Cambridgeshire, Suffolk and Norfolk: enquire how far the chalk vein runs in Suffolk and Norfolk?

From Devizes to the Derry Hill above Chippenham, red sand and ironstone: and in many places is found blue marl under the sand: and in autumn when the leaves fall into the ditches thereabouts, the water in the ditches is of a bluish colour, which I was much concerned at when a schoolboy.

In the vale by Devizes, i.e. between that and Redhone, about six miles or more broad, the earth is of an olive colour: it bears good corn. In some places, as about Foxhanger etc, the earth almost a *terre-vert*: and I believe if one did bore one might find good *terre-vert*. 'Tis certain it hath its green tincture from copper: but how deep that lies, let it be tried by those that are concerned. From Chippenham to Gloucester (south and north) stonebrash, and grey slates: the earth the colour of a hare. The like from Marsfield in Gloucestershire to Morton Hinmarsh: all good barley land. It runs from Northampton-shire to the north of Oxfordshire. In all this tract the plovers (green etc) take great delight to feed, and plenty of them.

Over all Cotswold (Gloucs) in the arable land, abundance of wild tansy, and likewise it is so plentiful in the moors in Somersetshire, though one region is dry, and the other wet; so that the earth must be of the same temper. In Cotswold are many good freestone quarries (under the stone-brash) and, indeed, the freestone vein runs all along northward from Bath to Edinburgh, over all Scotland. I find the hazel is a signature of freestone as well as minerals: e.g. at Haselbury quarry, Wilts, which takes its denomination from them; from this quarry was drawn most of the stone with which our churches and convents were built [i.e. in Wiltshire].

Between Chippenham and Malmesbury is a stiff blue clay: especially in the parish of Kington St Michael. Wormwood grows hereabout plentifully: as also woodwax (luteola), my ladies bedstraw, sorrel and abundance of lower plants: they make good cheese hereabout. Also maidenhair (Kington St Michael and Easton Piers),

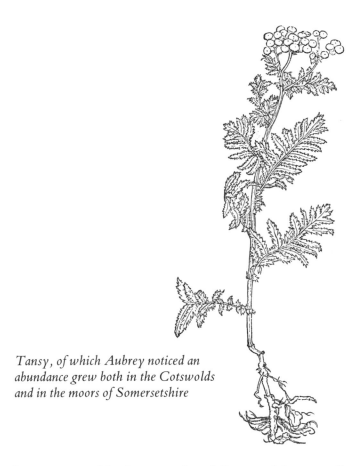

Tansy, of which Aubrey noticed an abundance grew both in the Cotswolds and in the moors of Somersetshire

hartstongue, adders'-tongue, brooklime etc: it is an excellent country for plants, and so farther southwest to Bath, nine miles.

From the isle of Purbeck (Dorset) to Egham in Surrey is all along heath: underneath which is red sand; here and there symptoms of iron ore. In some parts of Surrey little picos (volcanos).

Through the middle of Sussex runs a continued tract of downs (like a *spina dorsa*) from whence you have a most delightful prospect over the flat part of it to the sea: underneath the turf of the downs is chalk. Wheatears, and godwits (rare little birds) are most upon these downs.

The forest of Kingswood (Gloucs.) near Bristol, red earth, plenty of oaks; but I never saw or heard of anywhere else so great plenty of holly trees: underground full of coal: and I take from hence holly-trees to be a good indication of coal. 'Tis believed here may be coal enough to serve all England.

In the steep cliffs at Aust, by the river Severn, in the red earth, are great humps of alabaster: in some ploughed fields in Herefordshire, e.g. Burford and Burlton, are commonly found small pieces of it.

All the earth on the north side of the Severn, and likewise the stones, are of a dry nature, like smalt: it hath a kind of hungriness in it or rather thirstiness. How quickly it drinks up water or soil, as smalt doth. Herefordshire so: but Brecknockshire more: there is a barrenness or hungriness in the very stones thereabout.

From the river Severn northward, over all Wales, earth red. In the Forest of Dean great plenty of iron ore, and of red oaks. Here was before 1630 the greatest plenty of oaks of any part of England and the best for the building of ships: for the oaks here (as also in Wales) are tougher than the oaks of the south. North of Severn oaks plentiful, and much iron ore: and in some places red marl. The iron and the oak seem to have a kind of cognation: where the oaks do naturally abound, I account it to be an indication of iron: so in North Wilts, about Pewsham forest, etc. All Herefordshire and Shropshire red earth: whose red tincture is from Mars.

Between the Cotswold hills and the Vale of Evesham

Red earth, and iron-like stones from the vale of Gloucestershire to the Irish sea. People black hair'd, hard-eyed, choleric, and consequently active. From about Bath in Somersetshire to Northamptonshire, graystone and reddish earth.

From Redhone the ascent by the downs south from Devizes to the New Forest is down, namely Salisbury plain: underneath chalk and flints. New Forest red earth, gravel and pebbles.

Tewkesbury vale and Evesham vale breed fair lusty tough people. At Huntley in Gloucestershire, the nature of the people breaks with the soil; which there the sand leaves and the wet woodsere soil comes, and so the north part of Wiltshire. In the sandy part the natives are of muddy complexion, hard or black-eyed, quick; and the other slow, pale, long-visaged, drawling voice, spiteful, and as a result inhospitable, always cold in their feet, anxious, malicious, bigots and witches. According to the saying, you may as soon break your neck as your

thirst among 'em; on the other hand, in Herefordshire they will ask strangers as they ride along by their horses, invite them to drink.

Mendip hills (forest, in Somerset) limestone: much of which stone is full of the span of lead. Here in the mines is the greatest quantity of lead in England. The hills are very barren: but the hazel thrives pretty well, as likewise the yew trees upon the cliffs at Cheddar. As to the plants of this forest, consult *Gerard's Herbal*.

I have found by my own trial, that the wells in the city of Wells do yield upon precipitation the greatest quantity of limestone powder of any that I have tried, i.e. in a threefold or greater proportion, especially the water of the draught well at the Kings Arms (or Crown – enquire) Inn at Wells.

Make a map of Somersetshire, as to the meres, pastures, meadows, mountains and arable land, to guess what proportion they do bear to one another.

In Devonshire (they tell me) the earth is red: they have marl, with which they much improve their lands; and about Plymouth they have marble quarries.

In Cornwall is the greatest abundance of tin of any part of the world, so much that anciently the nation had its name from it.

Norfolk and Suffolk (towards the seaside) of a yellow, light sand (like that about Calais and Boulogne in Picardy) which is driven by the wind over the country and has encroached as far (almost) as Norwich.

Both in north and south Wales are petrified shells (from Mr Edward Lloyd) but the stones are all of a hard grit and full of little pocks as a grindstone. It is a very dry stone: both stones and casts quickly become dry. I do not remember that ever I saw gravel such as in England in Wales, but the earth and stones are full of exceeding small (atoms of) glistening sand. The stones in the mountains in north Wales look whetstonish, and a barrenness appears even in the very stones. I never saw or could hear of any freestone in Wales. In Anglesey, I remember the green blades of oats were as it were like rushes: and they tasted rusky. The plums in Wales are a great deal harder than ours.

A Welsh proverb, much observed by them:

Haf hyd galan
gaiaf hyd Fai

that is, if it be summerly weather till the Kalends of January, it will be winterly weather to May.

In south Wiltshire they observe if drops do hang on the hedges on Candlemas it will be a good pease year; much observed.

The stones and earth in Wales being of a dry nature by consequence their dwellings are dampish, as in clayy and marly and nitrous earth, inimical to the nerves, they are: this much conduces to their long life. At Dolgellau in Merionethshire (a great parish) Mr Meredith Lloyd hath seen a hundred (or more) of poor people of eighty years of age at church in a morning who come thither barefoot and barelegged a great way. 'Tis observed in Wales, that they that go barefoot and barelegged never have the king's evil (but they are begot of healthy and not luxurious parents).

About Birmingham the freestone is of a red colour, i.e. tinged by the effluvia of the iron: and (methinks) the deep red tincture of the soil and stone gives full evidence that there was a time when here great volcanoes caused that rubiginous colour.

Yellow ochre burnt becomes red: why may not this deep redness of the earth and stone proceed from a conflagration in the youth of the world? In the red sandy part of Surrey, it seems to be evident, as one may say reguluses of iron found in these sands: some like great tubes.

The series of rocky mountains from Snowdon hills in Carnarvonshire to Scotland, have (methinks) a resemblance of the ribs of arches in architecture.

In Yorkshire the earth and the stones full of very little atoms like silver no bigger than the smallest pins' heads, namely in the hollow way at Wentbrig, and at Dodington above Ferrybridge.

The natives of Yorkshire are tall, strong and long-legged. They call 'em opprobriously, long-legged tykes: a short man or woman very rare to be seen.

In these parts (and I presume all over the north) they do cast away all their L's if it comes before a consonant, as the French do cast off their s's. So they say not an old man but an owd man etc.

Plants

On the top of Netherdale hills, the earth, by time and rains, hath left the stones bare in the same posture nature placed them: out of their chinks grows plentifully graephalio.

Ragwort, *vulgo* swine-grass, grows too plentifully in good ground from Nottinghamshire to the bishopric of Durham.

Wormwood is plentiful in this country. The corn is mighty tall: they do reap their barley and oats, but their bread and beer is not right till you come to Grantham.

Wych-hazels plenty: at Fountains Abbey the leaves of young sprouts that grew out of the rocks were as long as my hand and more.

The whitty-tree (wayfaring tree) in the greatest abundance that ever I saw: and also the biggest, i.e. as big as ordinary ashes. In Hertfordshire they did plant them in their gardens near their houses when I was a boy, as a preservation against witchcraft and made pins for their yokes of it to keep their oxen from being forespoken.

When you are beyond Stamford you must bid farewell to elms; they call in the north wych hazels elms; enquire if the spinnies in Northamptonshire are not different from our southern elms, namely more slender and tender.

Old Captain Tooke of Kent, born in 1588 told me (1672) that cherries were first brought into Kent in the time of Henry VIII, who being in Flanders and liking cherries, his gardener brought them thence and propagated them in England, particularly in Kent, which soil is most proper for them.

Hops, a great commodity in Kent, most of any part of England: one said it is not above sixty years that they have taken to it; Captain Took saith about fourscore (1672).

Since the draining of the fens in Lincolnshire, it is observed that we have had dry summers; and that since that draining, Northampton-shire (heretofore very healthy) hath since been anguish and feverish and more infested with gnats. Sir Paul Neale said that in the bishopric of Durham is a coalery, which by reason of the damps, which did so frequently kill the workmen (sometimes ten in a month) that he could make little or nothing of it. It happened one time, that the workmen being merry with drink, fell to play with fire-brands and to throw live coals at one another by the head of the pit where they usually have fires. It fortuned that a firebrand fell into the bottom of the pit: whereat there proceeded such a noise as if it had been a gun: they, liking the sport, threw down more firebrands and there followed the like noise, for several times, and at length it ceased. They went to work after, and were free from damps. So having by good chance found out this experiment they do now, every morning, throw down some coals, and they work as securely as in any other mines. Memorandum: bitumen and sulphur are of a suffocating nature.

At Craven (in Yorkshire) where they eat scarce any flesh in a year, but feed on whey porridge and buttermilk, and milk-porridge; they are very tall and strong and live to be a hundred and twenty years old. Yorkshire men subtle and wary: no fools.

At Whitby (and thereabouts a good way) is great plenty of allum stone. There is a great allum work at Whitby, where they use a great deal of man's urine but the clerk of the works did assure me that the urine of these that drink nothing but water and butter-milk and eat whey porridge and milk porridge does weigh the heaviest: tried by their weighing glass to be heavier than the urine of the wine-drinkers at Whitby: the heaviest urine is the best.

About Ripon etc are white marl-pots; but no chalk.

In Yorkshire their cattle are larger than ours in the south: but the hares, blackbirds, pigeons etc not so big as ours.

The Scotch cows have many of them no horns: 'crumoc-cow'?

Beeches flourish in Buckinghamshire: from which tree (buc) it has its denomination, and so in Berkshire the birches (bic) which gives it its name. In Hertfordshire, hornbeam is the most common tree: in the west there are none. Black cherry-trees are there also extraordinary common. Wych hazels are very common in north Wilts: but not seen in the south of England. In Sir Neville Poole's park at Okesey are two wych hazels as big as most oaks: but in Yorkshire they are very common (they call 'em elms).

Petrified shells: as you ride from Cricklade to Highworth, Wilts, you find frequently roundish stones, as big, or bigger than one's head, which (I think) they call brain stones, for on the outside they resemble the ventricles of the brain; they are petrified sea mushrooms.

The free-stone of Haselbury [near Box] hath, amongst several other shells, perfect petrified scallop-shells. The rough stone about Chippenham (especially at Cockleborough) is full of petrified cockles. But all about the country between that and Tedbury, and about Malmesbury hundred, the rough stones are full of small shells like little cockles, about the bigness of a halfpenny.

At Dinton, on the hills on both sides, are perfect petrified shells in great abundance, something like cockles, but neither striated, nor invecked, nor any counter-shell to meet, but plain and with a long neck of a reddish gray colour, the inside part petrified sand; of which sort I gave a quantity to the Royal Society, about twenty years since; the species whereof Mr Hooke says is now lost.

At Portland (Dorset) the freestone is full of oyster-shells and a great deal of stuff like sugar candy, which Mr Hooke says is petrified salt water. Memorandum: this quarry hath not been discovered above fourscore years, that is, about 1590. The church of Portland, which is hard by the quarry (as likewise all the churches thereabout, even within ten miles of Salisbury) are built of Normandy freestone. The first Portland stone used about London was by Mr Inigo Jones for the building of the Banqueting house at Whitehall: which was after Dr Lamb was killed in the streets by the apprentices of London, for which the city was fined £10,000, which paid for the building of the banquetting house; since that building, Portland freestone is generally used at and about London.

At Long Lane (Somerset) and thereabouts between Kilmanton and Bruton are flints of a liver colour.

Pebbles are of an ovalish figure: how came they to be so? There was a time when they were *in fluore*: and as salts shoot into their respective figures, so pebbles into this oval; and they break according to their long diameter.

Essex is a great flat, from London to Colchester hardly any elevation. Matthew Paris says that in his time what is now the fens of Lincolnshire was counted the garden of England.

Winchelsea Haven now a great green meadow. Fossil salt in Cheshire and Worcestershire (as at Utica in Africa).

Memorandum: in the parabolical vaulture at Wookey Hole and in the caves at Cheddar rocks etc do hang down from the vaulture petrifications like icicles.

On Bannerdown, above Bath Easton near Bath, where a battle of King Arthur was fought, are great stones scattered in the same manner as they are on Durnhamdown, about Bristol, which was assuredly the work of an earthquake, when these great cracks and vallies were made.

The like dispersion of great stones is upon the hills by Cheddar rocks, as all about Charterhouse, and the like at the forest at Fontainebleau, in France; and so in several parts of England, and yet visible the remarks of earthquakes and volcanoes; but in time the husbandmen will clear their ground of them, as at Durnham down they are exceedingly diminished since my remembrance, by making lime of them.

The great inequality of the surface of the earth was rendered so by earthquakes: which when taking fire, they ran in trains several miles according to their caverns; so for instance at Yatton Keynell, Wilts, a crack begins which runs to Longdeanes, in the parish, and so to Slaughtonford, where are high steep cliffs of freestone, and opposite to it at Colerne the like cliffs; thence to Bath, where on the south side appear Claverdon, in the north, Lansdon cliffs, both downs of the same piece; and it may be at the same time the crack was thus made at St Vincent's rocks near Bristol, as likewise Cheddar rocks, like a street. From Castle Combe runs a valley or crack to Ford, where it shoots into that that runs from Yatton to Bath.

Gassendus, in the life of Monsieur Peiresc, hath this remark, that mountains (generally) run east-westish. So the hills from Roundway in Wilts (near Devizes) and also from Westbury eastwards to Berkshire, Oxfordshire, Buckinghamshire, and Bedfordshire.

So the tract of hills from Stinchcombe in Gloucestershire to Burdlop Hills, Stanway, etc and so to Warwickshire.

Snowdon Hills also run eastish and westish towards Scotland.

The chalky land of Wilts, Dorset, Hampshire, Isle of Wight, seem to have been all of a continuous piece: but now some intervals of valleys by earthquakes; e.g. between the hill called Redhone and Roundway Down and so to Marlborough: and the like one may see between these downs: and so between the south of Kent and Picardy, sc. chalky land.

In Jamaica, and in other plantations of America, e.g. in Virginia, the natives did burn down great woods, to cultivate the soil with maize and potato-rootes, which plains were there made by firing the woods to sow corn. They do call these plains Savannas. Who knows but Salisbury plains, etc might be made long time ago, after this manner, and for the same reason?

At Chepstow (where the bridge is) is a great crack of rocks. At this crack the river Wye disembogues into the Severn; and here at this bridge is the greatest difference between high water and low water mark of any places on the whole globe: except somewhere about the Strait of Aniam.

Edmund Waller Esq (the poet) made a query, I remember, at the Royal Society about 1666, whether Salisbury plains were always plains? He said then that he did cut down a beechwood at Beaconsfield, and afterward there came up a birch wood. In the county of Wiltshire are no beeches except in the south east, and at the forest of Graveley, belonging to the Earl of Pembroke: disafforested 1683 to be converted to pasture for profit's sake.

In time of old when this whole nation was but a forest, and encumbered with trees, why might not the Romans burn down the beeches on our downs to turn them to pasturage and corn ground, which is the best improvement for this tract of ground.

I do presume that the red land is three-quarters (or more) of England.

I have oftentimes wished for a map of England coloured according to the colours of the earth, with marks of the fossils and minerals.

The great snails of the downs at Albery in Surrey (twice as big as ours) were brought from Italy by the Earl Marshal about 1638.

In France the people are generally bigger-headed than in England: and their arms are shorter in proportion to their bodies than ours.

The Normans are the most litigious people of France.

The Virginians are very much given to law suits; and so are the Africans.

Of the Indoles of the Irish. Mr J. Stevens went from Trinity College in Oxford, 1647–8, to instruct the Lord Buckhurst in grammar; afterwards he was schoolmaster of the Free School at Camberwell; thence he went to be master of Merchant Taylors' School; next he was master of the school at Charter House; thence he went to the Free School at Liverpool, from whence he was invited to be a schoolmaster of the great school at Dublin, in Ireland; when he left that he was schoolmaster of Blandford, in Dorset; next of Shaftesbury; from whence he was invited by the city of Bristol to be master of the Free School there; from thence he went to be master of the Free School of Dorchester in Dorset, and thence he removed to be rector of Wylye in Wilts, 1666.

He is my old acquaintance, and I desired him to tell me freely if the Irish boys had as good wit as the English; because some of our severe wits have ridiculed the Irish understanding. He protested to me that he could not find but they had as good wits as the English; but generally speaking he found they had better memories. Dr James Usher, Lord Primate of Ireland, had a great memory: Dr Hayle (Dr of the Chair at Oxford) had a prodigious memory: Sir Lleonell Jenkins told me, from him, that he had read over all the Greek fathers three times, and never noted them but with his nail. Mr Congreve, an excellent dramatic poet. Mr John Dodwell hath also a great memory, and Mr Tolet hath a girl at Dublin, mathematic, who at eleven years old would solve questions in algebra to admiration. Mr Tolet told me he began to instruct her at seven years of age.

At Paris are many Irish religious, and they are accounted the best school-divines in Paris.

Complexions

Several nations have such and such peculiar constitutions (complexions) sc. eyes, hair, humour. Well now, in England we have all sorts of these, both excellently good and excellently ill.

Query: if aborigines of one country being transplanted to another, will not after some generations, degenerate, or the contrary, according to the nature of the soil. 'Tis said that the English, after they have lived a matter of several years in Ireland, become as lazy as the Irish. Nicholas Earl of Thanet had an Italian gardener that had lived with him about six years or better: he had a sharp wit: he had perfectly learned all our English airs, but retained indeed those of his own country.

At Blandford school (a great free school in Dorset) we observed that the country boys (labourers' sons) were more dull and unapt to take their learning than the gentlemen's sons and the town boys (tradesmen's sons).

The French have much better, stronger and clearer voices than the English: one may hear the singing from the French church in Threadneedle Street as far, or very near as far, as the upper end of the street at St Martin Outwich church.*

I remember Vitruvius has a pretty remark concerning voices in several climates: and the further south, the deeper and sweeter. The Africans and Arabians have admirable voices, and so have the negroes.

As to singing voices we have great diversity in several counties of this nation; and any one may observe that generally in the rich vales they sing clearer than on the hills, where they labour hard and breathe a sharp air. This difference is manifest between the vale of North Wilts and the South. So in Somersetshire they generally sing well in the churches, their pipes are smoother.

In North Wilts the milkmaids sing as shrill and clear as any swallow sitting on a berne:

> So lowdly she did yerne,
> Like any swallow sitting on a berne.
> Chaucer

Dr Muffet, in his book of meats, says that when Dr Caius was very old, he was suckled by two women: one a scold, the other good humoured: and accordingly he would become froward, or the contrary.

I remember Samuel Cowper the painter did remark that Frenchmen are all ingenious, few excellent and they (generally) want patience to go through knotty studies; and Bishop Wilkins was wont to say they did not write so close as the English.

The Africans have delicate subtle wits, and treacherous, and very litigious, much given to lawsuits. It was observed (Sir S. Petty) that the Fez ambassador did outwit all our statesmen here in managing his negotiation.

---

* At my return to London from France, I went to St Paul's church to prayers and hear an anthem: a French youth that waited on me then, told me that the singing men and boys had taken a cold: they sang 'enrouément': he spake it ignorantly. French men at arms are generally shorter than the Englishmen and their heads are generally bigger.

Our game-cocks and mastiff dogs do degenerate when carried into southern air. The hill country (chalky) fellows are more vigorous and courageous (generally) than the vale.

Now according to the several sorts of earth in England (and so all the world over) the *Indigenae* are respectively witty or dull, good or bad. Plants are made of the earth; by them we are nourished, and e.g. an apple-tree (which is a wholesome fruit) by applying of moulds of certain plants to the root, may be made to bring apples that will be poisonous.*

To write a true account of the several humours of our own country would be too sarcastical and offensive: this should be a secret whisper in the ear of a friend only, and I should superscribe here,

> *Pinge duos angues – locus est sacer: extra*
> *Mei ite.*
>
> Persius, *Satyr*

Well then! Let these memoirs lie concealed as a sacred arcanum.

I remember (upon the foresaid reason) that Capt. John Graunt did say, it was observed that there were no anchor-smiths fanatics; for it is a mighty laborious task and they must drink strong drink to keep up their spirits. So they never troubled their heads with curious notions of religion.

In North Wiltshire, and like the vale of Gloucestershire (a dirty clayey country) the *Indigenæ*, or Aborigines, speak drawling; they are phlegmatic, skins pale and livid, slow and dull, heavy of spirit: hereabout is but little tillage or hard labour, they only milk the cows and make cheese; they feed chiefly on milk meats, which cools their brains too much, and hurts their inventions. These circumstances make them melancholy, contemplative, and malicious; by consequence whereof come more law suits out of North Wilts, at least double to the southern parts. And by the same reason they are generally more apt to be fanatics: their persons are generally plump and feggy: gallipot eyes, and some black: but they are generally handsome enough. It is a woodsere country, abounding much with sour and austere plants, as sorrel, etc which makes their humours sour and fixes their spirits. In Malmesbury Hundred, etc (the wet clayey parts) there have ever been reputed witches.

On the downs, sc. the south part, where 'tis all upon tillage, and where the shepherds labour hard, their flesh is hard, their bodies

---

* In Spain they have an art to make figs poisonous by planting certain poisonous fruits at the root of the tree: hence comes the proverb of the 'Spanish fig'.

strong: being weary after hard labour, they have not leisure to read and contemplate of religion, but go to bed to their rest, to rise betime the next morning to their labour.

The vale of White Horse has the handsomest people of any part of England: and they are good-conditioned people: and it and Oxfordshire have a commendation at London for good faithful servants.

Somersetshire: large people, fair and a little too plump: without sinister designs, not litigious.

Now do but cross the river and travel into Herefordshire, to Radnorshire, Salop etc: you are in red, sandy, healthy country where the natives are of a brisk spirit, clear voices, speak quick, move quick, have clear warm skins and generally hazel eyes (or a bright red hazel) and chestnut hair: longaevous, not covetous and stingy, but hospitable; quick-witted but not of a contemplative wit, but nimble, quick upon the catch, and over-reacting.

So that to make a parallel of the humours of Trans-Sabrinians and Citra-Sabrinians, one has more of the toad, the other of the viper (their eyes are of the colour of a viper) which indicates a good wit, and the Africans that were here with the Morocco ambassador had such.

Let us divert into South Wales: and we shall observe they have generally dark hazel eyes, and black eyes are common among them; choleric, quickly moved to anger: according to the proverb, 'their Welsh blood will be up', very litigious,★ their skins well-coloured and of a very fine texture (not gooseskin, and lax as in the phlegmatic countries). The cherries in Wales are hard and harsh: and so are their plums.

There are characters in Welsh of several of the counties in south Wales which I have forgotten, but to this purpose: 'dissembling Glamorganshire', 'Brecknockshire – litigious, knavery.'

North Wales hath curious subtleties and more acute of the two than the south, but tending to over-react. But all of them have civility and are not stingy (chiche) which is an effect of a cold lurid complexion.

The astrologers and historians write that the ascendant as of Oxford is Capricornus, whose lord is Saturn, a religious planet, and patron of religious men. If it be so, surely this influence runs all along through North Wilts, the vale of Gloucestershire, and Somersetshire. In all changes of religions they are more zealous than other; where in the time of the Roman Catholic religion there were more and better

---

★ Dr David Rhesus in his preface to his Welsh grammar does much lament the great increase of attorneys in Brecknockshire (his native country) which destroys it by law-suits. In 1656, Judge Rumsey told there were 24 attorneys in this small county.

churches and religious houses founded than any other part of England could show, they are now the greatest fanatics, even to spiritual madness: e.g. the multitude of enthusiasts. Capt. Stokes, in his 'Wiltshire Rant', printed about 1650, recites the strangest extravagances of religion that were ever heard of since the time of the Gnostics. The rich wet soil makes them hypochondrical.

The Norfolk air is clear and fine. Natives, good clear wits, subtle, and the most litigious of England: they carry *Littleton's Tenures* at the plough tail. Sir Thomas Browne MD of Norwich, told me that their eyes in that county do quickly decay; which he imputes to the clearness and dryness (subtleness) of the air. Wormwood grows the most plentifully there of any part of England: which the London apothecaries do send for.

Memorandum: that North Wiltshire is very wormwoodish and more litigious than South Wilts.

Yorkshire, cunning wary people. The attorneys say that most causes are tried in Yorkshire and Norfolk of any counties of England: and that you still never draw out of a Yorkshire man any thing that may at least tend to his prejudice: and the like they say of Devonshire men. The common people have hard dry skins and not so clear.

Devonshire of a rough, gruff humour: very industrious (like the Gascons), sound judgements. They are strong stout men, and have bred a great many brave men both for sea and land. Now they say the Cornish humour is quite contrary to the Devonshire, as humane and courteous as can be.

Provincial pronunciations

The northern parts of England speak gutturally and in Yorkshire and the bishopric of Durham they have more of the cadence or Scottish tone than they have at Edinburgh: in like manner, in Herefordshire they have more of the Welsh cadence than they have in Wales. The western people cannot open their mouths, to speak *ore rotundo*. We pronounce *paal*, *pale* etc, and especially in Devonshire. The Exeter College men in dissertations when they allege *causa causa est causa causati* they pronounce it *caza caza est caza cazati*, very ungracefully. Now by contrast the French and Italians do pronounce *a* fully and *e* and even children of French born in England: and the further you go south the more fully. This must proceed from the earth, or air, or both.

One may observe that the speech (twang or accent) of the vulgar begins to alter something towards the Herefordshire manner even at Cirencester. Mr Hobbes told me that Sir Charles Cavendish did say that the Greeks do sing their words (as they in Herefordshire do in some degrees). From hence arose the accents, not used by the ancients.

I do believe that the Britons of the south part of this isle, e.g. the Trinobantes etc, did speak no more guttural or twanging than the inhabitants do now: the tone, accent etc, depends on the temper of the earth (and so to plants) and air.

Staffordshire: great part of the earth is of an ash-colour, and abounding in fern, with which burnt the poor people make balls to use in washing instead of soap. The ash trees here have large leaves that ones in the south. The air is very good, clear but not piercing.

> Proverbs: Cheshire chief of men
> Lancashire fair women.
> The North for largeness: the east for health.
> The South for buildings: the west for wealth.
>
> As false as a Scot – Mr John Ray's proverb.

The Cheshire men were reputed heretofore for good bowmen, when this kingdom got great glory by the gray-goose wing. They are strong men and draw the arrow near to the head: and outshot the French.

Cattle

Yorkshire: black, large headed
Lancashire: black and large-horned
Gloucestershire: brown
North Wiltshire: pied (at Hartham Warren the coneys are pied)
Picardy, sandy coloured: and so is the south part of Kent, Norfolk and Suffolk

In Kent the cows are of a yellowish-red, but not so faint and sandy colour as in Picardy.

In East Kent are several wells of sixty, seventy, some eighty, some an hundred fathom deep: from George Jenkins, steward to Nicholas Earl of Thanet.

Paddlesworth is the highest place in Kent.

The bread in Kent is not good, like that of Norfolk and Suffolk.

Air

Before I enter upon the discourse of the air of this county, it would not be amiss that I gave an account of the winds that most commonly blow in the western parts of England.

I shall first allege the testimony of Julius Caesar, who delivers to us thus: 'The western wind, which is wont to blow for a great part of the time in these regions'. – (*Commentaries*, Bk 5) To which I will subjoin this of Mr Thomas Ax, of Somersetshire, who hath made daily observations of the weather for these twenty-five years past, since 1661, and finds that, one year with another, the westerly winds, which do come from the Atlantic sea, do blow ten months of the twelve. Besides, he hath made observations for thirty years, that the manors in the eastern parts of the netherlands of Somersetshire do yield six or eight per cent of their value; whereas those in the western parts do yield but three, seldom four per cent, and in some manors but two per cent. Hence he argues that the winds carrying these unwholesome vapours of the low country from one to the other, do make the one more, the other less, healthy.

Now, although Mendip hills and Whitesheet, etc, are as a bar and screen to keep off from Wiltshire the westerly winds and rains, as they do in some measure repel those noxious vapours, yet we have a flavour of them; and when autumnal agues reign, they are more common on the hills than in the vales of this country.

The downs of Wiltshire are covered with mists, when the vales are clear from them, and the sky serene; and they are much more often here than in the lowest story or stage.

The leather covers of books, etc do mould more and sooner in the hill country than in the vale. The covers of my books in my closet at Chalke would be all over covered with a hoar mouldiness, that I could not know of what colour the leather was; when my books in my closet at Easton Piers (in the vale) were not touched at all with any mouldiness.

So the rooms at Winterslow, which is seated exceedingly high, are very mouldy and dampish. Mr Lancelot Moorehouse, Rector of Pertwood, who was a very learned man, said that mists were very frequent there: it stands very high, near Hindon, which one would think to stand very healthy: there is no river nor marsh near it, yet they do not live long there.

The wheat hereabout, namely towards the edge of the downs, is much subject to be smutty, which they endeavour to prevent by drawing a cart-rope over the corn after the mildews fall.

Besides that the hill country is elevated so high in the air, the soil doth consist of chalk and mawm, which abounds with nitre, which craddles the air, and turns it into mists and water.

On the east side of the south down of the farm of Broad Chalk are pitts called the Mearn-Pitts, which, though on a high hill, whereon is a sea mark towards the Isle of Wight, yet they have always water in them. How they came to be made no man knows; perhaps the mortar was digged there for the building of the church.

Having spoken of mists it brings to my remembrance that in December, 1653, being at night in the court at Sir Charles Snell's at Kington St Michael in this country, there being a very thick mist, we saw our shadows on the fog as on a wall by the light of the lanterns, namely about 30 or 40 foot distance or more. There were several gentlemen which saw this; particularly Mr Stafford Tyndale. I have been informed since by some that go bird-baiting in winter nights that the like hath been seen: but rarely.

The north part of this county is much influenced by the river Severn, which flows impetuously from the Atlantic Sea. It is a ventiduct, and brings raw gales along with it: the tides bringing a chilliness with them.

On the top of Chalk-down, 16 or 18 miles from the sea, the oaks are, as it were, shorn by the south and south-west winds; and do recline from the sea, as those that grow by the sea-side.

At Hullavington, about 1649, there happened a strange wind, which did not only lay down flat the corn and grass as if a huge roller had been drawn over it, but it flatted also the quickset hedges of two or three grounds of George Joe, Esq. – It was a hurricane.

Anno 1660, I being then at dinner with Mr Stokes at Titherton, news was brought in to us that a whirlwind had carried some of the hay-cocks over high elms by the house: which brings to my mind a story that is credibly related of one Mr J. Parsons, a kinsman of ours, who, being a little child was set on a hay-cock, and a whirlwind took him up with half the hay-cock and carried him over high elms, and laid him down safe, without any hurt, in the next ground.

Edward Saintlow, of Knighton, Esq. was buried in the church of Broad Chalk, May 6, 1578, as appeares by the register book. The snow did then lie so thick on the ground that the bearers carried his body over the gate at Knighton field, and the company went over the hedges, and they digged a way to the church porch. I knew some ancient people of the parish that did remember it. On a May day, 1655 or 1656, being then in Glamorganshire, at Mr John Aubrey's at Llanchrechid, I saw the mountains of Devonshire all white with snow. There fell but little in Glamorganshire.

Ignis fatuus, called by the vulgar 'Kit of the Candlestick' is not very rare on our downs about Michaelmas.

Riding in the north lane of Broad Chalk in the harvest time in the twilight, or scarce that, a point of light, by the hedge, expanded itself into a globe of about three inches diameter, or near four, as boys blow bubbles with soap. It continued but while one could say one, two, three, or four at the most. It was about a foot from my horse's eye; and it made him turn his head quick aside from it. It was a pale light as that of a glow-worm: it may be this is that which they call a blast of blight in the country.

Sounds

The top of one of the niches in the grot in Wilton gardens, as one sings there, doth return the note A re, louder, and clearer, but it doth not the like to the eighth of it. The diameter is 22 inches. But the first time I happened on this kind of experiment was when I was a scholar in Oxford, walking and singing under Merton College gate, which is a Gothic irregular vaulting, I perceived that one certain note could be returned with a loud hum, which was C.fa, ut, or D.sol, re; I do not now well remember which. I have often observed in quires that at certain notes of the organ the desk would have a tremulation under my hand. So will timber; so will one's hat, though a spongy thing, as one holds it under one's arm at a music meeting. These accidents do make me reflect on the brazen or copper tympana, mentioned by Vitruvius, for the clearer and farther conveying the sound of the *recitatores* and musicians to the auditors. I am from hence induced to be of opinion that these tympana were made according to such and such proportions, suitable to such and such notes.

Mersennus, or Kircher, sayes, that one may know what quantity of liquor is in the vessel by the sound of it, knowing before the empty note. I have several times heard great brass pans ring by the barking of a hound; and also by the loud voice of a strong man.

As I rode from Bristol to Wells down Dundery-hill, in the month of June, 1663, walking down the hill on foot, presently after a fine shower I sawe a little thin mist arise out of the ditch on the right hand by the highways side. But when I came near to the place I could not discern it: so I went back a convenient distance and saw it again; and then took notice of some flower or weed that grew in the ditch whence the vapour came. I came again to the mark, and could see nothing of a mist, as before; but my nose was affected with a smell which I knew; but immediately it came not to my mind; which was the smell of the canals that come from the baths at Bath. By this time my groom was come to me, who, though of a dull understanding, his senses were very quick; I asked him if he smelt nothing, and after a sniff or two, he answered me, he smelt the smell of the Bath. This place is about two parts of three of the descent of Dundery Hill.

The River Thames, as it runs to Cricklade passes by Ashton Keynes; from whence to Charleton, where the North Avon runs, is about three miles. Mr Henry Briggs (Savilian professor of Geometry at Oxford) observing in the map the nearness of these two streams, and reflecting on the great use that might accrue if a cut were made from the one to the other (of which there are many examples in the Low Countries), took a journey from Oxford to view it, and found the ground level and sappable and was very well pleased with his notion; for that if these two rivers were married by a canal between them, then might goods be brought from London to Bristol by water, which would be an extraordinary convenience both for safety and to avoid overturning. This was about the year 1626. But there had been a long calm of peace, and men minded nothing but pleasure and luxury. Knowledge of this kind was not at all in fashion, so that he had no encouragement to prosecute this noble design: and no more done but the mere discovery: and not long after he died, on January 31st 1631; and this ingenious notion had died too and been forgotten, but that Mr Francis Mathew (formerly of the county of Dorset, a captain in his majesty King Charles I's service) who was acquainted with him, and had the hint from him, and after the wars ceased revived this design. He took much pains about it; went into the country and made a map of it, and wrote a treatise of it, and addressed himself to Oliver the Protector, and Parliament. Oliver was exceedingly pleased with the design; and, had he lived but a little longer, he would have had it perfected: but upon his death it sank.

After his majesty's restoration, I recommended Captain Mathew to the Lord William Brouncker, then President of the Royal Society, who introduced him to his majesty: who did much approve of the design; but money was wanting, and public-spirited contributions; and the captain had no purse (undone by the wars), and the heads of the Parliament and Council were filled with other things. – Thus the poor old gentleman's project came to nothing.

He died about 1676, and left many good papers behind him concerning this matter, in the hands of his daughters; of which I acquainted Mr John Collins, RSS in 1682, who took a journey to Oxford (which journey cost him his life, by a cold), and first discoursed with the barge-men there concerning their trade and way:

then he went to Lechlade, and discoursed with the barge-men there; who all approved of the design. Then he took a particular view of the ground to be cut between Ashton Keynes and Charleton. From Malmesbury he went to Bristol. Then he returned to Malmesbury again and went to Wootton Bassett, and took a view of that way. Sir Jonas Moore told me he liked that way, but J. Collins was clearly for the cut between Ashton Keynes and Charleton.

At his return to London I went with him to the daughters of Mr Mathew, who showed him their father's papers, draughts, models, copper-plate of the map of the Thames, Acts of Parliament, and Bills prepared to be enacted, etc; as many as did fill a big portmanteau. He proposed the buying of them to the Royal Society, and took the heads of them, and gave them an abstract of them. The papers, etc were afterwards brought to the Royal Society; the price demanded for all was but five pounds (the plate of the map did cost eight pounds). The Royal Society liked the design; but they would neither undertake the business nor buy the papers. So that noble knight, Sir James Shaen, RSS, who was then present, slipped five guineas into J. Collins's hand to give to the poor gentlewomen, and so immediately became master of these rarities. There were at the Society at the same time three aldermen of the city of London, fellows of the Society, who when they heard that Sir James Shaen had got the possession of them were extremely vexed; and repented (when 'twas too late) that they had overslipped such an opportunity: then they would have given thirty pounds. This undertaking had been indeed most proper for the honourable city of London.

Jo. Collins wrote a good discourse of this journey, and of the feasibility, and a computation of the charge. Query, whether he left a copy with the Royal Society. Mr Win, mathematical instrument maker in Chancery Lane, had all his papers, and amongst many others is to be found this.

I have been the more full in this account, because if ever it shall happen that any public-spirited men shall arise to carry on such a useful work, they may know in whose hands the papers that were so well considered heretofore are now lodged.

Mr Jonas Moore, Surveyor of the Ordinance, told me that when the Duke of York sent him to survey the manor of Dauntsey, formerly belonging to Sir John Danvers, he did then take a survey of this design, and said that it is feasible; but his opinion was that the best way would be to make a cut by Wootton Bassett, and that the king himself should undertake it, for they must cut through a hill by Wootton Bassett; and that in time it might quit cost. As I remember, he told me that forty thousand pounds would do it.

But I think that Jo. Collins sayes in his papers, that the cut from Ashton Keynes to Charleton may be made for three thousand pounds.

The earth about Malmesbury hundred and Chippenham hundred, especially about Pewsham-forest, is vitriolate, or aluminous and vitriolate; which in hot weather the sun does make manifest on the banks of the ditches.

At Bradfield and Draycot Cerne is such vitriolate earth; which with galls will make inke. This makes the land so sour, it beares sour and austere plants: it is a proper soil for dairies. At summer it hunger-banes the sheep; and in winter it rots them.

These clay and marly lands are wet and dirty; so that to poor people, who have not change of shoes, the cold is very incommodious, which hurts their nerves exceedingly. Salts, as the Lord Chancellor Bacon sayes, do exert (irradiate) rays of cold. Elias Ashmole, Esq. got a dangerous cold by sitting by the salt sacks in a salter's shop, which was like to have cost him his life. And some salts will corrode papers, that were three or four inches from it. The same may be said of marble pavements, which have cost some great persons their lives.

The turf of our downs, and so east and west, is the best in the world for gardens and bowling-greens; for more southward it is burnt, and more north it is coarse.

Temple down in Preshute parish, belonging to the right honourable Charles Lord Seymour, worth twenty shillings per acre, and better, a great quantity of it.

As to the green circles on the downs, vulgarly called fairy circles (dances), I presume they are generated from the breathing out of a fertile subterraneous vapour. (The ring-worm on a man's flesh is circular. Excogitate a parallelism between the cordial heat and the subterranean heat, to elucidate this phenomenon.) Every tobacco-taker knows that 'tis no strange thing for a circle of smoke to be whiff'd out of the bowl of the pipe; but 'tis done by chance. If you dig under the turf of this circle, you will find at the roots of the grass a hoar or mouldiness. But as there are fertile streams, so contrarywise there are noxious ones, which proceed from some minerals, iron, etc; which also as the others, other things being equal, appear in a circular form.

In the common field of Winterbourn is the celebrated path called St Thomas Becket's path. It leads from the village up to Clarendon Park. Whether this field be sown or lies fallow, the path is visible to one that looks on it from the hill, and it is wonderful. But I can add yet farther the testimonies of two that I very well know (one of them my servant, and of an excellent sight) that will attest that, riding in the road from London one morning in a great snow, they did see this path visible on the snow. St Thomas Becket, they say, was sometime a cure priest at Winterbourn, and did use to go along this path up to a chapel in Clarendon Park, to say mass and very likely 'tis true: but I have a conceit that this path is caused by a warm subterraneous steam from a long crack in the earth, which may cause snow to dissolve sooner there than elsewhere: and consequently gives the dissolving snow a darker colour, just as we see the difference of whites in damask linen.

The right reverend father in God, Seth, Lord Bishop of Salisbury, avers to me that at Silchester in Hampshire, which was a Roman city, one may discern in the corn ground* the sign of the streets; nay, passages and hearths: which also Dr John Wilkins (since Lord Bishop of Chester) did see with him, and has affirmed the same thing to me. They were there, and saw it in the spring.

Stones

I will begin with freestone as the best kind of stone that this country doth afford.

The quarry at Haselbury was most eminent for freestone in the western parts, before the discovery of the Portland quarry, which was but about the year 1600. The church of Portland, which stands by the seaside upon the quarry, (which lies not very deep, namely ten foot), is of Caen stone, from Normandy. Malmesbury Abbey and the other Wiltshire religious houses are of Haselbury stone. The old tradition is that St Aldhelm, Abbot of Malmesbury, riding over the ground at Haselbury, did throw down his glove, and had them dig there, and they should find great treasure, meaning the quarry.

The common stone in Malmesbury hundred and thereabout is oftentimes bluish in the inside, and full of very small cockles, as at Easton Piers. These stones are dampish and sweat, and do emit a cold and unwholesome damp, namely, the vitriolate petrified salt in it exerts itself.

Pebbles – The millers in our country used to put a black pebble under the pin of the axis of the mill-wheel, to keep the brass underneath from wearing; and they do find by experience, that nothing doth wear as long as that. The bakers take a certain pebble, which they put in the vaulture of their oven, which they call the warning-stone; for when that is white the oven is hot.

There was a time when all pebbles were liquid. We find them all ovalish. How should this come to pass? As for salts, some shoot

* i.e. what a modern archaeologist would call 'crop marks'.

cubical, some hexagonal. Why might there not be a time, when these pebbles were making in embryo, for such a shooting as falls into an ovalish figure?

Pebbles do break according to the length of the greatest diameter: but those we do find broken in the earth are broken according to their shortest diameter. I have broken above an hundred of them, to try to have one broken at the shortest diameter, to save the charge and paines of grinding them for molers to grind colours for painters; and they all brake the long way as aforesaid.

Black flints are found in great plenty in the chalky country. They are a kind of pyrites, and are as regular; 'tis certain they have been *in fluore*.

Excellent fire-flints are digged up at Dun's Pit in Groveley, and fitted for guns by Mr Thomas Sadler of Steeple Langford.

Of plants

It were to be wished that we had a survey or inventory of the plants of every county in England and Wales, as there is of Cambridgeshire by Mr John Ray; that we might know our own store, and whither to repair for them for medicinal uses. God Almighty hath furnished us with plants to cure us, that grow perhaps within five or ten miles of our abodes, and we know it not.

Experience hath taught us that some plants have wonderful virtues; and no doubt all have so, if we knew it or could discover it. Homer writes sublimely, and calls them the hands of the gods: and we ought to reach them religiously, with praise and thanksgiving.

I am no botanist myself, and I think we have very few in our country that are; the more is the pity. But had Thomas Willisel lived, and been in England, I would have employed him in this search.

Sir William Petty surveyed the kingdom of Ireland geographically, by those that knew not what they did. Why were it impossible to procure a botanic survey of Wiltshire by apothecaries of several quarters of the county? Their profession leadeth them to an acquaintance of herbs, and the task being divided, would not be very troublesome; and, besides the pleasure, would be of great use. The apothecaries of Highworth, Malmesbury, Calne, and Bath (which is within three miles of Wilts) might give an account of the northern part of Wiltshire, which abounds with rare simples: the apothecaries of Warminster, the Devizes, and Marlborough, the midland part; and the apothecaries of Salisbury the south part, towards the New Forest.

At Mintie is an abundance of wild mint, from whence the village is denominated.

Drawing by Aubrey of Easton Piers, or Percy, before it was rebuilt, showing it surrounded by oaks

Argentina (wild tansey) grows the most in the fallows in Cotswold, and North Wilts adjoining, that I ever saw. It grows also in the fallows in South Wiltshire, but not so much.

About Priory St Mary's, and in the Minchin meadows there, but especially at Brown's hill, which is opposite to the house where, in an unfortunate hour, I drew my first breath, there is infinite variety of plants; and it would have tempted me to have been a botanist had I had leisure, which is a jewel I could be never master of. In the banks of the rivulet growes abundantly maiden-hair, hart's-tongue, phyllitis, brook-lime, etc, cowslip and primroses not inferior to Primrose Hills. In this ground calver-keys, hare-parsley, wild vetch, maiden's honesty, polypodium, fox-gloves, wild-vine, bayle. Here is wonderful plenty of wild saffron, carthamus, and many vulnerary plants, now by me forgotten. There grows also adder's-tongue, plenty – query if it is not the same with viper's-tongue?

Strawberries, in Colerne woods, exceeding plentiful; the earth is not above two inches above the free-stone. The poor children gather them, and sell them to Bath; but they kill the young ashes, by barking them to make boxes to put them in.

Strawberries have a most delicious taste, and are so innocent that a woman in childbed, or one in a fever, may safely eat them: but I have heard Sir Christopher Wren affirm, that if one that has a wound in his head eats them, they are mortal. Methinks 'tis very strange. Query the learned of this?

Oaks (the best of trees). – We had great plenty before the disafforestations. We had in North Wiltshire, and yet have, though not in the former plenty, as good oaks as any in England. The best that we have now (1670) are at Okesey Park, Sir Edward Poole's, in Malmesbury hundred; and the oaks at Easton Piers (once mine) were, for the number, not inferior to them. In my great-grandfather Lyte's time one might have driven a plough over every oak in the oak-close, which are now grown stately trees. The great oak by the dairy-house is the biggest oak now, I believe, in all the county. There is a commonwealth of rooks there. When I was a boy the two greatest oaks were, one on the hill at the parke at Draycot Cerne; the other at Mr Sadler's, at Longley Burrell. 'Twas of one of these trees, I remember, that the trough of the paper mill at Long-deane, in the parish of Yatton Keynell, in 1636, was made. In Garsden Park (now the Lord Ferrers's) is perhaps the finest hollow oak in England; it is not high, but very capacious, and well wainscotted; with a little table, which I think eight may sit round. When an oak is felling, before it falls, it gives a kind of shrieks or groans, that may be heard a mile off, as if it were the genius of the oak lamenting. E. Wyld, Esq. hath heard it several times.

In the New Forest, within the trenches of the castle of Molwood (a Roman camp) is an old oak, which is a pollard and short. It putteth forth young leaves on Christmas day, for about a week at that time of the year. Old Mr Hastings, of Woodlands, was wont to send a basket full of them every year to King Charles I. I have seen of them several Christmasses brought to my father.

Yew trees naturally grow in chalky countries. The greatest plenty of them, as I believe, in the west of England is at Nunton Ewetrees. Between Knighton Ashes and Downton the ground produces them all along; but at Nunton they are a wood. At Ewridge, in the parish of Colerne, in North Wilts (a stonebrash and a free stone), they also grow indifferently plentiful; and in the parish of Kington St Michael I remember three or four in the stonebrash and red earth.

When I learned my accidents [grammar], 1633, at Yatton Keynell, there was a fair and spreading yew-tree in the churchyard, as was common heretofore. The boys took much delight in its shade, and it furnished them with their scoops and nut-crackers. The clerk lopped it to make money of it to some bowyer or fletcher, and that lopping killed it: the dead trunk remaines there still.

Mr Anthony Hinton, one of the officers of the Earl of Pembroke, did inoculate, not long before the late civil wars (ten years or more), a bud of Glastonbury Thorn at his farm-house at Wilton, which blossoms at Christmas as the other did. My mother has had branches of them for a flower-pot several Christmasses, which I have seen. Elias Ashmole, Esq., in his notes upon *Theatrum Chymicum*, says that in the churchyard at Glastonbury grew a walnut tree that did put out young leaves at Christmas, as doth the king's oak in the New Forest. In Parham Park in Suffolk (Mr Boutele's), is a pretty ancient thorn that blossoms like that at Glastonbury; the people flock thither to see it on

Christmas day. But in the road that leads from Worcester to Droitwich is a blackthorn hedge at Clayn, half a mile long or more, that blossoms about Christmas day for a week or more together. The ground is called Longland. Dr Ezreel Tong said that about Romney marsh are thorns naturally like that at Glastonbury. The soldiers did cut down that near Glastonbury: the stump remains.

It is certain that no county of England had greater variety of game, etc, than Wiltshire, and our county hounds were as good, or rather the best of England; but within this last century the breed is much mixed with northern hounds. Sir Charles Snell, of Kington St Michael, who was my honoured friend and neighbour, had till the civil wars as good hounds for the hare as any were in England, for handsomeness and mouth (deep-mouthed) and goodness, and suited one another admirably well. But it was the Right Hon. Philip, Earl of Pembroke, that was the great hunter. It was in his lordship's time, that is, in the reigns of James I and Charles I, a serene calm of peace, that hunting was at its greatest height that ever was in this nation. The Roman governors had not, I think, that leisure. The Saxons were never at quiet: and the barons' wars, and those of York and Lancaster, took up the greatest part of the time since the Conquest: so that the glory of the English hunting breathed its last with this earl, who deceased about 1644, and shortly after the forests and parks were sold and converted into arable, etc.

'Twas after his lordship's decease [1650] that I was a hunter; that is to say, with the right honourable William, Lord Herbert, of Cardiff, the aforesaid Philip's grandson. Mr Christopher Wace then taught him Latin, and hunted with him; and 'twas then that he translated Gratius' *Cynegeticon*, and dedicated it to his lordship, which will be a lasting monument for him.

The Wiltshire greyhounds were also the best of England, and are still; and my father and I have had as good as any were in our times in Wiltshire. They are generally of a fallow colour, or black; but Mr Ditton's, of Shirburn in Gloucestershire, are some white and some black. But Gratius, in his *Cynegeticon*, adviseth:

> And chuse the grayhound py'd with black and white,
> He runs more swift than thought, or winged flight;
> But courseth yet in view, not hunts in traile,
> In which the quick Petronians never faile.

I have not seen so many pied cattle anywhere as in North Wiltshire. The country hereabout is much inclined to pied cattle, but commonly the colour is black or brown, or deep red. Some cow-stealers will make a hole in a hot loaf newly drawn out of the oven, and put it on an ox's horn for a convenient time, and then they can turn their softened hornes the contrary way, so that the owner cannot swear to his own beast. Not long before the king's restoration a fellow was hanged at Tyburn for this, and said that he had never come thither if he had not heard it spoken of in a sermon. Thought he, I will try this trick.

Birds

We have great plenty of larks, and very good ones, especially in Colerne fields and those parts adjoining to Cotswold. They take them by alluring them with a daring-glass, which is whirled about in a sun-shining day, and the larks are pleased at it, and strike at it, as at a sheep's eye, and at that time the net is drawn over them. While he plays with his glass he whistles with his lark-call of silver, a tympanum of about the diameter of a threepence. In the south part of Wiltshire they do not use daring-glasses but catch these pretty aetherial birds with trammels.

The buntings do accompany the larks. Linnets on the downs. Woodpeckers several sorts: many in North Wilts.

Sir Benet Hoskyns, Baronet, told me that his keeper at his park at Morehampton in Herefordshire, did, for experiment sake, drive an iron nail athwart the hole of the woodpecker's nest, there being a tradition that the dam will bring some leaf to open it. He laid at the bottom of the tree a clean sheet, and before many hours passed the nail came out, and he found a leaf lying by it on the sheet. Query the shape of figure of the leaf. They say the moonwort will do such things. This experiment may easily be tried again. As Sir Walter Raleigh says, there are stranger things to be seen in the world than are between London and Staines.

Of gardens

To write in the praise of gardens is besides my design. The pleasure and use of them were unknown to our great-grandfathers. They were contented with pot-herbs, and did mind chiefly their stables. The chronicle tells us, that in the reign of King Henry VIII pearmains were so great a rarity that a basketful of them was a present to the great Cardinal Wolsey.

Henry Lyte, of Lyte's Cary, in Somerset, Esq. translated Dodoens' Herbal into English, which he dedicated to Queen Elizabeth, about the beginning of her reign [1578]. He had a pretty good collection of plants for that age; some few whereof are yet alive, 1660: and no

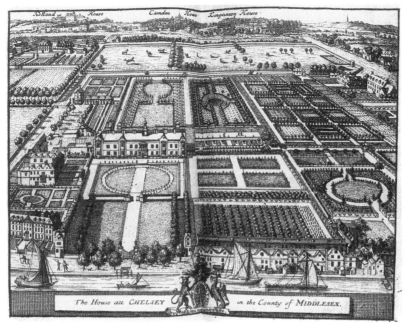

The house and garden at Chelsea

question but Dr Gilbert, etc did furnish their gardens as well as they could so long ago, which could be but meanly. But the first peer that stored his garden with exotic plants was William Earl of Salisbury, a catalogue whereof, fairly written in a skin of vellum, consisting of 830 plants, is in the hands of Elias Ashmole, Esq. at South Lambeth.

But 'twas Sir John Danvers, of Chelsea, who first taught us the way of Italian gardens. He had well travelled France and Italy, and made good observations. He had in a fair body an harmonical mind. In his youth his complexion was so exceeding beautiful and fine that Thomas Bond, Esq. of Ogbourne in Wiltshire, who was his companion in his travels, did say that the people would come after him in the street to admire him. He had a very fine fancy, which lay chiefly for gardens and architecture.

The garden at Lavington in this county, and that at Chelsea in Middlesex, as likewise the house there, do remain monuments of his ingenuity. The garden at Lavington is full of irregularities, both natural and artificial, i.e. elevations and depressions. Through the length of it there runneth a fine clear trout stream; walled with brick on each side, to hinder the earth from mouldering down. In this stream are placed several statues. At the west end is an admirable place for a grotto, where the great arch is, over which now is the market

The garden at Wilton

road. Among several others there is a very pleasant elevation of the south side of the garden, which steals, arising almost insensibly, that is, before one is aware, and gives you a view over the spacious corn-fields there, so to East Lavington: where, being landed on a fine level, letteth you descend again with the like easiness; each side is flanked with laurels. It is almost impossible to describe this garden, it is so full of variety and unevenness; nay, it would be a difficult matter for a good artist to make a draught of it. About 1686, the right honourable James Earl of Abingdon built a noble portico, full of water works, which is on the north side of the garden, and faceth the south. It is both portico and grotto, and was designed by Mr Rose of Oxfordshire.

Wilton Garden was the third garden after these two of the Italian mode; but in the time of King Charles II gardening was much improved and became common. I do believe I may modestly affirm that there is now (1691) ten times as much gardening about London as there was in 1660; and we have been, since that time, much improved in foreign plants, especially since about 1683, there have been exotic plants brought into England no less than seven thousand. (From Mr Watts, gardener of the Apothecary's garden at Chelsea, and other botanists.)

Till the breaking out of the civil wars, Tom o' Bedlams did travel about the country. They had been poor distracted men that had been put into Bedlam, where, recovering to some soberness, they were licentiated to go a-begging: e.g. they had on their left an armilla of tin, printed in some works, about four inches long; they could not get it off. They wore about their necks a great horn of an ox in a string or baldric, which, when they came to an house for alms, they did wind: and they did put the drink given them into this horn, whereto they did put a stopple. Since the wars I do not remember to have seen any one of them.

Salisbury Cathedral

'Tis strange to see how error hath crept in upon the people, who believe that the pillars of this church were cast, forsooth, as chandlers make candles; and the like is reported of the pillars of the Temple Church, London, etc: and not only the vulgar swallow down the tradition glibly, but several learned and otherwise understanding persons will not be persuaded to the contrary, and that the art is lost. Nay, all the bishops and churchmen of that church in my remembrance did believe it, till Bishop Ward came, who would not be so imposed on; and the like error runs from generation to generation concerning Stonehenge, that the stones are artificial. But, to return to the pillars of this church, they are all real marble, and show the grain of the Sussex marble (i.e. the little cockles), from whence they were brought. At every nine foot they are jointed with an ornament or band of iron or copper. This quarry hath been closed up and forgot time out of mind, and the last year, 1680, it was accidentally discovered by felling of an old oak; and it now serves London. (From Mr Bushnell, the stone-cutter.)

The old tradition is, that this church was built upon wool-packs, and doubtless there is something in it which is now forgotten. I shall endeavour to retrieve and unriddle it by comparison. There is a tower at Rouen in Normandie called the Butter Tower; for when it was built a toll was laid upon all the butter that was brought to Rouen, for and towards the building of this tower; as now there is a duty laid upon every chaldron of coals towards the building of St Paul's Church, London: so hereafter they may say that that church was built upon Newcastle coals. In like manner it might be that heretofore, when Salisbury Cathedral was building, which was long before wool was manufactured in England (the merchants of the staple sent it then in woolpacks beyond sea, to Flanders, etc), that an imposition might be put on the Wiltshire wool-packs towards the carrying on of this magnificent structure. There is a saying also that London Bridge was built upon wool-packs, upon the same account.

Sir William Dugdale told me, many years since, that about Henry III's time the Pope gave a bull or patents to a company of Italian freemasons to travel up and down over all Europe to build churches. From those are derived the fraternity of adopted masons. They are known to one another by certain signs and watch-words: it continues to this day. They have several lodges in several counties for their reception, and when any of them fall into decay the brotherhood is to relieve him, etc. The manner of their adoption is very formal, and with an oath of secrecy.

Memorandum: this day, May 18th, being Monday, 1691, after Rogation Sunday, is a great convention at St Paul's Church of the fraternity of the adopted masons, where Sir Christopher Wren is to be adopted a brother, and Sir Henry Goodric, of the Tower, and divers others. There have been kings of this sodality.

Sir William Dugdale told me he finds that painting in glass came first into England in King John's time. Before the Reformation I believe there was no county or great town in England but had glass painters. Old Mr Harding, of Blandford in Dorsetshire, where I went to school, was the only country glass painter that ever I knew. Upon play days I was wont to visit his shop and furnaces. He died about 1643, aged about 83, or more.

In St Edmund's church at Salisbury were curious painted glass windows, especially in the chancel, where there was one window (I think the east window) of such exquisite work that Gondomar, the Spanish Ambassador, did offer some hundreds of pounds for it, if it might have been bought. In one of the windows was the picture of God the Father, like an old man, which gave offence to H. Shervill, Esq., then Recorder of this city (this was about 1631), who, out of zeal, came and brake some of these windows, and clambering upon one of the pews to be able to reach high enough, fell down and brake his leg. For this action he was brought into the Star Chamber, and had a great fine laid upon him which, I think, did undo him.

Heretofore all gentlemen's houses had fish ponds, and their houses had moats drawn about them, both for strength and for convenience of fish on fasting days.

The architecture of an old English gentleman's house, especially in Wiltshire, and thereabout, was a good high strong wall, a gate house, a great hall and parlour, and within the little green court where you come in, stood on one side the barn: they then thought not the noise of the threshold ill music. This is yet to be seen at several old houses and seats.

Agriculture

Considering the distance of place where I now write, London, and the distance of time that I lived in this country, I am not able to give a satisfactory account of the husbandry thereof. I will only say of our husbandmen, as Sir Thomas Overbury does of the Oxford scholars, that they go after the fashion; that is, when the fashion is almost out they take it up: so our country-men are very late and very unwilling to learn or be brought to new improvements.

The Devonshire men were the earliest improvers. I heard Oliver Cromwell, Protector, at dinner at Hampton Court, 1657 or 8, tell the Lord Arundel of Wardour and the Lord Fitzwilliam that he had been in all the counties of England, and that the Devonshire husbandry was the best: and at length we have obtained a good deal of it, which is now well known and need not to be rehearsed. But William Scott, of Hedington, a very understanding man in these things, told me that since 1630 the fashion of husbandry in this country had been altered three times over, still refining.

Mr Bishop, of Merton, first brought into the south of Wiltshire the improvement by burn-becking or Denshiring, about 1639. He learnt it in Flanders; it is very much used in this parish, and their neighbours do imitate them: they say 'tis good for the father, but naught for the son, by reason it does so wear out the heart of the land.

The wheat and bread of this county, especially South Wilts, is but indifferent; that of the Vale of White Horse is excellent. King Charles II when he lay at Salisbury, in his progress, complained that he found there neither good bread nor good beer. But for the latter, 'twas the fault of the brewer not to boil it well; for the water and the malt there are as good as any in England.

The improvement by cinquefoil, which now spreads much in the stone-brash lands, was first used at North Wraxhall by Nicholas Hall, who came from Dundery in Somersetshire, about the yeare 1650.

George Johnson, Esq. counsellor-at-law, did improve some of his estate at Bowdon Park, by marling, from 6d. an acre to 25 s. He did lay three hundred loads of blue marl upon an acre.

Sir William Basset, of Claverdoun, hath made the best vineyard that I have heard of in England. He sayes that the Navarre grape is the best for our climate, and that the eastern sun does most comfort the vine, by putting off the cold. Mr John Ash, of Teffont Ewyas, has a pretty vineyard of about six acres, made in 1665. Sir Walter Erneley, Baronet, told me, a little before he died, that he was making one at Stert, I think, near Devizes.

The improvement of watering meadows began at Wylie, about
1635, about which time, I remember, we began to use them at Chalk.
Watering of meadows about Marlborough and so to Hungerford
was, I remember, about 1646, and Mr John Bayly, of Bishop's Down,
near Salisbury, about the same time made his great improvements by
watering there by St Thomas's Bridge. This is as old as the Romans.
Mr John Evelyn told me that out of Varro, Cato, and Columella are
to be extracted all good rules of husbandry; and he wishes that a good
collection or extraction were make out of them.

Enclosing. Anciently, in the hundreds of Malmesbury and Chippenham were but few enclosures, and that near houses. The north part of
Wiltshire was in those days admirable for fieldsports. All vast
champaign fields, as now about Sherston and Marsfield. King Henry
VII brought in depopulations, and that enclosures; and after the
dissolution of the abbeys in Henry VIII's time more enclosing. About
1695 all between Easton Piers and Castle Combe was a campania, like
Cotswold, upon which it borders; and then Yatton and Castle
Combe did intercommon together. Between these two parishes
much hath been enclosed in my remembrance, and every day more
and more. I do remember about 1633 but one enclosure to
Chippenham, which was at the north end, and by this time I think it is
all inclosed. So all between Kington St Michael and Draycot Cerne
was common field, and the west field of Kington St Michael between
Easton Piers and Haywood was inclosed in 1664. Then were a world
of labouring people maintained by the plough, as they were likewise
in Northamptonshire. 'Tis observed that the enclosures of Northamptonshire have been unfortunate since, and not one of them have
prospered.

Mr Toogood, of Harcot, has fenced his grounds with crab-tree
hedges, which are so thick that no boar can get through them.
Captain Jones, of Newton Tony, did the like on his downs. Their
method is thus: they first run a furrow with the plough, and then they
sow the cakes of the crabs, which they get at the verjuice mill. It
grows very well, and on many of them they do graff [make ditches].

Limeing of ground was not used but about 1595, some time after
the coming in of tobacco. (From Sir Edward Ford of Devon.)

Old Mr Broughton, of Herefordshire, was the man that brought in
the husbandry of soap ashes. He living at Bristol, where much soap is
made, and the haven there was like to have been choked up with it,
considering that ground was much meliorated by compost, etc did
undertake this experiment, and having land near the city, did
accordingly improve it with soap ashes. I remember the gentleman

very well. He dyed about 1650, I believe near 90 years old, and the handsomest, well limbed, strait old man that ever I saw, had a good witt and a graceful elocution. He was the father of Bess Broughton, one of the greatest beauties of her age.

Proverb for apples, pears, hawthorns, quicksets, oaks:

> Set them at All-Hallow-tyde, and command them to grow;
> Set them at Candlemas, and entreat them to grow.

Butter and Cheese. At Pertwood and about Lidyard as good butter is made as any in England, but the cheese is not so good. About Lidyard, in those fat grounds, in hot weather, the best huswives cannot keep their cheese from heaving. The art to keep it from heaving is to put in cold water. Sour wood-sere grounds do yield the best cheese, and such are Cheshire, Bromefield, in the parish of Yatton, is so, sour and wet, and there I had better cheese made than anywhere in all the neighbourhood.

Somerset proverb:

> If you will have a good cheese, and hav'n old,
> You must turn'n seven times before he is cold.

John Shakespeare's wife, of Worplesdown in Surrey, a North Wiltshire woman, and an excellent huswife, does assure me that she makes as good cheese there as ever she did at Wraxhall or Bitteston, and that it is merely for want of art that her neighbours do not make as good; they send their butter to London. So it appears that, some time or other, when there in the vale of Sussex and Surrey they have the North Wiltshire skill, that half the cheese trade of the markets of Tedbury and Marlborough will be spoiled.

Now of late, about 1680, in North Wiltshire, they have altered their fashion from thin cheeses about an inch thick, made so for the sake of drying and quick sale, called at London Marlborough cheese, to thick ones, as the Cheshire cheese. At Marlborough and Tedbury the London cheesemongers do keep their factors for their trade.

The Downs

We now make our ascent to the second elevation or the hill country, known by the name of the Downs, or Salisbury Plains; and they are the most spacious plains in Europe, and the greatest remains that I can hear of the smooth primitive world when it lay all under water.

These downs run into Hampshire, Berkshire, and Dorsetshire; but as to its extent in this county, it is from Redhone, the hill above

Salisbury Plain. A watercolour by Aubrey showing himself hawking with Sir James Long (centre).

Urchfont, to Salisbury, north and south, and from Mere to Ludgershall, east and west. The turf is of a short sweet grass, good for the sheep, and delightful to the eye, for its smoothness like a bowling green, and pleasant to the traveller; who wants here only variety of objects to make his journey less tedious: for here is 'nought save field and air', not a tree, or rarely a bush to shelter one from a shower.

The soil of the downs I take generally to be a white earth or mawm. More south, about Wilton and Chalke, the downs are intermixed with boscages that nothing can be more pleasant, and in the summer time to excel Arcadia in verdant and rich turf and moderate air, but in winter indeed our air is cold and raw. The innocent lives here of the shepherds do give us a resemblance of the golden age. Jacob and Esau were shepherds; and Amos, one of the royal family, asserts the same of himself, for he was among the shepherds of Tecua [Tekoa] following that employment. The like, by God's own appointment, prepared Moses for a sceptre, as Philo intimates in his life, when he tells us that a shepherd's art is a suitable preparation to a kingdom. The same he mentions in his life of Joseph, affirming that the care a shepherd has over his cattle very much resembles that which a king hath over his subjects. The Romans, the worthiest and greatest nation in the world, sprang from shepherds. The augury of the twelve vultures placed a sceptre in Romulus's hand, which held a crook before; and as Ovid says:

His own small flock each senator did keep.

Lucretius mentions an extraordinary happiness, and as it were divinity, in a shepherd's life:

Thro' shepherd's care, and their divine retreats.

And, to speak from the very bottom of my heart, not to mention the integrity and innocence of shepherds, upon which so many have insisted and copiously declaimed, methinks he is much more happy in a wood that at ease contemplates the universe as his own, and in it the sun and stars, the pleasing meadows, shades, groves, green banks, stately trees, flowing springs, and the wanton windings of a river, fit objects for quiet innocence, than he that with fire and sword disturbs the world, and measures his possessions by the waste that lies about him.

These plains do abound with hares, fallow deer, partridges, and bustards.

Sheep. As to the nature of our Wiltshire sheep, negatively, they are not subject to the shaking; which the Dorsetshire sheep are. Our sheep about Chalke do never die of the rot. My cousin Scott does assure me that I may modestly allow a thousand sheep to a tything, one with another. Mr Rogers was for allowing of two thousand sheep, one with another, to a tything, but my cousin Scott says that is too high.

Shepherds. The Britons received their knowledge of agriculture from the Romans, and they retain yet many of their customs. The festivals at sheep-shearing seeme to be derived from the Parilia. In our western parts (I know not what is done in the north), the sheep-masters give no wages to their shepherds, but they have the keeping of so many sheep, pro rata; so that the shepherd's lambs do never miscarry.

Their habit, I believe (let there be a draught of their habit), is that of the Roman or Arcadian shepherds; as they are delineated in Mr Michael Drayton's *Poly-olbion*: a long white cloak with a very deep cape, which comes halfway down their backs, made of the locks of the sheep. There was a sheep-crook (*vide* Virgil's *Eclogues*, and Theocritus,) a sling, a scrip, their tar-box, a pipe or flute, and their dog. But since 1671, they are grown so luxurious as to neglect their ancient warm and useful fashion, and go à la mode. T. Randolph in a Pastoral says:

> What clod-pates, Thenot, are our British swaines,
> How lubber-like they loll upon the plaines.

Before the civil wars I remember many of them made straw hats, which I think is now left off, and our shepherdesses of late years (1680) do begin to work point, whereas they before did only knit coarse stockings.

Mr Ferraby, the minister of Bishop's Cannings, was an ingenious man, and an excellent musician, and made several of his parishioners good musicians, both for vocal and instrumental music; they sung the Psalms in consort to the organ which Mr Ferraby procured to be erected.

When King James the First was in these parts he lay at Sir Edward Baynton's at Bromham. Mr Ferraby then entertained his majesty at the Bush, in Cotefield, with bucolics of his own making and composing, of four parts; which were sung by his parishioners, who wore frocks and whips like carters. While his majesty was thus diverted, the eight bells (of which he was the cause) did ring, and the organ was played on for state; and after this musical entertainment he entertained his majesty with a football match of his own parishioners. This parish in those days would have challenged all England for music, football, and ringing. For this entertainment his majesty made him one of his chaplains in ordinary.

When Queen Anne [i.e. King James's wife] returned from Bath, he made an entertainment for her majesty on Canning's-down, at Shepherd's-shard, at Wensditch, with a pastoral performed by himself and his parishioners in shepherds' weeds. A copy of his song was printed within a compartment excellently well engraved and designed, with goates, pipes, sheep hooks, cornucopias, etc.

Wool. This nation is the most famous for the great quantity of wool of any in the world; and this country hath the most sheep and wool of any other. The down-wool is not of the finest of England, but of about the second rate. That of the common-field is the finest.

Query: if Castle Combe was not a staple for wool, or else a very great wool-market?

Mr Ludlowe, of Devizes, and his predecessors have been wool brokers 80 or 90 years, and hath promised to assist me.

Query: if it would not be the better way to send our wool beyond the sea again, as in the time of the staple? For the Dutch and French do spin finer, work cheaper, and dye better. Our clothiers combine against the wool-masters, and keep their spinners but just alive: they steal hedges, spoil coppices, and are trained up as nurseries of sedition and rebellion.

Falling of Rents. The falling of rents is a consequence of the decay of the Turkey trade; which is the principal cause of the falling of the price of wool. Another reason that conduces to the falling of the prices of wool is our women's wearing so much silk and Indian ware as they do. By these means my farm at Chalk is worse by sixty pounds per annum than it was before the civil wars.

The gentry living in London, and the daily concourse of servants out of the country to London, makes servants' wages dear in the country, and makes scarcity of labourers.

Sir William Petty told me, that when he was a boy a seedsman had five pounds per annum wages, and a country servant-maid between 30 and 40s. wages.

Memorandum: great increase of sainfoin now, in most places fit for it; improvements of meadows by watering; ploughing up of the King's forests and parks, etc. But as to all these, as ten thousand pounds is gained in the hill barren country, so the vale does lose as much, which brings it to an equation.

The Indians do work for a penny a day; so their silks are exceeding cheap; and rice is sold in India for four pence per bushel.

Eminent Clothiers of this County. Mr Sutton of Salisbury, was an eminent clothier: what is become of his family I know not. [John]

Hall, I do believe, was a merchant of the staple, at Salisbury, where he had many houses. His dwelling house, now a tavern, (1669), was in the Ditch, where in the glass windows are many escutcheons of his arms yet remaining, and several merchant marks. Query, if there are not also woolsacks in the panels of glass?

The ancestor of Sir William Webb of Odstock, near Salisbury, was a merchant of the staple in Salisbury. As Grevill and Wenman bought all the Cotswold wool, so did Hall and Webb the wool of Salisbury plains; but these families are Roman Catholic.

The ancestor of Mr Long, of Rood Ashton, was a very great clothier. He built great part of that handsome church, as appears by the inscription here, between 1480 and 1500.

[William] Stump was a wealthy clothier at Malmesbury, in the time of Henry VIII. His father was the parish clarke of North Nibley, in Gloucestershire, and was a weaver, and at last grew up to be a clothier. This clothier at Malmesbury, at the dissolution of the abbeys, bought a great deal of the abbey lands thereabout. When King Henry VIII hunted in Bradon forest, he gave his majesty and the court a great entertainment at his house (the abbey). The King told him he was afraid he had undone himself; he replied that his own servants should only want their supper for it. Leland says that when he was there the dortures and other great rooms were filled with weavers' looms.

Mr Paul Methwin of Bradford succeeded his father-in-law in the trade, and was the greatest clothier of his time (in the time of Charles II). He was a worthy gentleman, and died about 1667. Now (in the time of James II) Mr Brewer of Trowbridge driveth the greatest trade for medleys of any clothier in England.

Fairs and markets

Fairs. The most celebrated fair in North Wiltshire for sheep is at Castle Combe, on St George's Day (23 April), whither sheep-masters do come as far as from Northamptonshire. Here is a good cross and market-house; and heretofore was a staple of wool, as John Scrope, Esq. Lord of the manor, affirms to me. The market here is now very inconsiderable.

At Wilton is a very noted fair for sheep, on St George's Day also; and another on St Giles's Day, September the first. Graziers, etc from Buckinghamshire come hither to buy sheep.

Wilton was the head town of the county till Bishop Bingham built the bridge at Harnham which turned away the old Roman way (in the Ledger book of Wilton called the 'herepath', i.e. the army path), and brought the trade to New Sarum, where it hath ever since continued.

At Chilmark is a good fair for sheep at St Margaret's day, 20th July.

Burford, near Salisbury, a fair on Lammas day; 'tis an eminent fair for wool and sheep, the eve is for wool and cheese.

At the city of New Sarum is a very great fair for cloth at Twelfth Tide, called Twelfth Market. In the parish of All-Cannings is St Anne's Hill, vulgarly called Tann Hill, where every year on St Anne's day (26th July), is kept a great fair within an old camp, called Oldbury. The chief commodities are sheep, oxen and fineries. This fair would be more considerable, but that Bristol Fair happens at the same time.

At Devizes several fairs; but the greatest is at the Green there, at Michaelmas: it continues about a week.

Markets. Warminster is exceeding much frequented for a round corn-market on Saturday. Hither come the best teams of horses, and it is much resorted to by buyers. Good horses for the coach: some of £20 or more. It is held to be the greatest corn-market by much in the West of England. My bailiff has assured me that twelve or fourteen score loads of corn on market-days are brought thither: the glovers that work in their shops at the town's end do tell the carts as they come in; but this market of late years has decayed; the reason whereof I had from my honoured friend Henry Millburne, Esq. Recorder of Monmouth.

My bailiff, an ancient servant to our family, assures me that, about 1644, six quarters of wheat would stand, as they term it, Hindon Market, which is now perhaps the second best market after Warminster in this county.

I have heard old men say long since that the market at Castle Combe was considerable in the time of the staple: the market day is Monday. Now only some eggs and butter, etc.

Marlborough Market is Saturday: one of the greatest markets for cheese in the west of England. Here do reside factors for the cheesemongers of London.

King Edgar granted a charter to Steeple Ashton.

At Highworth was the greatest market, on Wednesday, for fat cattle in our county, which was furnished by the rich vale; and the Oxford butchers furnished themselves here. In the late civil wars it being made a garrison for the King, the graziers, to avoid the rudeness of the soldiers, quitted that market, and went to Swindon, four miles distant, where the market on Monday continues still, which before was a petty, inconsiderable one. Also, the plague was at Highworth before the late wars, which was very prejudicial to the market there; by reason whereof all the country sent their cattle to Swindon market, as they did before to Highworth.

Devizes: on Thursday a very plentiful market of every thing: but the best for fish in the county. They bring fish from Poole hither, which is sent from hence to Oxford.

Of hawks and hawking

[From Sir James Long, Draycot.] Memorandum: between the years 1630 and 1634 Henry Poole, of Cirencester, Esquire (since Sir Henry Poole, Baronet), lost a falcon flying at Brook, in the spring of the year, about three o'clock in the afternoon; and he had a falconer in Norway at that time to take hawks for him, who discovered this falcon, upon the stand from whence he was took at first, the next day in the evening. This flight must be 600 miles at least.

Dame Julian Barnes, in her book of hunting and hawking, says that the hawk's bells must be in proportion to the hawk, and they are to be equiponderant, otherwise they will give the hawk an unequal ballast: and as to their sound they are to differ by a semitone, which will make them heard better than if they were unisons.

William of Malmesbury says that in the year 900, in the time of King Alfred, hawking was first used. Cotswold is a very fine country for this sport, especially before they began to enclose about Malmesbury, Newton, etc. It is a princely sport, and no doubt the novelty, together with the delight to behold King Athelstan's figure in his monument at Malmesbury Abbey Church, with a falconer's glove on his right hand, with a knob or tassel to put under his girdle, as the falconers use still; but this chronological advertisement clears it. Sir George Marshal of Cole Park, equerry to King James I, had no more manners or humanity than to have his body buried under this tomb. The Welsh did King Athelstan homage at the city of Hereford, and covenanted yearly payment of £20 in gold, in silver £300, oxen 2,500, besides hunting dogs and hawks. He died in 941, and was buried with many trophies at Malmesbury. His laws are extant to this day among the laws of other Saxon kings.

The race

Henry Earl of Pembroke instituted Salisbury Race; which hath since continued very famous, and beneficial to the city. He gave [fifty] pounds to the corporation of Sarum to provide every year, in the first Thursday after Mid-Lent Sunday, a silver bell of value; which, about 1630, was turned into a silver cup of the same value. This race is of two sorts: the greater, fourteen miles, begins at Whitesheet and ends on Harnham Hill, which is very seldom run, not once perhaps in twenty years. The shorter begins at a place called the Start, at the end of the edge of the north down of the farm of Broad Chalk, and ends at the standing at the hare-warren, built by William Earl of Pembroke, and is four miles from the start.

It is certain that Peacock used to run the four mile course in five minutes and a little more; and Dalavill since came but little short of him. Peacock was first Sir Thomas Thynne's of Longleat; who valued him at £1000. Philip Earl of Pembroke gave £5 but to have a sight of him: at last his lordship had him; I think by gift. Peacock was a bastard barb. He was the most beautiful horse ever seen in this last age, and was as fleet as handsome. He died about 1650.

> Here lies the man whose horse did gain
> The bell in race on Salisbury plain;
> Reader, I know not whether needs it,
> You or your horse rather to read it.

At Everly is another race. Query: if the Earl of Abingdon hath not set up another?

At Salisbury a phantom appeared to Dr Turbervill's sister several times, and it discovered to her a writing or deed of settlement that was hid behind the wainscot.

Phantoms: Though I myself never saw any such things, yet I will not conclude that there is no truth at all in these reports. I believe that extraordinarily there have been such apparitions; but where one is true a hundred are figments. There is a lechery in lying and imposing on the credulous; and the imagination of fearful people is to admiration; e.g. Not long after the cave at Bathford was discovered (where the *opus tessellatum* was found), one of Mr Skreen's plough-boys lying asleep near to the mouth of the cave, a gentleman in a boat on the River Avon, which runs hard by, played on his flageolet. The boy apprehended the music to be in the cave, and ran away in a lamentable fright, and his fearful fancy made him believe he saw spirits in the cave. This Mr Skreen told me, and that the neighbour-hood are so confident of the truth of this, that there is no undeceiving of them.

Aubrey on education

An Idea of Education of Young Gentlemen

Note: this was edited by J. E. Stephens in 1972, (in *An Idea of Education*, published by Routledge and Kegan Paul plc) and the excerpts which follow are from his text, reprinted here with thanks.

PREFACE

Plato says that the education of children is the foundation of government: it will follow then that the education of the nobles must be the pillars and ornament of it. 'Tis true there is an ample provision made in both our universities for the education of divines, but no care has been taken of the right breeding up gentlemen of quality, than which there is not anything of greater moment in a nation; for it is the root and source of their good administration of justice. It may perhaps seem paradoxical to aver that no nobleman's son in England is so ill-bred (or can have so good a breeding) as the King's mathematical boys at Christchurch Hospital in London, but it is certainly so. About 167–, King Charles II erected that Mathematical School for forty boys to be made fit for navigation, but their teacher is on the king's order to teach no other. But we want such a nursery, or way of instruction, for the children of the gentry.

As for grammar learning, the commonest way of teaching it is so long, tedious and preposterous that it breaks the spirits of the fine, tender, ingenious youths and makes them perfectly to hate learning; and they are not to be blamed for it. Most of their rules which they commonly learn are as difficult to be understood as a logic or a metaphysic lecture, and the authors they read as hard to be understood as any they read when they come to be men. Besides, there is a tyrannical beating and dispiriting of children from which many tender and ingenious do never recover again. I have known some that forty years old and upwards when anything troubled them, they dreamed they were under the tyranny of their schoolmaster. So strong an impression does the horror of the discipline leave.

This tyranny at Blandford School was so great that yet, upon any trouble Captain Baynard dreams he is there at *Hic, haec, hoc,* with fear and trembling, which was about thirty years hence. The like for twenty years by dreams, frequently happened to myself.

It was a most ridiculous and imprudent way of breeding up youth in King James's time or before, and at Bristol much used as yet, viz. to damp poor lads' spirits, and so daunting them with shipping, cuffing and brow-beating that oftimes a spirit thus broken never recovers itself again. This way made not only a strangeness between parents and children, but made the child absolutely to hate the parent, as a rogue the beadle. What a sad thing it is to see youths or girls come before strangers, hanging down their heads, sneaking and void of spirits; whereas nature intended at this age their eyes should dance with joy. One thus spoiled, 'tis well if he recovers his understanding faculties but to speak in public without being confounded with fear.

Being scared, and having other ideas than which he should have at that present presenting themselves to his imagination, he will never be able, but either do it with angry ill-grace or leave off in the middle of it.

Now rather a child of mine should undergo such slavery, he should never learn the Latin tongue, but be content with that of his mother, and be mathematically informed. John Newton, DD, minister at Ross in Herefordshire, kept a mathematical school there for youths who did profit exceedingly under him. He protested to me that, after they were a little entered, they took so great a delight in their studies that they would learn as fast as one could teach them. But he was utterly against the learning of the Latin tongue at this school: he would not have the studies mixed. Methinks he was too straight-laced and magisterial in that point, for since it is so that Latin is the universal language, and that one cannot be said to be a well-bred man that is ignorant of it, I should think it fit that their studies be inter-mixed and changed with delight. But their Latin should be learned after an easier manner. Mr Martindale, a nonconformist schoolmaster in Cheshire, teaches both and with a very good success, and is the only person that I hear of that does so. They take a great delight in it and on play days make it their pastime.

Arithmetic and geometry are the keys that open unto us all mathematical and philosophical knowledge, and by consequence, all other knowledge: namely by teaching us to reason aright and carefully, and not to conclude hastily and make a false step. These two sciences ought to be instilled into boys and they will joyfully imbibe such demonstrative delightful and useful learning. And being learnt so young, it sticks by them as long as they live, and becomes habitual. Otherwise, when these two sciences are learnt by men of good years, as commonly it falls out, it turns the edge of their wits, and they give it off. Or, if not, they make no great matter of it. For example, Mr Thomas Hobbes, who was forty years old or better when he began to study Euclid's *Elements*. 'Tis as though a man of thirty or forty should learn to play on the lute when the joints of his fingers are knit. There may be something analogous to this in the brain and understanding. Sir Jonas More told me that he had a Fellow of a house in Cambridge that was one of the best humanists and orators in that university to be his scholar for mathematics, thirty years old and more. He protested he could not make him understand or learn division, and so he gave it off as incapable.

Without a doubt, it was of great advantage to the learned Mr W. Oughtred's natural parts that his father taught him common arithmetic perfectly while he was a schoolboy. The like advantage might be reported of the reverend and learned Edward Davenant, DD, whose father, a merchant of London, taught him arithmetic

Thomas Hobbes, the philosopher

when he was a schoolboy. The like may be said of Sir Christopher Wren, Mr Edmond Halley and Mr Thomas Ax, whose father taught him the table of multiplication at seven years old.

As for private education, though great persons are able to maintain able instructors, the inconveniences are so many and so obvious that 'tis needless to recount them. Young heirs, bred at home, are so flattered by the servants and dependents of the family that they think themselves to be the best men in the nation, and they are not to be blamed for it, for they know nothing to the contrary. So when they make their entry into the world amongst their equals and superiors they give offence and become ridiculous, till time, and affronts, and perchance some beatings, have more civilised them. Besides, being bred at home, their minds are advocated with continual suggestions of trivial divertisements as coursing, hawking, setting and conversation with their sisters and relations, domestic differences – all which are alien in this way of education that I propose, and where they will be weaned from their nursery.

The French academies seem to me not able to perform the generous education promised thence, and so much cried up. 'Tis like the shearing of hogs: they make a great cry and little wool. The most considerable thing learned there is to fit to be a man, a French chevalier, to manage the great horse; that is in plain English, to be a complete trooper. 'Tis true, there are masters for mathematics, for logic, for the lute and guitar, and all these are learnt and jumbled together when they are great fellows at an age more proper for matrimony, when their minds do chiefly run on propagating their race. Nature will be nature still at eighteen. So that at this age, and with these circumstances, their information is like writing on greasy parchment: it will not stick and leave an imprint. Or, like painting anew on an old picture, the new colours will not be imbibed. However, the boys at St Omer have an aptitude at grammar that indeed they have very well. The like is at La Flèche and the rest of the schools of that Society [the Jesuits]. The reason is plain. Because they are not made acquainted with the sweets and illicibrations of the sciences (e.g. arithmetic and geometry), nor are they well introduced into the knowledge of the passions, but pick up scraps out of the old poets.

'Twas a great disadvantage to me in my childhood to be bred up in a kind of park, far from neighbours, and no child to converse withall, so that I did not speak till late. I was eight years old before I knew what theft was, for I had a fine top which was stolen from me. My father had one to teach me in the house, and I was pent up in a room by myself, melancholy. At twelve years old I was put to public school at Blandford under Mr W. Sutton, BD, I was like a bird that was got out of his cage amongst the free citizens of the air. It was the first time I knew the world and the wickedness of boys. The boys mocked me and abused me that were stronger than myself so I was fain to make friendship of a strong boy to protect me. I am sensible of the inconvenience of my former private education to this very day; besides, it impaired my health. Sir Christopher Wren said also the same of himself; wherefore he has sent his son to a great school, Eton, not much caring what Latin he learned, but to learn how to shift and live in the world.

Now for the remedying of a private or pedantic education there must be taken a quite contrary way of institution for breeding up youths of that rank. Gentlemen, and youth of this quality ought to be bred up among their equals. Here at school are laid the fundamentals of friendships and acquaintance which last till death. A cobbler's son may have a good wit and may perchance be a good man, but he would not be proper for a friend to a person of honour. It is of ill consequence for a youth to be sent to a great school in his own country, which contracts an acquaintance never to be shaken off, and this will be chargeable as well as perpetually troublesome. Most men do not desire to have a glass before their hearts that all people might know their minds and affections. What is the disposition of a boy is the same when he is a man, only he covers it with a vizor of cunning and dissembling. Schoolfellows know one another's foibles, as they say, and some come to be their servants who were their playfellows at school.

Relaxation and bodily exercise

For exercise, the tops and gig, but especially the shuttlecock, which is an introduction to tennis, quickens the eye and prepares to fencing. Besides it is not too violent, yet robust enough; and children ought to be exercised to digest their phlegm and [dispel] their moisture, consequently amending the temperature of their brains. Let anyone observe when he has played at shuttlecock or tennis (I mean moderately) whether, when he comes to study, he does not find his understanding and apprehension clearer than usual. It disperses the fog which in England is frequent.

Wherefore, let every Thursday (especially in the afternoon) be a time of relaxation from their other tasks. Let 'em walk in the fields, or ride, but still to be kept strictly to speak good Latin: sometimes (rarely), in their short journeys to visit persons of quality, but never to lie out except upon extraordinary reason.

Here should be kept half a dozen or more little horses for the young gentlemen, the gentleman of the horse to be a well-bred Swiss who speaks good Latin as most of them do and had seen the wars, to teach the young gentlemen to sit a horse gracefully and discourse to them of the world and of wars, and to delight them: to mind them of N. Machiavelli's observation in his *Prince*, which is what Philopoemen did long ago, namely, when he did ride abroad he would consider the ground, so, and so; if an enemy were there how should he order his strength.

Young men do much want airing, especially those of sulphurious complexion: they are apt to kindle a fever without it. Good air is a 'food to the mind': when they do air themselves, either riding or walking, let them be informed in the botanics and husbandry (good or bad) as also antiquities if they lie in their way; and therefore let an old antiquary or botanist travel with a young man to inform him. Some of them will catch at these things. Let 'em carry in their coat pockets Mr John Ray's *Synopsis of English Plants* or Mr Paschal's *Botanic Tables* from Mr Ray's book done in the Real Character in three sheets. The Duke of Orleans and several great princes and persons have made it their delight and recreation. Methinks it is a kind of irreligion to be ignorant of the names and virtues of those plants that grow about our dwellings, which we daily see and with which we are daily nourished. Those who are easy enough may read Virgil's *Georgics* and Servius's *Notes* and let 'em peruse Columella and Varro that they may be the better acquainted with them hereafter if they have a mind to it. Mr John Evelyn affirms that none have writ better.

John Evelyn, the diarist and fellow antiquary

Let 'em never be idle; nay, let their every play be instructive. Let 'em always have in their pockets some dialogues, and Euclid's *Elements* as religiously a monk his breviary. Let 'em be told how to excerpt, for which purpose let every one have a little 12 mo pocket book to enter excerpts, either of reading or of observations either of men's knowledge, or men's manners, or natural things, poignant sayings or antiquities. This will create in them the habit of doing and continuing this way, and finding daily more and more use of it, they will continue it as long as they live. It was a considerable advantage to Sir Francis North, now Lord Keeper, besides his own good parts and excellence of wit, that his tutor (as his Lordship told me) made him properly to understand what he read to him before he left him, so no doubt was left upon him. Let this method be used through all the arts.

These hints will be as a mustard seed – nest eggs. Their excerpts of observations in their note books will be repositories or stories from observations and experience, away beyond the common way of precepts as the knowledge of a traveller exceeds that which is gotten by a map. I know not where are to be found better specimens of this kind than in Ben Jonson's *Underwoods*.

He deeply read men and made his observations as he walked along the streets. Had he not done that, he had never wrote so well. He has outdone all men yet in dramatic poetry. Nature is the best guide and the best pattern: 'tis better to copy Nature than books, as the best painters imitate Nature, not copy it. This will put life and vigour into youths of ingenious spirits to see that by these steps the old writers came by their mastership. Drexilius inculcated, 'Always excerpt'. Then, as for notions which it shall please God to dart into their minds, those winged fugitives to be entered and so to become fixed, or otherwise, perhaps, they may be eternally lost.

Whilst invention is in the flux, let it run; for if it be checked, 'tis like the stopping of a patient's breathing sweat, which is not easily regained. Let them exercise to make unpenned speeches, declamations or addresses. This way of exercise to the Lord Chancellor Bacon does much appear of all most useful. A Spanish Jesuit told a friend of mine that 'tis a good way, before one was to speak to a prince, or in a great assembly, to speak it first in one's chamber, to your bedpost, or to a picture. My Lord William Brereton, my honoured friend, told me has asked Dr Burnet how he obtained that extraordinary mastership in preaching. The Doctor told him that when he began to be a preacher, he would go up into the mountains where he was sure nobody could hear him and speak aloud and by much practice he obtained this perfection.

Geometry

When I was at Blandford, there was at the Bowling Green a gentleman, a German, that was driven out of his estate and country by the wars that raged there. He was forced to maintain himself by surveying land. He told the gentleman that it was good to have a little learning; no one knew to what straits or shifts he might be brought. 'Before the wars,' he said, 'I had as good an estate as any of you;' which expression I took much notice of. Had this gentleman been bred only to understand genus and species, he might have wanted bread; and besides his want of mathematics, he would not have had the address, or been conversable, è contra. The Right Honourable Edward, Earl of Hertford, was wont to say that if he were to earn his living, he had no way but that of the fiddler, and thus were several great persons bred in those days. Music is a great thief of time and if one love it never so well and has a genius for it, a common fiddler, or barber, or footman must needs outdo him; they making it their continual practice. The late King of Spain [Philip IV] spent the great part of his time in playing on the tenor-viol: as for matters of estate he left that to be managed by his minister of estate. It argued a most magnanimous soul in the present Louis, King of France, of whom the Archbishop of Paris in the life of Henry IV says of him, being then but a youth, that he had rather have no crown than not to govern himself. He (his majesty of France) cannot play on the fiddle, but he can make little towns great cities and make devastations of great cities and countries. He understands perfectly fortifications, the besiegings and making approaches to cities or castles which he was taught when young, not only by linear draughts but by works raised in earth. And he has in his cabinet at the Louvre very curious models of fortifications in cabinet work. It ought not to be forgotten that his majesty, King Charles II, though a prince of peace, did understand fortifications as well as any man. He had a mathematical genius, but wanted early education. He was wont to divertise himself at Windsor with such military draughts and designs and did invent a new device in fortification unknown before. Mr N. Mercator has proved ingeniously to me that his majesty understands fortifications as well as he did.

Foreign travel

The cursus of this school being now finished, I would in the next place have them travel beyond the sea, unless they would go through a cursus of chemistry. The martialists may go from hence to a campaign. Travel does much open the understanding, and besides gives a good address. I have heard an old friend, Fabian Philipps, say that Queen Elizabeth did cut out so many ingenious young gentlemen out of the universities to send to travel *pro bono publico* in order to make them ministers of state. This the learned Society of Jesus knew right well, who send their company from one college to another. No doubt but there are some men of as good natural parts in other colleges, but being acquainted one with another seven years or more, to converse with them is like thinking oneself; besides it makes them speak Latin well. Mr Lascelles has writ the best directions for European travels. His opinion is 'tis the best way to begin with Holland and Germany, or Switzerland and return by Italy and France, for he says the frippery of France, especially Paris, would too much allure them to vanity and make them disrelish their more serious and useful studies. Let them stay in Germany so long that they understand a Dutch [i.e. German] author. For chemistry and mixed mathematics no language does afford so many good books. No nation is so much addicted to chemistry in so much that the very country people do understand distillation and can make extracts, especially in Tyrol and Meissen, and above all Goslar in Low Saxony. (This good note I had from my honoured friend, Mr D[ethlevus] Cluverus, RSS.)

Let them in their travels observe husbandry and economy and all ingenious and useful engines; of architecture of rooms of use, as kitchens, barns and stables, cow-houses and pigsties; and in these things Holland does most excel. They are now entered into the dangerous time of temptation of love, which by staying at home they would infallibly fall into – lawful or unlawful – but being kept in action, body and mind, in a strange country they will not be at leisure to be attacked by Cupid.

When they return home, I would have them travel several parts of England where they may make curious remarks. Scarce any country has greater variety of natural things. When they are twenty-one years of age, or on their return home, let 'em read John Norden's *Dialogues*, between the lord of a manor and the steward, between the lord of a manor and his bailiff and between the lord of a manor and his surveyor.

Some fathers do send their sons abroad to travel and they do well in it, but few do take care to train them up to understand their estates, as if afraid to let them be acquainted with that mystery, the want of which proves often of very bad consequence. They ought to be well-informed in the buying and selling of timber. The Lord Lovelace's father, who aggrandised the estate, advised Sir Robert Henley's father to make his purchases in a woodland country. I have heard a friend of mine, say, who had great woods, that selling timber by the foot was not the best way. 'Tis better, he said, to sell by the lump; that is, top, lop and bark – to every 50 feet of timber, ten shillings for top, lop and bark. The heaving and carriage is pretty considerable.

Epilogue: or the Conclusion

By this education, when they are eighteen or nineteen years old, their genius will appear, to what it is inclined. Boys have as many, or more, maggots (as they call 'em) in their heads, than men. Now this way of education will find work for them and matter enough for 'em to bite and feed on – drawing, mechanics, chemistry, perspective and the rest.

God almighty is the giver of gifts: to excel in any art or invention is God's gift. We have it from our genitures and from the stars. Sir Anthony Van Dyck or Sir Peter Lely could not teach his disciples to be equal to himself. So in mechanics, of all gifts the most useful to mankind, oratory, poetry, etc. 'Tis true, those that are dull, or of ordinary understanding, may obtain to some degree of skill for their way of living, calling or station; as every man cannot attain to the skill of dancing on a rope, but as my Lord Bacon says, he may learn to walk on the rope.

All have not parts to be scholars, but those to whom nature has not given to be such, will like this institution well, that they will breed up their sons after this way, and recommend children of their friends to be thus informed. A dunce may have a prodigious wit in his son, and vice versa, as we many times see. Sir William Petty told me when he was a boy, he did understand all trades in Rumsey, his native place, a market town in Hampshire – namely, watchmakers, smiths, dyers, and the rest. Now as to this institution, I think it would be very fit to have them see chemical operations, as, suppose, the physician of the college at his laboratory, to become in love with it, which will be a useful and ingenious diversion and excitement to them; namely, to make their own medicines, especially if they live in the country. And this they will learn in one month.

Now the gentlemen thus instituted are qualified for lawyers, ambassadors, commanders by land or sea, architects, solicitors, chemists and surveyors. Astrology is the best guide, to direct us as to what professions or callings children are by nature most fit or most inclined to.

My friend Sir Edward Harley, Knight of the Bath, was wont to say that he had rather trust his estate to an ingenious education than to a sheepskin (meaning a deed of entail). It will make 'em disrelish and contemn base and ignorant conversation.

Methinks it is a great pleasure to me to consider and foresee how many young gentlemen's minds would be cultivated and improved and their understandings opened by good information of sciences, as the sweet rose-buds are opened by the morning dew. How much would learning receive an advancement in this way, and how many patrons and Maecenases would spring up to encourage learning and learned men. Whereas, on the contrary hitherto, seed has been sown on a rock, which has generally either withered or degenerated into wild oats, unless by God's wonderful providence, five or six in an age come to be eminent in mathematics. And but few are economical to their country, or themselves and their concerns.

But now, methinks, I see a black squadron marching from Oxford, set up by a crozier staff to discomfit this pretty little flock. And so this pleasing dream is at an end.

Aubrey and the supernatural

Miscellanies

The *Miscellanies* were published in 1696, and in a second posthumous edition in 1721; the latter contains some corrections by Aubrey.

To The Right Honourable James, Earl of Abingdon,
Lord Chief Justice in Eyre of all his majesty's Forests and Chases on
this side Trent.

My Lord, When I enjoyed the contentment of solitude in your
pleasant walks and gardens at Lavington the last summer, I reviewed
several scattered papers which had lain by me for several years; and
then presumed to think, that if they were put together, they might be
somewhat entertaining: I therefore digested them there in this order,
in which I now present them to your lordship.

The matter of this collection is beyond human reach: we being
miserably in the dark, as to the economy of the invisible world, which
knows what we do, or incline to, and works upon our passions, and
sometimes is so kind as to afford us a glimpse of its prescience.

My lord, it was my intention to have finished my *Description of
Wiltshire* (half finished already) and to have dedicated it to your
lordship: but my age is now too far spent for such undertakings: I
have therefore devolved that task on my country man, Mr Thomas
Tanner, who hath youth to go through with it, and a genius proper
for such an undertaking.

Wherefore, I humbly beseech your lordship to accept of this small
offering, as a grateful memorial of the profound respect which I have
for you, who have for many years taken me into your favour and
protection.

My lord, may the blessed Angels be your careful guardians: such
are the prayers of
Your lordship's most obliged and humble servant,

John Aubrey 1696

Hermetic philosophy

Natural philosophy hath been exceedingly advanced within fifty
years last past; but, methinks 'tis strange that *Hermetic Philosophy* hath
lain so long untouched. It is a subject worthy of serious consideration:
I have here, for my own diversion, collected some few remarks,
within my own remembrance, or within the remembrance of some
persons, worthy of belief, in the age before me. Those, who desire to
know more of things of this nature, may be pleased to peruse *Histoire
Prodigieuse*, written by Père Arnault: as also a book entitled *Lux è
Tenebris*, which is a collection of modern visions and prophesies in
Germany, by several persons; translated into Latin by Jo. Amos
Comenius, printed at Amsterdam, 1655.

Thomas Flud, Esq. in Kent, told me that it is an old observation, which was pressed earnestly to King James I, that he should not remove the Queen of Scots' body from Northamptonshire, where she was beheaded and interred: for that it always bodes ill to the family, when bodies are removed from their graves. For some of the family will die shortly after, as did Prince Henry, and I think Queen Anne.

A little before the death of Oliver, Protector, a whale came into the river Thames, and was taken at Greenwich. 'Tis said Oliver was troubled at it.

When I was a freshman at Oxford, 1642, I was wont to go to Christ Church, to see King Charles I at supper; where I once heard him say, 'That as he was hawking in Scotland, he rode into the quarry, and found the covey of partridges falling upon the hawk; and I do remember this expression further; viz. and I will swear upon the book 'tis true.' When I came to my chamber, I told this story to my tutor; said he, that covey was London.

The bust of King Charles I carved by Bernini, as it was brought in a boat upon the Thames, a strange bird (the like whereof the bargemen had never seen) dropped a drop of blood, or blood-like upon it; which left a stain not to be wiped off. This bust was carved from a picture of Sir Anthony van Dyck's drawing: the sculptor found great fault with the forehead as most unfortunate. There was a seam in the middle of his forehead, (downwards) which is a very ill sign in metoposcopy.

Colonel Sharington Talbot was at Nottingham, when King Charles I did set up his standard upon the top of the tower there. He told me, that the first night, the wind blew it so, that it hung down almost horizontal; which some did take to be an ill omen.

The day that the Long Parliament began, 1641, the sceptre fell out of the figure of King Charles in wood, in Sir Thomas Trenchard's hall at Wullich, in Dorset, as they were at dinner in the parlour: Justice Hunt then dined there.

The picture of Archbishop Laud, in his closet, fell down (the string broke) the day of the sitting of that Parliament. This is mentioned in *Canterbury's Doom* by W. Prynne.

The psalms for the eleventh day of the month, are 56, 57, 58, etc. On the eleventh day of one of the months in summertime, the citizens came tumultuously in great numbers in boats and barges over against Whitehall, to show they would take the Parliament's part. The psalms aforesaid, both for morning and evening service, are as prophesies of the troubles that did ensue.

When the high court of justice was voted in the parliament house, as Birkenhead (the mace bearer) took up the mace to carry it before the Speaker, the top of the mace fell off. This was avowed to me by an eye witness then in the house.

The head of King Charles I's staff did fall off at his trial: that is commonly known.

The second lesson for the 30th of January in the calendar before the common prayer, is concerning the trial of Christ: which, when Bishop Duppa read, the king was displeased with him, thinking he had done it of choice; but the bishop cleared himself by the calendar, as is to be seen.

King Charles II was crowned at the very conjunction of the Sun and Mercury; Mercury being then *in corde solis* [the heart of the sun]. As the King was at dinner at Westminster Hall, it thundered and lightened extremely. The cannons and the thunder played together.

King Charles II went by long sea to Portsmouth or Plymouth, or both; an extraordinary storm arose, which carried him almost to France. Sir Jonas Moore (who was then with his Majesty) gave me this account, and said, that when they came to Portsmouth to refresh themselves, they had not been there above half an hour, but the weather was calm, and the sun shone: his Majesty put to sea again, and in a little time had the like tempestuous weather as before.

Not long before the death of King Charles II a sparrow-hawk escaped from the perch, and pitched on one of the iron crowns of the White Tower, and entangling its string in the crown, hung by the heels and died. Not long after, another hawk pitched on one of the crowns. From Sir Edward Sherborne, knight.

The Gloucester frigate cast away at the Lemanore, and most of the men in it; the Duke of York escaping in a cock boat, 1682, May the 5th, on a Friday.

When King James II was crowned, (according to the ancient custom, the peers go to the throne, and kiss the king) the crown was almost kissed off his head. An earl did set it right; and as he came from the Abbey to Westminster Hall, the crown tottered extremely.

The canopy (of cloth of gold) carried over the head of King James II by the Wardens of the Cinque Ports, was torn by a puff of wind as he came to Westminster Hall; it hung down very lamentably: I saw it.

When King James II was crowned, a signal was given from Westminster Abbey to the Tower, where it was Sir Edward Sherborne's post to stand to give order for firing the cannons, and to hoist up the great flag with the king's arms. It was a windy day, and the wind presently took the flag half off, and carried it away into the Thames. From Sir Edward Sherborne.

The top of his sceptre (fleur-de-lis) did then fall.

Upon Saint Mark's day, after the coronation of King James II were prepared stately fireworks on the Thames: it happened, that they took fire all together, and it was so dreadful, that several spectators leaped into the river, choosing rather to be drowned than burned. In a yard by the Thames, was my Lord Powys's coach and horses; the horses were so frightened by the fireworks, that the coach man was not able to stop them, but ran away over one, who with great difficulty recovered.

When King James II was at Salisbury, 1688, the iron crown upon the turret of the council house was blown off. This has been often confidently asserted by persons who were then living.

I did see Mr Christopher Love beheaded on Tower Hill, in a delicate clear day; about half an hour after his head was struck off, the clouds gathered blacker and blacker; and such terrible claps of thunder came, that I never heard greater.

'Tis reported, that the like happened after the execution of Alderman Cornish, in Cheapside, October 23, 1685.

Anno 1643. As Major John Morgan of Wells, was marching with the king's army into the west, he fell sick of a malignant fever at Salisbury, and was brought dangerously ill to my father's at Broad Chalk, where he was lodged secretly in a garret. There came a sparrow to the chamber window, which pecked the lead of a certain panel only, and only one side of the lead of the lozenge, and made one small hole in it. He continued this pecking and biting the lead, during the whole time of his sickness; (which was not less than a month) when the Major went away, the sparrow desisted, and came thither no more. Two of the servants that attended the Major, and sober persons, declared this for a certainty.

Sir Walter Long's (of Draycot in Wilts) widow, did make a solemn promise to him on his death-bed, that she would not marry after his decease, but not long after, one Sir ... Fox, a very beautiful young gentleman did win her love; so that notwithstanding her promise aforesaid she married him: she married at South Wraxall, where the picture of Sir Walter, hung over the parlour door, as it doth now at Draycot. As Sir ... Fox led his bride by the hand from the church, (which is near to the house) into the parlour, the string of the picture broke, and the picture fell on her shoulder, and cracked in the fall. (It was painted on wood, as the fashion was in those days). This made her ladyship reflect on her promise, and drew some tears from her eyes.

In the life of Monsieur Periesc, writ by Gassendus, it is said, that Monsieur Periesc, who had never been at London, did dream, that he was there, and as he was walking in a great street there, espied in a goldsmith's glass desk, an antique coin, he could never meet with (I think an Otho). When he came to London, walking in (I think) Cheapside, he saw such a shop, and remembered the countenance of the goldsmith in his dream, and found the coin desired, in his desk. See his life.

When Doctor Hamey (one of the physicians' college in London) being a young man, went to travel towards Padua, he went to Dover, (with several others) and showed his pass as the rest did, to the governor there. The governor told him, that he must not go, but must keep him prisoner. The doctor desired to know for what reason? How had he transgressed? Well, it was his will to have it so. The packet-boat hoisted sail in the evening (which was very clear) and the doctor's companions in it. There ensued a terrible storm, and the packet-boat and all the passengers were drowned: the next day the same news was brought to Dover. The doctor was unknown to the governor, both by name and face; but the night before, the governor had the perfect vision in a dream, of Doctor Hamey, who came to pass over to Calais; and that he had a warning to stop him. This the governor told the doctor the next day. The doctor was a pious, good man, and has several times related this story to some of my acquaintance.

My Lady Seymour dreamt, that she found a nest, with nine finches in it. And so many children she had by the Earl of Winchelsea, whose name is Finch.

The Countess of Cork (now Burlington) being at Dublin, dreamt, that her father, (the Earl of Cumberland) who was then at York, was dead. He died at that time.

'Tis certain, that several had monitory dreams of the conflagration of London.

Sir Christopher Wren, being at his father's house, in the year 1651, at Knahill in Wilts, (a young Oxford scholar) dreamt, that he saw a fight in a great market-place, which he knew not; where some were flying, and others pursuing; and among those that fled, he saw a kinsman of his, who went into Scotland to the king's army. They heard in the country, that the king was come to England, but whereabout he was, they could not tell. The next night his kinsman came to his father at Knahill, and was the first that brought the news of the fight at Worcester.

Captain Wingate told me, that Mr Edmund Gunter, of Gresham College, did cast his nativity, when about seventeen or eighteen years old; by which he did prognosticate that he should be in danger to lose his life for treason. Several years before the civil wars broke out, he

had dreamt that he was to be put to death before a great castle, which
he had never seen; which made a strong impression in his memory. In
1642, he did oppose the church ceremonies, and was chosen a member
of Parliament, then was made a Captain, and was taken prisoner at
Edge Hill, by Prince Rupert, and carried to Kenilworth Castle, and
condemned to die: but they did better consider of it, and spared his
life; for that he being so considerable a person, might make an
exchange for some of the king's party*; and he was exchanged for the
right honourable Montague, Earl of Lindsey (heir of the general).
Since the Restoration, he was made one of the commissioners of the
excise office in London. He did protest that Kenilworth castle was the
very castle he saw in his dream.

Sir Roger L'Estrange was wont to divertise himself with cocking in
his father's (Sir Hammond L'Estrange's) park; he dreamt that there
came to him in such a place of the park, a servant, who brought him
news, that his father was taken very ill. The next day going to his
usual recreation, he was resolved for his dream's sake to avoid that
way; but his game led him to it, and in that very place the servant
came and brought him the ill news according to his dream.

Mr Edmund Halley, RSS was carried on with a strong impulse to
take a voyage to St Helena, to make observations of the southern
constellations, being then about twenty four years old. Before he
undertook his voyage, he dreamt that he was at sea, sailing towards
that place, and saw the prospect of it from the ship in his dream,
which he declared to the Royal Society, to be the perfect representation of that island, even as he had it really when he approached to it.

1690. One, in Ireland, dreamed of a brother or near relation of his,
(who lived at Amesbury in Wiltshire) that he saw him riding on the
downs, and that two thieves robbed him and murdered him. The
dream awaked him, he fell asleep again and had the like dream. He
wrote to his relation an account of it, and described the thieves'
complexion, stature and clothes; and advised him to take care of
himself. Not long after he had received this monitory letter, he rode
towards Salisbury, and was robbed and murdered; and the murderers
were discovered by this letter, and were executed. They hang in
chains on the road to London.

Mrs Cl———, of S———, in the county of S———, had a
beloved daughter, who had been a long time ill, and received no
benefit from her physicians. She dreamed that a friend of hers,
deceased, told her that if she gave her daughter a drench of yew
pounded, that she would recover; she gave her the drench, and it

---

* Captain Wingate was a prisoner in Oxford, after Edgehill fight, 1642.

killed her. Whereupon she grew almost distracted: her chamber maid to complement her, and mitigate her grief, said surely that could not kill her, she would adventure to take the same herself; and did so, and died also. This was about the year 1670, or 1671. I knew the family.

A gentlewoman of my acquaintance, dreamed that if she slept again, the house would be in danger of being robbed. She kept awake, and anon thieves came to break open the house, but were prevented.

J. H. Esq. being at West Lavington with the Earl of Abingdon, dreamed, on December 9th, that his mother rose up in mourning: and anon the Queen appeared in mourning. He told his dream the next morning to my Lord, and his Lordship imparted it to me (then there) Tuesday, December 11th. In the evening came a messenger, post from London, to acquaint Mr H. that his mother was dangerously ill: he went to London the next day; his mother lived but about eight days longer. On Saturday, December 15th, the Queen was taken ill, which turned to the smallpox, of which she died, December 28th, about two o'clock in the morning.

Sir Thomas White, Alderman of London, was a very rich man, charitable and public spirited. He dreamt that he had founded a college at a place where three elms grow out of one root. He went to Oxford, probably with that intention, and discovering some such tree near Gloucester Hall, he began to repair it, with a design to endow it. But walking afterwards by the Convent where the

Gloucester Hall, Oxford, showing the elm tree that Sir Thomas White saw in his dream

Bernardines formerly lived, he plainly saw an elm with three large bodies rising out of the same root: he forthwith purchased the ground, and endowed his college there, as it is at this day, except the additions which Archbishop Laud made, near the outside of which building in the garden belonging to the president, the tree is still to be seen. He made this discovery about the year 1557.

William Penn, proprietor of Pennsylvania, told me, that he went with his mother on a visit to Admiral Dean's wife, who lived then in Petty-France; the Admiral was then at sea. She told them, that, the night before, she had a perfect dream of her husband, whom she saw walking on the deck, and giving directions, and that a cannon bullet struck his arm into his side. This dream did much discompose her, and within forty-eight hours she received news of the fight at sea, and that her husband was killed in the very manner aforesaid.

Apparitions

There is a tradition, (which I have heard from persons of honour) that as the Protector Seymour and his Duchess were walking in the gallery at Sheen, (in Surrey) both of them did see a hand with a bloody sword come out of the wall. He was afterwards beheaded.

Sir John Burroughes being sent envoy to the Emperor by King Charles I did take his eldest son Caisho Burroughes along with him, and taking his journey through Italy, left his son at Florence, to learn the language; where he having an intrigue with a beautiful courtisan, (mistress of the Grand Duke) their familiarity became so public, that it came to the duke's ear, who took a resolution to have him murdered; but Caisho having had timely notice of the duke's design, by some of the English there, immediately left the city without acquainting his mistress with it, and came to England; whereupon the duke being disappointed of his revenge, fell upon his mistress in most reproachful language; she on the other side, resenting the sudden departure of her gallant, of whom she was most passionately enamoured, killed herself. At the same moment that she expired, she did appear to Caisho, at his lodging in London; Colonel Remes was then in bed with him who saw her as well as he; giving him an account of her resentments of his ingratitude to her, in leaving her so suddenly, and exposing her to the fury of the duke, not omitting her own tragical exit, adding withal, that he should be slain in a duel, which accordingly happened; and thus she appeared to him frequently, even when his younger brother (who afterwards was Sir

John) was in bed with him. As often as she did appear, he would cry out with great shrieking, and trembling of his body, as anguish of mind, saying, 'Oh God! Here she comes,' and at this rate she appeared till he was killed; she appeared to him the morning before he was killed. Some of my acquaintances have told me, that he was one of the most beautiful men in England, and very valiant, but proud and blood-thirsty.

This story was so common, that King Charles I sent for Caisho Burroughes's father, whom he examined as to the truth of the matter; who did (together with Colonel Remes) aver, the matter of fact to be true, so that the king thought it worth his while to send to Florence, to enquire at what time this unhappy lady killed herself; it was found to be the same minute that she first appeared to Caisho, being in bed with Colonel Remes. This relation I had from my worthy friend Mr Monson, who had it from Sir John's own mouth, brother of Caisho; he had also the same account from his own father, who was intimately acquainted with old Sir John Burroughes and both his sons, and says, as often as Caisho related this, he wept bitterly.

In 1647, the Lord Mohun's son and heir, (a gallant gentleman, valiant, and a great master of fencing and horsemanship) had a quarrel with Prince Griffin; there was a challenge, and they were to fight on horse-back in Chelsea fields in the morning; Mr Mohun went accordingly to meet him; but about Ebury Farm, he was met by some who quarrelled with him and pistoled him, it was believed by the order of Prince Griffin; for he was sure, that Mr Mohun, being so much the better horseman would have killed him had they fought.

In James Street, in Covent Garden, did then lodge a gentlewoman, a handsome woman, but common, who was Mr Mohun's sweetheart. Mr Mohun was murdered about ten o'clock in the morning; and at that very time, his mistress being in bed, saw Mr Mohun come to her bedside, draw the curtain, look upon her and go away: she called after him but no answer: she knocked for her maid, asked her for Mr Mohun; she said she did not see him, and had the key of her chamber door in her pocket. This account my friend aforesaid, had from the gentlewoman's own mouth, and her maid's.

To one Mr Towes, who had been schoolfellow with Sir George Villiers, the father of the first Duke of Buckingham, (and was his friend and neighbour) as he lay in his bed awake, (and it was daylight), came into his chamber the phantom of his dear friend Sir George Villiers: said Mr Towes to him, 'Why, you are dead, what make you here?' Said the knight, 'I am dead, but cannot rest in peace for the wickedness and abomination of my son George, at court. I do appear to you, to tell him of it, and to advise and dehort him from his evil

ways.' Said Mr Towes, 'The Duke will not believe me, but will say,
that I am mad, or dote.' Said Sir George, 'Go to him from me, and tell
him by such a token:' (a mole) that he had in some secret place, which
none but himself knew of. Accordingly Mr Towes went to the Duke,
who laughed at his message. At his return home, the phantom
appeared again; and told him, that the duke would be stabbed (he
drew out a dagger) a quarter of a year after: 'and you shall outlive him
half a year; and the warning that you shall have of your death, will be,
that your nose will fall a-bleeding.' All which accordingly fell out so.
This account I have had (in the main) from two or three; but Sir
William Dugdale affirms what I have here taken from him to be true,
and that the apparition told him of several things to come, which
proved true, e.g. of a prisoner in the Tower, that shall be honourably
delivered. This Mr Towes had so often the ghost of his old friend
appear to him, that it was not at all terrible to him, He was surveyor of
the works at Windsor, (by the favour of the duke): being then sitting
in the hall, he cried out, 'The Duke of Buckingham is stabbed': he was
stabbed that very moment.

This relation Sir William Dugdale had from Mr Pine, (neighbour
to Mr Towes without Bishopsgate): they were both great lovers of
music, and sworn brothers. Mr W. Lilly, astrologer, did print this
story false, which made Sir Edmund Wyndham (who married Mr
Pine's daughter) give to Sir George Hollis this true account contrary
to Mr Lilly.

Mr Thomas Ellyot, Groom of the bed-chamber, married Sir
Edmund Wyndham's daughter, and had the roll (of near a quire of
paper) of the conferences of the apparition and Mr Towes. Mr Ellyot
was wont to say that Mr Towes was not a bigot, or did trouble
himself much about religion, but was a man of great morals.

Sir William Dugdale did farther inform me that Major General
Middleton (since Lord) went into the highlands of Scotland, to
endeavour to make a party for King Charles I. An old gentleman (that
was second-sighted) came and told him, that his endeavour was good;
but he would be unsuccessful, and moreover, 'that they would put the
King to death.' And that several other attempts would be made, but
all in vain: but that his son would come in, but not reign; but at last
would be restored. This Lord Middleton had a great friendship with
the Laird Bocconi, and they had made an agreement, that the first of
them that died should appear to the other in extremity. The Lord
Middleton was taken prisoner at Worcester fight, and was prisoner in
the Tower of London, under three locks. Lying in his bed pensive,
Bocconi appeared to him; my Lord Middleton asked him if he were
dead or alive. He said, dead, and that he was a ghost; and told him,

that within three days he should escape, and he did so, in his wife's clothes. When he had done his message, he gave a frisk, and said,

> Givenni Givanni 'tis very strange,
> In the world to see so sudden a change.

And then gathered up and vanished. This account Sir William Dugdale had from the Bishop of Edinburgh.

In 1670, not far from Cirencester, was an apparition; being demanded, whether a good spirit, or a bad? returned no answer, but disappeared with a curious perfume and most melodious twang. Mr W. Lilly believes it was a fairy. So Propertius:

> Here, her speech ending, fled the beauteous fair,
> Melting th' embodied form to thinner air,
> Whom the remaining scent a goddess did declare.

The learned Henry Jacob, fellow of Merton College in Oxford, died at Dr Jacob's house in Canterbury. About a week after his death, the doctor being in bed and awake, and the moon shining bright, saw his cousin Henry standing by his bed, in his shirt, with a white cap on his head, and his beard-mustachoes turning up, as when he was alive. The doctor pinched himself and was sure he awake: he turned to the other side, from him; and, after some time, took courage to turn the other way again towards him; and Henry Jacob stood there still; he should have spoken to him but he did not; for which he has been ever since sorry. About half an hour after, he vanished. Not long after this, the cook-maid, going to the wood-pile to fetch wood to dress supper, saw him standing in his shirt upon the wood-pile. This account I had in a letter from Doctor Jacob, 1673, relating to his life, for Mr Anthony Wood; which is now in his hands.

T.M. Esq., an old acquaintance of mine, hath assured me, that about a quarter of a year after his first wife's death, as he lay in bed awake with his grandchild, his wife opened the door, and came into the chamber by the bedside, and looked upon him and stooped down and kissed him; her lips were warm, he fancied they would have been cold. He was about to have embraced her, but was afraid it might have done him hurt. When she went from him he asked her when he should see her again. She turned about and smiled, but said nothing. The closet door striked as it uses to do, both at her coming in and going out. He had every night a great coal fire in his chamber, which gave a light as clear almost as a candle. He was hypochondriacal; he married two wives since, and the latter end of his life was uneasy.

A Dutch prisoner at Woodbridge in Suffolk, in the reign of Charles II, could discern spirits; but others that stood by could not.

Anthony à Wood's bookplate, comprising a portrait of himself

The bell tolled for a man newly deceased. The prisoner saw his phantom, and did describe him to the parson of the parish, who was with him; exactly agreeing with the man for whom the bell tolled. Says the prisoner, 'Now he is coming near to you, and now he is between you and the wall'; the parson was resolved to try it, and went to take the wall of him,* and was thrown down; he could see nothing. This story is credibly told by several persons of belief.

There is a very remarkable story of an apparition, which Martin Luther did see, mentioned in his Commensalia or Table-Talk, which see.

The beautiful Lady Diana Rich, daughter to the Earl of Holland, as she was walking in her father's garden at Kensington, to take the fresh

---

* i.e. go between him and the wall. *Ed.*

air before dinner, about eleven o'clock, being then very well, met with her own apparition, habit, and everything, as in a looking-glass. About a month after, she died of the small-pox. And it is said that her sister, the Lady Isabella Thynne, saw the like of herself also, before she died. This account I had from a person of honour.

Voices

One Mr Smith, a practitioner of physic at Tamworth in Warwickshire, an understanding sober person, reading in Holinshed's *Chronicle*, found a relation of a great fight between Vortigern and Hengest, about those parts, at a place called Colemore: a little time after, as he lay awake in his bed, he heard a voice, that said unto him, 'You shall shortly see some of the bones of those men and horses slain, that you read of:' he was surprised at the voice, and asked in the name of God, who it was that spoke to him. The voice made answer, that he should not trouble himself about that; but what he told him should come to pass. Shortly after, as he went to see Colonel Archer (whose servants were digging for marl) he saw a great many bones of men and horses; and also potsherds; and upon the view it appeared to be according to the description in Holinshed's *Chronicle*; and it was the place where the fight was; but it is now called Blackmore.

Impulses

One that I knew, that was at the battle of Dunbar, told me that Oliver was carried on with a divine impulse; he did laugh so excessively as if he had been drunk; his eyes sparkled with spirits. He obtained a great victory; but the action was said to be contrary to human prudence. The same fit of laughter seized Oliver Cromwell, just before the battle of Naseby; as a kinsman of mine, and a great favourite of his, Colonel J.P., then present, testified. Cardinal Mazarin said that he was a lucky fool.

In one of the great fields at Warminster in Wiltshire, in the harvest, at the very time of the fight at Bosworth field, between King Richard III and Henry VII, there was one of the parish took two sheaves, crying (with some intervals) now for Richard, now for Henry; at last lets fall the sheaf that did represent Richard; and cried, now for King Henry, Richard is slain. This action did agree with the very time, day and hour. When I was a schoolboy I have heard this confidently delivered by tradition, by some old men of our country.

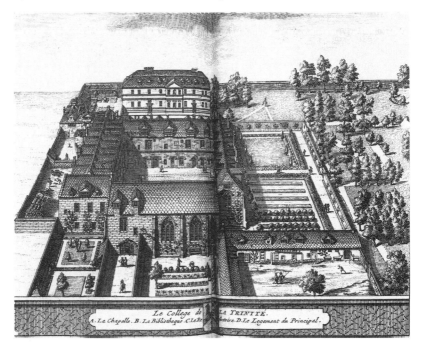

Trinity College, Oxford

A very good friend of mine and old acquaintance, hath had frequent impulses; when he was a commoner at Trinity College, Oxford, he had several. When he rode towards the West one time in the stage coach, he told the company, 'We shall certainly be robbed,' and they were so. When a brother of his, a merchant, died, he left him with other effects, a share of a ship, which was returning from Spain, and of which news was brought to the Exchange at London of her good condition; he had such an impulse upon his spirit, that he must needs sell his share, though to loss; and he did sell it. The ship came safe to Cornwall, (or Devon) and somewhere afterwards fell upon the rocks and sunk: not a man perished; but all the goods were lost except for some parrots, which were brought for Queen Katherine.

Knockings

Three or four days before my father died, as I was in my bed about nine o'clock in the morning perfectly awake, I did hear three distinct knocks on the bed's head, as if it had been with a ruler or ferula.

Mr Hierome Banks, as he lay on his death bed, in Bell-yard, said, three days before he died, that Mr Jennings of the Inner-temple, (his great acquaintance, dead a year or two before) gave three knocks, looked in, and said, 'Come away.' He was as far from believing such things as any man.

Magic

In Barbary are wizards, who do smear their hands with some black ointment, and then do hold them up to the sun, and in a short time you shall see delineated in that black stuff, the likeness of what you desire to have an answer of. It was desired to know, whether a ship was in safety, or no: there appeared in the woman's hand the perfect lineaments of a ship under sail. This Mr W. Cl. a merchant of London, who was factor there several years, protested to me that he did see. He is a person worthy of belief.

The last summer, on the day of St John the Baptist, 1694, I accidentally was walking in the pasture behind Montagu House, it was 12 o'clock. I saw there about two or three and twenty young women, most of them well habited, on their knees very busy, as if they had been weeding. I could not presently learn what the matter was; at last a young man told me, that they were looking for a coal under the root of a plantain, to put under their head that night, and they should dream who would be their husbands. It was to be sought for that day and hour.

Mr Ashmole told me, that a woman made use of a spell to cure an ague, by the advice of Dr Napier; a minister came to her, and severely reprimanded her for making use of a diabolical help, and told her she was in danger of damnation for it, and commanded her to burn it. She did so, and her distemper returned severely; insomuch that she was importunate with the doctor, to use the same again; she used it, and had ease. But the parson hearing of it, came to her again, and thundered hell and damnation, and frighted her so that she burnt it again. Whereupon she fell extremely ill, and would have had it a third time; but the doctor refused, saying, that she had despised and slighted the power and goodness of the blessed spirits (or Angels) and so she died. The cause of Lady Honywood's desperation, was that she had used a spell to cure her.

In Herefordshire, and other parts, they do put a cold iron bar upon their barrels, to preserve their beer from being soured by thunder. This is common practice in Kent.

To hinder the nightmare, they hang in a string, a flint with a hole in it (naturally) by the manger; but best of all they say, hung about their necks, and a flint will do it that hath not a hole in it. It is to prevent the nightmare, viz. the hag, from riding their horses, who will sometimes sweat all night. The flint thus hung does hinder it.

Mr Sp. told me that his horse, which was bewitched, would break bridles and strong halters, like Samson. They filled a bottle of the horse's urine, stopped it with a cork and bound it fast in, and then buried it under ground: and the party suspected to be the witch, fell ill, that he could not make water, of which he died. When they took up the bottle, the urine was almost gone; so that they did believe that if the fellow could have lived a little longer, he had recovered.

It is a thing very common to nail horse-shoes on the thresholds of doors: which is to hinder the power of witches that enter into the house. Most houses of the west end of London, have the horse-shoe on the threshold. It should be a horse-shoe that one finds. In the Bermudas, they use to put an iron into the fire when a witch comes in.

At Paris when it begins to thunder and lighten, they do at once ring out the great bell at the Abbey of St Germain, which they do believe makes it cease. The like was wont to be done heretofore in Wiltshire when it thundered and lightened, they did ring St Aldhelm's bell, at Malmesbury Abbey. The curious do say that the ringing of bells exceedingly disturbs spirits.

Transportation by an invisible power

A letter from the Reverend Mr Andrew Paschal, BD, Rector of Chedzoy in Somersetshire, to John Aubrey, Esq. at Gresham College, London.

Sir,

I last week received a letter from a learned friend, the minister of Barnstaple in Devon, which I think worthy your perusal. It was dated May 3, 1683, and is as follows. (He was of my time in Queen's College, Cambridge.)

There having been many prodigious things performed lately in a parish adjoining to that which Bishop Sparrow presented me to, called Cheriton-Bishop, by some discontented demon, I can easily remember that I owe you an account thereof, in lieu of that which you desired of me, and which I could not serve you in.

About November last, in the parish of Spreyton in the county of Devon, there appeared in a field near the dwelling house of Philip

Furze, to his servant Francis Fry, being of the age of twenty-one, next August, an aged gentleman with a pole in his hand, and like that he was wont to carry about with him when living, to kill moles withal, who told the young man he should not be afraid of him; but should tell his master, i.e. his son, that several legacies that he had bequeathed were unpaid, naming ten shillings to one, ten shillings to another, etc. Fry replied, that the party he last named was dead. The spectrum replied, he knew that, but said it must be paid to (and named) the next relation. There things being performed, he promised he would trouble him no further. These small legacies were paid accordingly. But the young man having carried twenty shillings ordered by the spectrum to his sister Mrs Furze, of the parish of Staverton near Totness, which money the gentlewoman refused to receive, being sent her, as she said, from the Devil. The same night Fry lodging there, the spectrum appeared to him again, whereupon Fry challenged his promise not to trouble him, and said he had done all he desired him; but that Mrs Furze would not receive the money. The spectrum replied, that is true indeed; but bid him ride to Totnes and buy a ring of that value, and that she would take. Which was provided for her and received by her. Then Fry rode homewards attended by a servant of Mrs Furze. But being come into Spreyton parish, or rather a little before, he seemed to carry an old gentlewoman behind him, that often threw him off his horse, and hurried him with such violence, as astonished all that saw, or heard how horridly the ground was beaten; and being come into his master's yard, Fry's horse (a mean beast) sprung at once twenty five feet. The trouble from the man-spectre ceased from this time. But the old gentlewoman, Mrs Furze, Mr Furze's second wife, whom the spectre at his first appearance to Fry, called 'that wicked woman my wife' (though I knew her, and took her for a very good woman) presently after appears to several in the house, viz. to Fry, Mrs Thomasin Gidley, Anne Langdon, born in my parish, and to a little child which was forced to be removed from the house; sometimes in her own shape, sometimes in shapes more horrid, as of a dog belching fire, and of a horse, and seeming to ride out of the window, carrying only one pane of glass away, and a little piece of iron. After this Fry's head was thrust into a narrow space, where a man's fist could not enter; between a bed and a wall; and forced to be taken thence by the strength of men, all bruised and bloody; upon this it was thought fit to bleed him; and after that was done, the binder was removed from his arm, and conveyed about his middle, and presently was drawn so very straight, it had almost killed him, and was cut asunder, making an ugly uncouth noise. Several other times with handkerchiefs, cravats and other things he was near strangled, they were drawn so close upon his throat. He lay one night in his periwig (in his master's chamber, for the more safety) which was torn all to pieces. His best periwig he enclosed in a little box on the inside with a joined stool, and other weight upon it; the box was snapped asunder, and the wig torn all to flitters. His master saw his buckles fall all to pieces on his feet. But first I should have told you the fate of his shoe-strings, one of which a gentlewoman (greater than all exception⋆) assured me, that she saw it come out of his shoe, without any visible hand, and fling itself to the farther end of the room; the other was coming out too, but that a maid prevented and helped it out, which crisped and curled about her hand like a living eel. The clothes worn by Anne Langdon and Fry, (if their own) were torn to pieces on their backs. The same gentlewoman, being the daughter of the minister of the parish, Mr Roger Specott, showed me one of Fry's gloves, which was torn in his pocket while he was by. I did view it near and narrowly, and do seriously confess that it is torn so very accurately in all the seams and in other places, and laid abroad so artificially, and it is so dexterously tattered, (and all done in the pocket in a minute's time) as nothing human could have done it; no cutler could have made an engine to do it so. Other fantastical freaks have been very frequent, as the marching of a great barrel full of salt out of one room into another; an andiron laying itself over a pan of milk that was scalding on the fire, and two flitches of bacon descending from the chimney where they hung, and laid themselves over that andiron: the appearing of the spectrum (when in her own shape) in the same clothes, to seeming, which Mrs Furze her daughter-in-law has on. The entangling of Fry's face and legs about his neck, and about the frame of the chairs, so as they have been with great difficulty disengaged.

But the most remarkable of all happened in that day that I passed by the door in my return hither, which was Easter Eve, when Fry, returning from work (that little he can do), was caught by the woman spectre by the skirts of his doublet, and carried into the air; he was quickly missed by his master and the workmen, and great enquiry was made for Francis Fry, but no hearing of him; but about half an hour after Fry was heard whistling and singing in a kind of a quagmire. He was now affected as he was wont to be in his fits, so that none regarded what he said; but coming to himself an hour after, he solemnly protested, that the demon carried him so high that he saw his master's house underneath him no bigger than a hay-cock, that he was in perfect sense, and prayed God not to suffer the devil to destroy

⋆ i.e. whose word could not be doubted. *Ed.*

him; that he was suddenly set down in that quagmire. The workmen found one shoe on one side of the house, and the other shoe on the other side; his periwig was espied next morning hanging on the top of a tall tree. It was soon observed, that Fry's part of his body that had laid in the mud, was much benumbed, and therefore the next Saturday, which was the eve of Low Sunday, they carried him to Crediton to be let blood; which being done, and the company having left him for a little while, returning they found him in a fit, with his forehead all bruised and swollen to a great bigness, none able to guess how it came, till he recovered himself, and then he told them, that a bird flew in at the window with a great force, and with a stone in its mouth flew directly against his forehead. The people looked for it, and found in the ground just under where he sat, not a stone, but a weight of brass or copper, which the people were breaking, and parting it among themselves. He was so very ill, that he could ride but one mile or little more that night, since which time I have not heard of him, save that he was ill handled the next day, being Sunday. Indeed Sir, you may wonder that I have not visited that house, and the poor afflicted people; especially since I was so near, and passed by the very door: but besides that, they have called to their assistance none but nonconforming ministers. I was not qualified to be welcome there, having given Mr Furze a great deal of trouble the last year about a conventicle in his house, where one of this parish was the preacher. But I am very well assured of the truth of what I have written, and (as more appears) you shall hear from me again.

I had forgot to tell you that Fry's mother came to me, grievously bewailing the miserable condition of her son. She told me, that the day before he had five pins thrust into his side. She asked; and I gave her the best advice I could. Particularly, that her son should declare all that the spectre, especially the woman, gave him in charge, for I suspect, there is something hidden; and that she should remove him thence by all means. But I fear that she will not do it. For I hear that Anne Langdon is come into my parish to her mother, and that she is grievously troubled there. I might have written as much of her, as of Fry, for she had been as ill treated, saving the aerial journey. Her fits and obsessions seem to be greater, for she screeches in a most hellish tone. Thomasin Gidley (though removed) is in trouble I hear.

Sir, this is all my friend wrote. This letter came enclosed in another from a clergyman, my friend, who lives in those parts. He tells me all the relations he receives from divers persons living in Spreyton and the neighbouring parishes, agree with this. He spake with a gentleman of good fashion, that was at Crediton when Fry was blooded, and saw the stone that bruised his forehead; but he did not call it copper or brass, but said it was a strange mineral. That gentleman promised to make a strict inquiry on the place into all particulars, and to give him the result: which my friend also promises me; with hopes that he shall procure for me a piece of that mineral substance, which hurt his forehead.

The occasion of my friend's sending me this narrative, was my entreating him sometime since, to inquire into a thing of this nature, that happened in Barnstaple, where he lives. An account was given to me long since, it fills a sheet or two, which I have by me. I desired to have it well attested, it being full of very memorable things; but it seems he could meet only a general consent as to the truth of the things, the reports varying in the circumstances.

Sir, Yours.

Visions in a beryl or crystal

A beryl is a kind of crystal that hath a weak tincture of red; it is one of the twelve stones mentioned in *Revelations*. I have heard, that spectacles were first made of this stone, which is the reason that the Germans do call a spectacle-glass (or a pair of spectacles) a 'Brill'.

I have here set down the figure of a consecrated beryl, now in the possession of Sir Edward Harley, Knight of the Bath, which he keeps in his closet at Brampton Bryan in Herefordshire, amongst his collections I saw there. It came first from Norfolk; a minister had it there, and a call was to be used with it. Afterwards a miller had it, and both did work great cures with it, (if curable) and in the beryl they did see, either the receipt in writing, or else the herb. To this minister, the spirits or angels would appear openly, and because the miller (who was his familiar friend) one day happened to see them, he gave him the aforesaid beryl and call: by these angels the minister was forewarned of his death. This account I had from Mr Ashmole. Afterwards this beryl came into somebody's hand in London, who did tell strange things by it; insomuch that at last he was questioned for it, and it was taken away by authority, (it was about 1645).

This beryl is a perfect sphere, the diameter of it I guess to be something more than an inch: it is set in a ring, or circle of silver resembling the meridian of a globe: the stem of it is about ten inches high, all gilt. At the four quarters of it are the names of four angels, viz. Uriel, Raphael, Michael, Gabriel. On the top is a cross patée.

Converse with angels and spirits

Dr Richard Nepier, rector of Lynford, was a good astrologer, and so was Mr Marsh of Dunstable; but Mr Marsh did seriously confess to a friend of mine, that astrology was but the countenance; and that he did his business by the help of the blessed spirits; with whom only men of great piety, humility and charity, could be acquainted; and such a one he was. He was an hundred years old when my friend was with him; and yet did understand himself very well.

Good spirits are delighted and allured by sweet perfumes, as rich gums, frankincense, salts etc which was the reason the priests of the Gentiles, and also the Christians, used them in their temples, and sacrifices: and on the contrary, evil spirits are pleased and allured and called up by suffumigations of henbane etc, stinking smells etc which the witches do use in their conjuration. Toads (saturnine animals) are killed by putting of salt upon them; I have seen the experiment. Magical writers say that cedar-wood drives away evil spirits; it was, and is much used in magnificent temples.

Ecstasy

In 1670, a poor widow's daughter in Herefordshire, went to service not far from Harwood (the seat of Sir John Hoskins, Bart. RSS). She was aged near about twenty; fell very ill, even to the point of death; her mother was old and feeble, and her daughter was the comfort of her life; if she should die, she knew not what to do: she besought God upon her knees in prayer, that he would be pleased to spare her daughter's life, and take her to him: at this very time, the daughter fell into a trance, which continued about an hour: they thought she had been dead: when she recovered out of it, she declared the vision she had in this fit, viz. that one in black habit came to her, whose face was so bright and glorious she could not behold it; and also he had such brightness upon his breast, and (if I forget not) upon his arms. And he told her, that her mother's prayers were heard, and that her mother should shortly die, and she should suddenly recover; and she did so, and her mother died. She hath the character of a modest, humble, virtuous maid. Had this been in some Catholic country, it would have made a great noise.

Accidents

(From *The Natural History of Wiltshire*)

In the reign of King James I, as boys were at play in Amesbury Street, it thundered and lightened. One of the boys wore a little dagger by his side, which was melted in the scabbard, and the scabbard not hurt. This dagger Edward Earl of Hertford kept amongst his rarities. I have forgotten if the boy was killed. (From Mr Bowman and Mr Gauntlett.)

Dr Ralph Bathurst, Dean of Wells, and one of the chaplains to King Charles I, who is no superstitious man, protested to me that the curing of the king's evil by the touch of the king doth puzzle his philosophy: for whether they were of the house of York or Lancaster, it did. 'Tis true indeed there are prayers read at the touching, but neither the king minds them nor the chaplains. Some confidently report that James Duke of Monmouth did it.

Imposture: Richard Heydock, MD, a former fellow of New College in Oxford, was an ingenious and a learned person, but much against the hierarchy of the Church of England. He had a device to gain proselytes, by preaching in his dream; which was much noised abroad, and talked of as a miracle. But King James I being at Salisbury went to hear him. He observed that his harangue was very methodical, and that he did but counterfeit a sleep. He surprised the doctor by drawing his sword, and swearing, 'God's waunes, I will cut off his head': at which the doctor startled and pretended to awake; and so the cheat was detected.

In the time of King Charles II the drumming at the house of Mr Mompesson, of Tydworth, made a great talk over England, of which Mr Joseph Glanvill, rector of Bath, hath largely written; to which I refer the reader. But as he was an ingenious person, so I suspect he was a little too credulous; for Sir Ralph Bankes and Mr Anthony Ettrick lay there together one night out of curiosity, to be satisfied. They did hear sometimes knockings; and if they said 'Devil, knock so many knocks', so many knocks would be answered. But Mr Ettrick sometimes whispered the words, and there was then no return: but he should have spoke in Latin or French for the detection of this.

Another time Sir Christopher Wren lay there. He could see no strange things, but sometimes he should hear a drumming, as one may drum with one's hand upon the wainscot; but he observed that this drumming was only when a certain maidservant was in the next room: the partitions of the rooms are by borden-brass, as we call it. But all these remarked that the devil kept no very unseasonable hours: it seldom knocked after 12 at night, or before 6 in the morning.

Aubrey on folklore and superstition

Remains of Gentilism and Judaism

This was published for the Folklore Society in 1881 by James Britten, whose text I have followed. There is a more recent and systematically arranged edition by John Buchanan-Brown (*John Aubrey: Three Prose Works*, 1972).

When children shaled their teeth the women use to wrap, or put salt about the tooth, and so throw it into a good fire. Cramer saith that in Germany, in his native country, some women will bid their children to take the tooth, which is fallen or taken out, and go to a dark corner of the house or parlour, and cast the same into it thereby saying these words:

> Mouse! Here I give the a tooth of bone,
> But give thou me an iron one

(or iron tooth), believing that another good tooth will grow in its place.

'Tis commonly said, in Germany, that the witches do meet in the night before the first day of May upon an high mountain, called the Blocksberg, situated in Ascanien, where they together with the devils do dance, and feast, and the common people do the night before the said day fetch a certain thorn, and stick it at their house-door, believing the witches can then do them no harm.

At Oxford the boys do blow cows' horns and hollow caxes all night; and on May Day the young maids of every parish carry about their parish garlands of flowers, which afterwards they hang up in their churches.

The holy maul which (they fancy) hung behind the church door, which when the father was seventy the son might fetch, to knock his father in the head, as effete, and of no more use.

The seamen will not endure to have one whistle on shipboard: believing that it raises winds. On Malvern Hills, in Worcestershire, etc, thereabout when they fan their corn, and want wind, they cry Youle! Youle! Youle! to invoke it, which word (no doubt) is a corruption of Æolus (the God of the winds).

This Cramer affirms to be done likewise in Germany. He, being once upon the River Elbe, began accidentally to whistle, which the watermen presently disliked, and would have him rather to forbear.

When I was a little boy (before the civil wars) I have seen (according to the custom then) the bride and bridegroom kiss over the bride-cakes at the table: it was about the later end of dinner: and the cakes were laid one upon another, like the picture of the sew-bread in the old bibles. The bridegroom waited at table all dinner.

In Shropshire (All Souls' Day, November 2nd) there is set on the board a high heap of soul cakes, lying one upon another like the picture of the sew-bread in the old Bibles. They are about the bigness of twopenny cakes, and nearly all the visitants that day take one; and there is an old rhythm or saying,

> A Soul-cake, a Soul-cake,
> Have mercy on all Christian souls for a Soul-cake.

This custom is continued to this time.

Offertories at funerals: these are mentioned in the rubric of the Church of England Common prayer books: but I never saw it used, but once at Beaumaris, in Anglesey; but it is used over all the counties of North Wales. But before when the corpse is brought out of doors, there is cake and cheese, and a new bowl of beer, and another of milk, with the year engraved on it, and the name of the deceased, which one accepts of on the other side of the corpse; and this custom is used to this day, 1686, in North Wales.

When I was a boy in North Wilts (before the civil wars) the maid-servants were wont at night (after supper) to make smooth the ashes on the hearth, and then to make streaks on it with a stick; such a streak signified privately to her that made it such an unmarried man, such a one such a maid: the like for men. Then the men and the maids were to choose by this kind of way, their husbands and wives: or by this divination to know whom they should marry. The maids I remember were very fond of this kind of magic, which is clearly a branch of geomancy. Now the rule of geomancy is that you are not to go about your divination, but with a great deal of seriousness, and also prayers; and to be performed in a very private place; or on the sea shore.

Another remainder of geomancy to divine whether such a one will return this night or no, is by the sheath of a knife, which one holds at the great end with his two forefingers, and says 'he comes', then slips down his upper finger under his lower, and then the lower under that and says, 'he comes not', and so on till he is come to the bottom of his sheath, which gives the answer.

Also, I remember, the maids (especially the cook maids and dairymaids) would stick up in some chinks of the joists midsummer-men, which are slips of orpins. They placed them by pairs, one for such a man, the other for such a maid his sweetheart, and accordingly as the orpin did incline to, or recline from the other, that there would be love, or aversion; if either did wither, death.

So in Germany in the night before Christmas they take a trencher, and put upon it a little heap of salt, as big as a walnut, more or less, for such and such a one, and for themselves too, and set it in a safe place, in the morning when they find the heap or heaps entire, all will live the following year, but if any or more are melted down a little, they take it that the same man or woman will die, for which it was designed.

It was a custom for some people that were more curious than ordinary, to sit all night in the church porch of their parish on midsummer-eve, St John Baptist's eve; and they should see the apparitions of those that should die in the parish that year come and knock at the door: and still in many places on St John's night they make fires, bonfires, on the hills etc: but the civil wars coming on have put all these rites or customs quite out of fashion. Wars do not only extinguish religion and laws; but superstition: and no sufflamen is a greater fugator of phantoms, than gunpowder.

From my old cousin Ambrose Brown: Old Simon Brunsdon of Winterborne Basset, in Wilts: he had been parish clerk there in the time of Queen Mary. The tutelar saint of that church is Saint Katharine; he lived down till the beginning of King James I's reign: when the gadfly had happened to sting his oxen, or cows, and made them to run away in that champaign country, he would run after them, crying out, praying, 'good Saint Katharine of Winterborne stay my oxen, good Saint Katharine of Winterborne stay my oxen,' etc. This old Brunsdon was wont in the summer-time to leave his oxen in the field, and go to the church to pray to Saint Katharine. By that time he came back to his oxen, perhaps the gadfly might drive them away: upon such an occasion he would cry out to Saint Katharine as is already here said. We must not imagine that he was the only man that did so heretofore; and the like invocations were to other saints and martyrs, e.g. at St Oswald's Down and Ford down. Thereabout the shepherds prayed at night and at morning to St Oswald (that was martyred there) to preserve their sheep safe in the fold. St Oswald was slain by Penda on the great down east of Marsfield in Gloucestershire as you ride to Castlecombe, from whence it is called St Oswald's down: in these parts, nay as far as Auburne chase (and perhaps a great deal further) when they penned their sheep in the fold, they did pray to God and St Oswald to bring the sheep safe to the fold: and in the morning, they did pray to God and St Oswald, to bring their sheep safe from the fold. The country folk call St Oswald St Twosole.

In those days, when they went to bed, they did rake up their fire and make a cross in the ashes, and pray to God and St Sythe (St Osyth) to deliver them from fire, and from water and from all misadventure.

When the bread was put into the oven, they prayed to God and Saint Stephen, to send them a just batch and an even.

They were wont to please the fairies, that they might do them no shrewd turns, by sweeping clean the hearth and setting by it a dish whereon was set a mess of milk sopped with white bread. And on the morrow they should find a groat; if they did speak of it they never had any again. That they would churn the cream etc. Mrs H., of Hereford had as many groats, or three-pences this way as made a little silver cup or bowl, of (I think) £3 value, which her daughter preserves still.

That the fairies would steal away young children and put others in their places; verily believed by old women of those days: and by some yet living.

Some were led away by the fairies, as was a hind riding upon Hackpen with corn, led a dance to Devizes. So was a shepherd of Mr Brown, of Winterborne-Basset: but never any afterwards enjoy themselves. He said that the ground opened, and he was brought into strange places underground, where they used musical instruments, viols, and lutes, such (he said) as Mr Thomas did play on.

At the funerals in Yorkshire, to this day, they continue the custom of watching and sitting up all night till the body is interred. In the interim some kneel down and pray (by the corpse), some play at cards, some drink and take tobacco: they have also mimical plays and sports, e.g. they choose a simple young fellow to be a judge, then the suppliants (having first blacked their hands by rubbing it under the bottom of the pot), beseech his lordship and smut all his face. They play likewise at hotcockles.

The Fellows of New College in Oxford have time out of mind every Holy Thursday betwixt the hours of eight and nine gone to the Hospital called Bartholomews near Oxford: where they retire into the chapel, and certain prayers are read and an Anthem sung: from thence they go to the upper end of the grove adjoining to the chapel (the way being beforehand strewed with flowers by the poor people of the hospital), they place themselves round about the well there, where they warble forth melodiously a song of three or four, or five parts; which being performed, they refresh themselves with a morning's draught there, and retire to Oxford before the sermon.

A prayer used when they went to bed.

> Matthew, Mark, Luke and John,
> Bless the bed that I lie on.
> And blessed Guardian-angel keep
> Me safe from danger whilst I sleep.

I remember before the civil wars, ancient people when they heard the clock strike, were wont to say, 'Lord grant, that my last hour may be my best hour.'

They had some pious ejaculation too, when the cock did crow which did put them in mind of the trumpet at the Resurrection.

Home harvests are observed (more or less) in most counties of England, e.g. South Wilts, Herefordshire etc: when they bring home the last load of corn; it is done with great joy and merriment: and a fiddler rides on the loaded cart, or wain, playing: a barrel of good beer is provided for the harvestmen, and some good rustic cheer.

Sin-eaters. In the county of Hereford was an old custom at funerals to hire poor people, who were to take upon them all the sins of the party deceased. One of them I remember lived in a cottage on Ross highway. (He was a long, lean, ugly, lamentable poor rascal.) The manner was that when the corpse was brought out of the house and laid on the bier, a loaf of bread was brought out, and delivered to the sin-eater over the corpse, as also a mazer bowl of maple (gossip's bowl) full of beer, which he was to drink up, and sixpence in money, in consideration whereof he took upon him (*ipso facto*) all the sins of the defunct, and freed him (or her) from walking after they were dead. This custom alludes (methinks) something to the scape-goat in the old law. This custom (though rarely used in our days) yet by some people was observed even in the strictest time of the Presbyterian government: as at Dynder, whether the parson of the parish wished it or not, the kindred of a woman deceased there had this ceremony punctually performed according to her will: and also the like was done at the city of Hereford in these times, when a woman kept many years before her death a mazer bowl for the sin-eater; and the like in other places in this county; as also in Brecon, e.g. at Llangorse, where Mr Gwin the minister, about 1640, could not hinder the performing of this ancient custom. I believe this custom was heretofore used over all Wales.

In North Wales, the sin-eaters are frequently made use of; but there, instead of a bowl of beer, they have a bowl of milk.

Methinks, doles to poor people with money at funerals have some resemblance of that of the sin-eater. Doles at funerals were continued at gentlemen's funerals in the west of England till the civil wars. And so in Germany at rich men's funerals doles are in use, and to every one a quart of strong and good beer. – Cramer.

In Scotland (especially among the Highlanders) the women do make a curtsey to the new moon; I have known one in England do it, and our English women in the country do retain (some of them) a touch of this gentilism still, e.g.

> All haile to thee Moon, all haile to thee!
> I prithee good Moon, declare to me,
> This night, who my Husband must be.

This they do sitting astride on a gate or stile the first evening the new moon appears. In Herefordshire the vulgar people at the prime of the moon, say, 'tis a fine moon, God bless her.

Despite the change of religion, the ploughboys, and also the schoolboys will keep up and retain their old ceremonies and customs and privileges, which in the west of England is used still (and I believe) in other parts. So in Somersetshire when they wassail (which is on Twelfth Night I think) the ploughmen have their twelve-cake, and they go into the ox-house to the oxen, with the wassail-bowl and drink to the ox with the crumpled horn that treads out the corn; they have an old conceived rhyme; and afterwards they go with their wassail bowl into the orchard and go about the trees to bless them, and put a piece of toast upon the roots.

And the school-days in the west still religiously observe St Nicholas' day (December 6th); he was the patron of the school-boys. At Curry Yeovil in Somersetshire, where there is a school in the church, they have annually at that time a barrel of good ale brought into the church; and that night they have the privilege to break open their masters' cellar door.

Item, for cock-fighting, the schoolboys continue that custom still: and have their victors, that is, he whose cock conquers or beats the rest, is victor, and he hath the privilege, during that Lent, to save what boy he pleases from whipping.

On Shrove Tuesday shroving when the victor boy went through the streets in triumph decked with ribbons, all his school fellows following with drum and a fiddle, to a feast at their master's school house. The custom (I think) has now left off.

'Tis a common use in London, and perhaps over great part of England, for apple women, oyster women, etc, and some butchers, to spit on the money which they first receive in the morning, which they call good handsel.

Some persons' eyes are very offensive: I cannot say why; there is something divine in it, more than every one understands. I have heard English merchants say, that in Spain they are very shy, and wary, who they let look on children's eyes for fear of this.

Virgil speaks somewhere (I think in the *Georgics*) of voices heard louder than a man's. Mr Lancelot Morehouse did aver to me that he did once hear such a loud laugh on the other side of a hedge, and was sure that no human voice could afford such a laugh.

This relates something to Robin Goodfellow.

Before the civil wars in Staffordshire, at and about Coventry, Warwickshire, and those parts, there went along with the fiddlers, rhymers (who perhaps were fiddlers too), that upon any subject given would versify *extempore* half an hour together.

These rhymers were of great antiquity in England, as appears by many families called by that name: and like enough the custom was derived from the old bards. In Wales are some bards still who have a strange gift in versifying: but the fit will sometimes leave them, and never return again. The vulgar sort of people in Wales have a humour of singing *extempore* upon occasion.

Mrs Clarke (a Herefordshire woman): Bury the head of a black cat with a Jacobus or a piece of gold in it, and put into the eyes two black beans (what was to be done with the beans she hath forgotten) but it must be done on a Tuesday at twelve o'clock at night, and that time nine nights later the piece of gold must be taken out; and whatsoever you buy with it (always reserving some part of the money) you will have money brought into your pocket, perhaps the same piece of gold again.

Not far from Sir Bennet Hoskyns, there was a labouring-man, that rose up early every day to go to work; who for a good while many days together found a ninepence in the way that he went. His wife wondering how he came by so much money, was afraid he got it not honestly; at last he told her, and afterwards he never found any more.

The Jews have strange fancies concerning the invisible bean. Take the head of a man that dies of a natural death, and set it in the ground, and in his eye, set a bean, cover it with earth, and enclose it about, that nobody may look into it, and without the enclosure set another bean, or two; when those without the enclosure are ripe, that within will be ripe also; then take the bean-stalk within the enclosure, and take a child, which hold fast by the hand, and the child must shell the beans; there will be but one invisible bean of them all, which when the child has, the other party cannot see her: 'let the Jew Apella believe it, not I.' But thus much I am morally certain of, that about 1680 two (or three) Jews, merchants, did desire Mr Wyld Clarke, merchant of London, leave to make this following experiment in his garden at Mile End; which he saw them do, and who told me of it. As I remember, 'twas much after this manner. They took a black cat, and cut off its head, at a certain aspect of the planets, and buried it in his garden by night with some ceremonies, that I have forgot, and put a bean in the brain of the cat; but about a day or two after, a cock came and scratched it all up. Mr Clarke told me, that they did believe it, and yet they were crafty, subtle merchants. This brings to my remembrance a story that was generally believed when I was a schoolboy (before the civil wars) that thieves when they broke open a house, would put a candle into a dead man's hand, and then the people in the chamber would not awake. There is such a kind of story somewhere amongst the magical writers.

We have a custom, that when one sneezes, every one else puts off his hat, and bows, and cries 'God bless you, Sir.' I have heard, or read a story that many years since, that sneezing was an epidemical disease and very mortal, which caused this yet received custom.

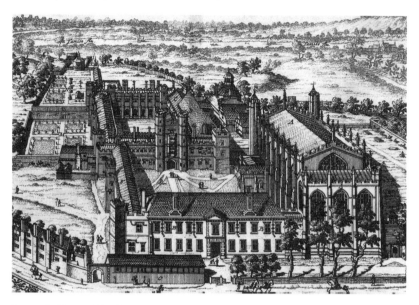

Eton College, Windsor

Some customs of Eton School: Eton College and school were founded by King Henry VI. They do hold some lands by a custom of offering to the travellers salt; 'tis on (I think) the first day of Hilary Term. The schoolmaster and all his scholars go to a tumulus (or barrow) by the road, near to Slough, which is about a mile from the college.

Also, about Whitsuntide, I think, on Holy Thursday, the school-boys do hunt a ram, till they kill him; and then they have a venison feast made of him; they use to overheat themselves, and get the small-pox.

Also, on Shrove Tuesday, as soon as ever the clock strikes nine, all the boys in the school cry 'Bacchus, Bacchus, Bacchus', as loud as they can yell; and stamp, and knock with their sticks; and then they do all run out of the school.

I am not acquainted with the schoolmaster here, but I have a good mind to write to him for a more particular account of these customs.

Captain Carlo Fantom (a Croatian) spoke thirteen languages, was a captain under the Earl of Essex. Sir Robert Pye was his colonel, who shot at him for not returning a horse which he took away before the regiment. This was done near in a field near Bedford, where the army then was, as they were marching to the relief of Gainsborough. Many are yet living that saw it. Captain Hamden was by; the two bullets went through his buff-coat, and the captain saw his shirt on fire. Captain Carlo Fantom took the bullets and said to Sir Robert 'Here, take your bullets again.' None of the soldiers would dare to fight with him, they said they would not fight with the devil. E. Wyld Esq. was very well acquainted with him and gave me many a treat: and at last he prevailed with him so far, towards the knowledge of this secret, that Fantom told him that the keepers in their forests did know a certain herb, which they gave to children, which made them to be shot-free (they call them hard-men). He had a world of cuts about his body with swords. He was very quarrelsome, and a great ravisher. He left the Parliament party, and went to King Charles I at Oxford, where he was hanged for ravishing.

Robert Earl of Essex, General for the Parliament, had this Captain Fantom in high esteem: for he was an admirable horse-officer, and taught the cavalry of the army the way of fighting with horse; the General saved him from hanging twice for ravishing, once at Winchester, secondly at St Albans, and he was not content only to ravish himself, but he would make his soldiers do it too, and he would stand by and look on. He met (coming, late at night, out of the Horseshoe Tavern, in Drury Lane) with a Lieutenant of Colonel Rossiter's, who had great jingling spurs on; said he, 'The noise of your spurs do offend me, you must come over the kennel [i.e. gutter] and give me satisfaction.' They drew, and passed at each other and the lieutenant was run through and died within an hour or two: and 'twas not known, who killed him.

Said he, 'I care not for your cause, I come to fight for your half-crown and your handsome women; my father was a Roman Catholic and so was my grandfather. I have fought for the Christians against the Turks, and for the Turks against the Christians.'

At Fausby (near Daventry) in Northamptonshire a raven did build her nest on the leads between the tower and the steeple. By the placing of her nest towards a certain point of the compass the inhabitants did make their prognostic as to the dearness or cheapness of corn; the oldest people's grandfathers here did never remember but that this raven yearly made her nest here, and in the late civil wars the soldiers killed her. I am sorry for the tragical end of this old church bird, that lived in so many changes of government and religion, ways of worship in the church. But our shepherds and ploughmen do make as useful considerable observations of a mousehole of a fieldmouse: which way it points; if it points eastward it is a sign of a wet winter, for here the wet comes from the west for the most part.

In the year 1659, on Saturday afternoon, as Mr George Crake and Mr Whorwood were passing over from Southampton to the Isle of Wight, a conglomerated substance in the air easily observed and resembling in some measure a chain-shot, was first taken notice of by a thatcher, who was at work on a house near the seaside, and seeing the boat where those two gentlemen, their men and horses, with two boatmen were, said to the man that served him, 'That Dwy' (for so this meteor is vulgarly called) 'will endanger that boat,' pointing towards it. And in very short time after, he saw the men in the boat labouring to lower sail, and lay all flat, who not being able to effect their design, the Dwy presently overset the boat and all were drowned. A few days after, being at my father's house at Lymington, at dinner, a master of a ship that was then in Cowes road dined with us, and was telling us news, that some dead bodies arose lately by his vessel's side, which I presently suspected to be the gentlemen mentioned, whom I left well, and found it true. Doctor Walter Pope, then Fellow of Wadham College, Oxon, Mr John Smart, Fellow of Trinity College, Oxon, and Mr Cripps, Fellow of Merton College, were then with me, and had gone with Mr Crake and Mr Whorwood had not my invitation prevailed with 'em. The nature of this Dwy is such that if it meet with opposition it destroys all, but to anything that yields it does no hurt; of a very swift motion, and certain mischief where it falls, and very usual there, if not peculiar to the place.

Illustrations

Set in 'Monophoto' Bembo 11 point spaced 1 point
by Keyspools Ltd, Golborne, Lancs
Printed lithographically at
The Bath Press, Avon
on Archive Long Life paper
Bound at the Bath Press
in Berkeley cloth
blocked with a special design by
Malcolm Harvey Young